LOVE TOGETHER

LONGTIME MALE COUPLES ON HEALTHY INTIMACY AND COMMUNICATION

LOVE TOGETHER

LONGTIME MALE COUPLES
ON HEALTHY INTIMACY AND
COMMUNICATION

TIM CLAUSEN

ISBN: 978-1492822257
ISBN-10: 1492822256

LCCN:2014920386

Printed in the United States of America.

To Jim Doran,
for introducing me
to my love of interviewing

TABLE OF CONTENTS

Foreword by Bob Barzan i
Acknowledgements... iii
Preface vii

Introduction 1
A Reading Suggestion 13
The Interview Questions 15

THE INTERVIEWS
Section I: Couples Together Ten to Twenty Years
1. Kurt & Dean, Costa Rica—Together 12 Years 23
2. Gary & Dan Ross, California—Together 13 Years 35
3. Ryan Levy & Ian Eastveld, Texas—Together 18 Years 47
4. Martin & Robert, Massachusetts—Together 16 Years 57
5. Patrick & Fraser, British Columbia—Together 11 Years 71
6. Jason Warner & deMarco Deciccio, Tennessee—Together 13 Years ... 85

Section II: Couples Together Twenty to Thirty Years
7. Matt & Scott, California—Together 24 Years 101
8. Steve Habgood & Mark Sadlek, Texas—Together 24 Years 113
9. Rob Dorgan & Steve Bolia, Kentucky—Together 26 Years 125
10. Willie Docto & Greg Trulson, Vermont—Together 21 Years 135
11. Craig & Paul, Connecticut—Together 24 Years 145
12. Stuart Gaffney & John Lewis, Cailfornia—Together 27 Years 157

Section III: Couples Together Thirty to Forty Years
13. Larry Duplechan & Greg Harvey, California—Together 37 Years 169
14. Chris & Andy, Oregon—Together 35 Years 179
15. Brian McNaught & Ray Struble, Florida—Together 38 Years 185

Section IV: Couples Together Forty to Fifty Years
16. Byron Roberts & Dennis Merrill, California—Together 46 Years 199
17. John McNeill & Charles Chiarelli, Florida—Together 48 Years 211

Section V: Couples Together Fifty to Sixty Years

18. Ward Stewart & George Vye, Washington—Together 56 Years 219
19. George Harris & Jack Evans, Texas—Together 52 Years 225

Section VI: Couples Together Sixty to Seventy Years

20. Johnny Dapper & Lyman Hollowell, California—Together 65 Years 235
21. Eric Marcoux & Eugene Woodworth, Oregon—Together 60 Years 239
22. Eugene Woodworth & Eric Marcoux, Oregon—Together 60 Years 251
23. Eric Marcoux—On Losing a Partner of 60 Years 263

About the Author 277

FOREWORD

You will find this an insightful, thought provoking, and entertaining collection of interviews compiled by a man who is unusually skilled in getting gay men to reveal intimate details about their lives. In these interviews, Tim Clausen breaks open for us the joys, disappointments, struggles, mysteries, and amusements of longtime relationships between men. What he uncovers is a wonder.

Despite every effort to destroy these relationships, to deny their existence, to make them impossible, to offer little or no support for them from society, religion, finance, or tradition, somehow, they survive and thrive. As one man says, "When I came out, I just assumed I was going to be alone, and then I met Andy and we've been together longer than anybody else in either one of our families, including our parents. And we've worked at it. It's not like we've never fought, but we just somehow complete each other."

The men in these relationships share how they work at it, how they have put together for themselves, usually with no models to draw from, a satisfying and joyful life as a couple.

Tim's work couldn't be timelier. Never have gay men's relationships received so much attention in the media, the courts, the ballot box, and in society at large. In the last year, several states have acknowledged and ratified our relationships by granting equal access to the benefits of marriage. In Seattle, Washington, Catholic high school students challenged their church to a higher moral standard by protesting the expulsion of their vice principal for loving and marrying his same sex partner.

The first gay male couple was married in the chapel at West Point with the usual military honors. For most of the men in these interviews, however, their relationships go back long before there was any hope for official recognition from the government or religion, some back to the 1940s and 1950s. Their stories are inspiring.

Tim Clausen and I have been in a longtime and long-distance friendship for more than twenty years. I met Tim via telephone when I lived in San Francisco and was publishing *White Crane Newsletter*, the gay men's spirituality journal. I personally experienced Tim's gentle interviewing style when he was working on a project exploring gay men's spirituality. I was one of several men he interviewed and eventually I published a couple of those interviews in *White Crane*.

I find the interviews in this collection to have the same perceptive and intimate quality that led me to publish the earlier interviews years ago. I hope you find them as enjoyable and revelatory as I did.

Bob Barzan
Modesto, California
12 January 2014

ACKNOWLEDGEMENTS

To restate a popular saying, it takes a village to write a book. Sometimes several villages. I was incredibly fortunate to have so many great people pitch in to assist in the slow, steady birth of *Love Together*.

From inception to finish, it was remarkable the way so many individuals appeared at just the right moments to offer encouragement, ideas, and assistance throughout the long, three-year gestation of this work.

My deep gratitude goes out to all who lent a helping hand. I would especially like to thank the following: Bob Barzan and Darrell Schramm each had excellent suggestions, which helped to refine and improve the interview questions. A longtime mentor and friend, Bob was also kind enough to pen the fine foreword. Readers Mary Lutz, Steve Franzen, Ellen Zipf, Harry Banzhaf, Evan Schmidt, and June Kurzon each read dozens of interviews and provided much-needed objectivity and many helpful suggestions.

Eric Marcoux, John McNeill, Brian McNaught, Larry Duplechan, Jack & George, Jason Warner, Kathy Schmidt, Brandon Best, Laurie Solomon, Jim Doran, Bob & Doris Laitinen, Steve Meyer, Kerry Heinze, Greg Lebrick, Ada & Phil Vogel, Bob Happach, Melinda Marsh, Elliot Czaplewski, Lisa Laham, Tom Sherbrook, Kinza Christenson, Beverly & Richard Weeden, and Bob Segedi all offered constructive ideas and encouragement.

Author Paul Boynton (*Begin With Yes*) explained to me in great detail why it makes so much sense these days to self-publish and helped steer me definitively in that direction. Since this book was produced on a shoestring budget, I profoundly appreciated the generous contributions made by friends Fred Hersch, Jim Maloney, Martin & Robert, Betsy Peterson, John Moore, Steve Franzen, and Marcos Montagnini, toward the editing and typesetting costs.

Special thanks to photographer Joel Benjamin for allowing me to use his magnificent photo of Willie and Greg as the ideal central image on the cover of *Love Together*. More of Joel's fine work can be found at www.joelbenjamin.com.

Big thanks to the many interviewing couples who sent me warm and wonderful photos of themselves—a number of these are featured prominently on the front cover—and to photographer Pamela Duncan for allowing me to include her terrific photo of Jason and deMarco. Thanks also to Three Birds Photography for the excellent Patrick and Fraser photo.

My very talented cousin Paul Westermann did a fantastic job on the cover art and was a real trooper in putting up with my endless questions and ideas. More of Paul's distinctive fine art can be found at http://www.redbubble.com/people/paulwestermann.

I'm very grateful to my friend Diane Weymier-Dodd for creating such a beautiful website for the book and also for giving my own site a much-needed makeover.

Thanks to photographer friend Rick Wood for taking the time this past January to snap the fine author photo.

Special thanks to writers Daniel Helminiak, Mark Matousak, Joe Kort, and Chris Glaser for their hearty recommendations of this work. I have greatly admired their own writings for years, and their strong affirmations of the material in *Love Together* pleased me more than I can say.

The one and only Kira Henschel of HenschelHAUS Publishing, www.henschelhausbooks.com, did the final editing and typesetting and was a godsend in helping me navigate the publishing process with her gentle wisdom and many years of experience.

Of course, without the many outstanding couples I was so fortunate to be able to interview for this project, this book wouldn't exist at all. Each of these wonderful men so well understood the purpose of this book: to address the need for healthy examples of committed, lasting, love relationships between men. I am deeply grateful to each couple for sharing their life experience so generously, for understanding how their own example might light the way for others to find encouragement and hope for their own journey.

A special thanks to my playful cat, Pepper, for napping frequently and endearingly on or near my lap throughout the slow process of writing this book.

Finally, I am especially grateful to my Higher Power for giving me both the idea for this book and the sustained enthusiasm needed to bring it into being. In addition to being a mountain of work, this entire project has been an extraordinarily wonderful learning experience. I hope it will make a positive difference in the lives of many.

Tim Clausen
Milwaukee, Wisconsin
November, 2014

PREFACE

Love Together is a decidedly unscientific work. You won't find any dry pronouncements here along the lines of "88.7% of couples polled said..." This author is not a scientist or a sociologist, but a simple, garden-variety jazz pianist. I am not a Ph. D. nor do I have a graduate degree.

What I do have are several decades worth of total inexperience in the realm of healthy, long-term love relationships. (There have been some good relationships of briefer duration.) Besides playing jazz, I'm fortunate to have been able to conduct hundreds of in-depth interviews with leading figures in the jazz world and elsewhere, including a humbling series of interviews I completed for sixteen families who lost loved ones in the September 11, 2001 disaster.

The interview process is for me a joy and I feel great respect for the importance of mankind's vast oral history/storytelling tradition. Combining this love for interviewing with a keen desire to learn more about the dynamics of longtime love relationships between men made the adventure of creating *Love Together* a natural and deeply compelling one for me.

Over the years, I've been both intrigued and mystified by certain longtime male couples I've met who appear to be extremely well matched, who seem to have this good, upbeat flow of energy between them. If, as author Kent Nerburn says, the key seems to be in choosing well, these pairs appear to have done just that.

I have often wondered, "Gee, how do they do it? Don't they get bored with one another? Run out of things to talk about? How do they keep things interesting in the bedroom, or did sex together as a couple go by the wayside long ago? How do they maintain harmony together for decades on end? Do they ever feel limited and stuck and miss their former freedom?"

Of course, not all men are interested in or inclined towards long-term relationships. Many men, gay and straight, prefer a variety of partners and relish the freedom of being single and not having to answer to anyone but themselves. It may be, as some have speculated, that there are two basic types of wiring in males, where some are naturally geared toward marriage and others are not. It is also likely that there is some overlap between these types, so that a man who prefers single life might fall deeply in love with a guy he finds himself wanting to make a life together with, and their love relationship may or may not also include a degree of negotiated openness to being sexual with others.

I find it surprising that nowadays, with the stunningly rapid rise in acceptance of gay and lesbian relationships, when same-sex marriage is so prominent in the American consciousness, that there is still such a noticeable lack of positive role models—healthy examples of longtime male couples—in books, film, and other media. Progress has certainly been made, but much more is still needed. I have known plenty of single gay men who are interested in finding a life partner who say, "I'd like to be in a healthy long-term relationship, but I really haven't a clue how they work for the men already in them..."

As wonderful as it is to see images of Elton John and his partner of many years in the media, how does their relationship actually work day to day? Singles, quite understandably, want to know things about longtime couples like: How did they meet? How did they know their partner was the right one for them? Were they sexual right away or did they take their time? How long did they wait before moving in together? How do they keep from taking each other for granted? Have they ever sought out counseling together, and was it helpful for them? Did they ever want to end the relationship and how did they get through that? Do they communicate about absolutely everything together or not?

Using a simple analogy, if one is interested in baking a cake, it is very helpful to read actual cake recipes and to learn in detail what kinds of recipes other bakers have used successfully. Just seeing pictures of beautiful cakes and hearing others talk about how wonderful and special their own cake happens to be is, of course, not as helpful.

And that's where this book comes in. *Love Together* presents nearly two dozen in-depth, real-life portraits of healthy long-term love relationships between men, which I hope will provide honest inspiration and encouragement to single gay men who are interested in finding a life partner. While this volume is my personal offering in the genre, many more books of this type are still needed. Certainly there is also a place for the female counterpart to this book, which I will leave to some enterprising woman to produce. She will find a good template for it in these pages.

It is my hope that *Love Together* will be genuinely helpful to established gay couples, and also educational for non-gay people who wish to better understand how longtime love relationships between men actually work day to day, to discover in what ways gay partnerships are similar to straight ones and in what ways they may differ.

It has been a labor of love and a great privilege to bring this book to fruition. The remarkable couples I was able to interview and get to know became my teachers and mentors throughout this journey. Each in their own way inspired me through their generous and open sharing and through the humanity of their example. I have learned a great deal in the process, and if it happens that I am someday fortunate enough to meet the right guy for me, it will be nice to be able to bring along all the helpful things I've learned from these admirable men to my own experience of love together.

Whether a future husband comes along or not, I'm truly delighted to make this book available to readers everywhere. If through reading it, even a handful of individuals are helped to experience more love in their lives, all my work will have been more than worthwhile.

INTRODUCTION

Henry Ford once famously quipped, "The air is full of ideas." So it is. One December afternoon in 2011, while outdoors stretching my pale Wisconsin legs, the idea for this book came drifting down from a bright ribbon of cirrus cloud and perched atop my shoulder.

It whispered in my ear, "*Hey, you! T. Clausen! I've got this big, overarching project for you to do, which will take up large amounts of your free time for the next several years. It will be a book of interviews with dozens of geographically diverse male couples you've never met or heard of before who have been together for decades, on how they communicate in a healthy way and manage to love each other and not kill each other. Your planet seems to be evolving lately in terms of understanding same-sex love relationships and could really use a book like this. It may help educate a bunch of people, and you're just the guy to do it. This project will give you something productive to do besides working full-time, exercising, meditating, and playing piano. You might even meet someone yourself through this process you adore who really loves you. Or you might not. When can you start?*"

When can I what? Seriously? The presumption! OK, I loved the idea. Especially the part about meeting someone I adore, and I'd always known in my heart that Jake Gyllenhaal and I would make a totally happening couple. Fortunately, I was then in between large, overarching projects and I do feel passionately about contributing meaningfully to the world, too. But before diving willy-nilly into such a grand adventure without a road map or compass, some general market research and deep soul-searching would need to take place. If it turned out that I couldn't be one hundred percent on board with this thing then I would simply take a pass, and my insistent, airborne friend could go find himself another writer.

Three factors brought about my "yes":

1. A chorus of thumbs-ups from friends;

2. The stunning lack of books in print on the subject of longtime male couples and their relationships and,

3. Some oddly persistent enthusiasm which kept welling up within me about the concept ever since my celestial visitor had first whispered it in my ear.

All right. Okay then... Onward! Now to just find those dozens of geographically diverse male couples I had never met or heard of before to do the interviews with. But where? How? Should I consult the master clairvoyants at *The Psychic Hotline*? Get the Oiuji Board out of mothballs? Clearly this was going to require a mountain of networking on my part, and an equal amount of blind faith that the right doors would open for me along the way. (They have.)

Luckily for me, I know some wonderful gay men around the country, and I had previously interviewed writer Larry Duplechan and had communicated as well with author/theologian John McNeill a number of times. So I already knew some great guys in long-term relationships whom I could ask. But before getting too far ahead of myself, it would be necessary to get clear on certain definitions...

What constitutes a longtime couple? I decided early on that ten years together would be a good starting point for the couples I wanted to interview. Though arbitrary, I reasoned that any couple who had cleared a decade together had weathered enough life experience to be able to impart some helpful wisdom from the journey to others. Certainly twenty, thirty, forty, fifty, or sixty years together would be even better, and I'd want to include the entire spectrum from ten years on up.

I also decided early on to only include pairs who have reasonably healthy and functional relationships. We've all met couples who bicker frequently and who seem to have a surplus of negativity between them. Those were definitely not the types I was seeking. ("OK, next question!

Which heavy household objects do you prefer to club each other with?") Although I understand that no perfect individuals or couples exist, the pairs on the healthiest end of the spectrum were definitely my demographic of choice.

I strove to find maximum variety and diversity in my interviewees regarding specifics like age, geographic location, racial/ethnic heritage, occupation, monogamy/non-monogamy status, spiritual-religious views, married or non-married, and with or without children. As wonderful as it would have been to interview every longtime male couple in North America, I just did not have enough vacation days to do so, so I scaled back my sights a bit.

Ultimately, I ended up completing just over one hundred interviews and was fortunate to get to know and work with a terrifically varied and exceptional group of couples. My guys (I've adopted them all) range in age from early thirties to early nineties, and are predominately Caucasian, Hispanic, African-American, or Asian. Several mixed race couples were included. In a few of the couples, there was a decade or two difference in the ages of the partners.

More than a few of my interviewees are fathers who had children either through a prior marriage, through adoption, or through surrogacy. One couple chanced upon an abandoned baby in the New York subway system and adopted the boy when no one came forward to claim him. Many of the couples have married, while others still wait for the right to do so legally in their state. Several pairs had no interest in marriage at all, if only because it would be financially disadvantageous for them to do so.

Most all the men I interviewed make their home in the United States, although two couples hail from Canada, while another pair resides in Costa Rica. I spoke at length with couples in New York, California, Texas, Alaska, Wisconsin, Massachusetts, Kentucky, Florida, Iowa, Oregon, New Jersey, Illinois, Vermont, Washington, Minnesota, New Mexico, and Connecticut. The greatest number of interviewees by far were in California and Texas.

The couples varied widely in terms of how they address the issue of sexual monogamy. Strict exclusivity works best for many, while other couples enjoy varying degrees of sexual openness. It's not at all uncommon for male couples to change their place along the open/closed continuum—sometimes several times—over the years, so that a couple might start out being sexually exclusive, then later on open the relationship up to being sexual with others, and still later opt for exclusivity once again.

My interviewees also varied tremendously regarding spirituality, and their stances ranged from strict atheism to agnosticism to more eclectic, New Age approaches to yoga to 12-Step spirituality to actively participating in Buddhism, Judaism, or various branches of Christianity. Daily prayer and meditation were important practices for several interviewees. Many of the couples continue to be strongly altruistic and are devoted to helping others, often rendering prodigies of service to their communities.

How did I find my interviewees? As previously mentioned, I already knew a few of the men who, when asked, generously agreed to interview with me. One East Coast couple, who met years ago at the gay fathers group I ran, interviewed with me. Active networking was especially productive in finding quality candidates, and high school classmates, various friends, and people I know from all walks of life introduced me to family members, friends, neighbors, and coworkers. Facebook also proved to be extremely helpful.

While on vacation, a casual conversation with the owner of an out-of-state health food store led to my being introduced to a wonderful Connecti-cut couple who have an interview included in Section Two of this book. Of course, not everyone I asked to interview said "yes." For instance, my attempts to contact Elton John, Neil Patrick Harris, and George Takei went nowhere, although I'm satisfied that I at least made the effort. As they say, if you don't ask the answer is always no. Anyway, they had their chance!

The refreshingly high degree of candor I was able to get in these interviews was truly gratifying. Each interviewee understood how his own honestly shared experience could be uniquely encouraging—life-saving even—for young, single men hungry for positive role models and healthy examples of enduring love relationships. My decision to offer full or partial anonymity to the couples played a huge and helpful role in this process.

As a longtime member of a 12-Step community where anonymity is held sacred, I early on decided to give all of my couples any level of anonymity they wished regarding their interviews. This approach opened some otherwise closed doors to me, and gave interviewing couples a greater level of comfort with the process, allowing them to share more freely, when they knew upfront that I wouldn't be using their actual names.

Many couples were totally fine with my including their full names. Others preferred I use only their first names. For those preferring complete anonymity I have changed their names altogether, and in a few cases also changed some minor details at their request. Incorporating anonymity into the interview process from the start helped make *Love Together* a far better book than it might otherwise have been.

Rather than interviewing both partners in a couple simultaneously, I chose to interview each partner separately. This approach gave each individual uninterrupted time and space to answer each interview question fully and, in my opinion, resulted in more complete and satisfying interviews. I have found that in speaking with both partners in a couple simultaneously, it is often easy for one partner to talk over the other or do most of the sharing. Often one partner is simply more extroverted, while the other is more introverted. But when each partner has the space to reflect without interruptions, it is easier for that person to really focus and share his own unique experience and perspective.

One-on-one has always been my format of choice when doing interviews, and it worked well in interviewing the many dozens of couples I spoke with for *Love Together*. The two-year process of interviewing the men for this book was both a pleasure and an honor, due to the fact that the couples I interviewed were all so consistently exceptional and interesting. I truly could not have asked for a finer group of guys.

Since I am not an Evelyn Wood graduate and have not yet mastered shorthand, I recorded all of the interviews on cassette tape. Later, they were transcribed the old-fashioned way by hand, which is both extremely tedious and time-consuming. (I actually enjoy the transcribing process. Maybe I just don't get out enough.)

While doing the transcriptions, I took myself and the interview questions out of the transcripts, so that what remains is a conversational, stream of consciousness piece on the part of each interviewee. I really like this approach and have used it for years in all the jazz interviewing I have done. Every effort has been made to keep each interview completely authentic to the voice of the narrator, although small details like grammar and sentence structure have been edited occasionally for improved clarity and readability. You will find the list of the main interview questions I asked the interviewees included separately in this book.

As each interview took place on a particular date, each one is also, in a sense, a time capsule. A given couple may have been together twenty-eight years at the time of our interview, and may speak, for instance, of looking forward to their twenty-ninth anniversary coming up in October. Today, with the passage of time, that couple may now actually be in their thirtieth year together.

For simplicity's sake, I have kept the original number of years together as stated in each interview in place. The only exception I made to this rule was for Eric and Eugene, who were together just shy of sixty years when I first interviewed them, and who did make their sixtieth anniversary soon thereafter. So, the number of years any couple had been together at the time of our interviews was changed only once for this book, to honor Eric and Eugene's reaching the remarkable milestone of six decades together.

These interviews are love stories that have weathered the tests of time. A number of the men I interviewed experienced major health crises and went through life-threatening illnesses, so these are also stories of endurance and survival. Two of the men I interviewed are caring for partners now in the late stages of Alzheimer's. One said, "Alzheimer's or not, I don't find that my feelings about Vince have changed throughout his illness. He has changed radically and is literally a fraction of the person he used to be—incoherent, incontinent, needs to be fed—and throughout the illness, all the things I loved about him sort of drained out of his feet. He no longer recognizes me. His intelligence, his humor, his education, his culture, and any memories of his life and what we shared are all gone. He has no capacity to communicate. But who he is as a person is still there, and so that's how I love Vince and that's why I'm dedicated to taking care of him." This is real love in action, and it is easy to assume that, had the shoes been reversed, the afflicted partner would be there just as solidly for his husband. Several months after that interview, Vince passed away, and my interviewee is now beginning a new chapter of life in his late fifties.

Since all the various stages of adult life together are represented here, the same event might mean something entirely different to a given couple, depending upon which stage of life they are in. For two lovers together a decade and now getting married in their early thirties, marriage is an entirely different affair than it is for a couple getting married after fifty years together. Now in their fifty-seventh year as a couple, Tom and Ron recently married in Palm Springs. Tom shared with me, "After fifty-seven years, marriage is just a formality and a way of protecting one another. The clerk was not very happy with me when she said, 'In sickness and in health..,' and I just had to laugh. It was like we have already been there. When she said, 'May you have a long and happy life together..,' I laughed again. She wanted to know what was so funny, and I said, 'At eighty-four and eighty-five, how much time do you think we have left?' My dark sense of humor, I guess. But we have made all the arrangements, cremation services, Columbarium, Celebration of Life, trust, and wills. While we were making arrangements at the mortuary, the guy asked what kind of box we want our ashes in. I picked a brass box with name and dates. Then he asked Ron, who said he would take the cardboard box.

I looked at Ron and said, 'You are NOT going to be next to me in a cardboard box...'. The look on the guy's face making the arrangements was really funny. Needless to say, Ron is also going to be in a brass box."

These are typical issues and concerns for couples in the winter of life. For a young couple getting married in their thirties, huge, promising vistas still stretch out before them; they may be brand new parents, fondly envisioning the day when they can bounce their first grandchild on their knee. Or to a twenty-year-old, whose longest love relationship has been only three weeks, ten years with a partner sounds like an eternity. A couple together thirty-five years may tell you that they were really just beginning to hit their stride at the ten-year mark. It's all, as they say, relative. Life's successive seasons find us at different places in our lives, and each one offers it's own unique tapestry of opportunities, rewards, sorrows, and joys.

As far as we know, every love relationship has a beginning and an end point. Though it's certainly possible that both life and love may continue on beyond this realm, we cannot really know for sure. But to sign onto the privilege of a shared life and deep love with another human being is to enter love's mysterious terrain, where along with the bliss of union is the pain of separation and loss.

As healthy couples get on in years, they begin to think about the prospect of losing each other. Contemplating loss sharpens our perception of the preciousness of those we love and of the beauty of each moment we are given together. Many of the couples I interviewed, especially those who have been together for many decades, talk freely to each other about what it will be like to lose each other. Johnny Dapper, a gentle man who had been with his partner sixty-five years, talked about what it was like to lose his husband and about how he is coping with his immense grief.

One of the most remarkable and touching interviews I have ever done was the three-part follow-up interview with Eric Marcoux, after Eugene Woodworth, his lover of sixty years, died. I had been fortunate to have interviewed Eugene a year prior, and his superb interview is also included in this collection. A Buddhist teacher and a man of profound reflection, Eric shared with me openly what their last weeks and days and minutes together were like and what it's been like for him to carry on after Eugene's passing. This magnificent interview is also included in the book, and it offers Eric's stunningly articulate and unguarded sharing of his experience of love's loss. It is an extraordinary high point of this collection.

Still it is playfulness, joy, and a profound zest for living and loving that most characterize these pieces. Humor is abundant throughout. Even Eric and Eugene had a sublimely funny moment in their final minutes together; one could not have asked for a more perfect parting than the two longtime lovers shared that December afternoon.

A much newer couple, Rich and Tommy, had been together for several years when they decided to move ahead with their plan to have children via surrogacy. Rich shared: "When Tommy and I met our surrogate, we met her husband as well, who was ex-military, and we were a little concerned about how he would receive all this and deal with a gay couple wanting to have a baby, and using his wife's womb to do it. One of the questions that came up was about 'What is everyone's family support situation for going through this process?' He said, 'I haven't told my family yet but I'm very excited to, to let them know that Joyce is pregnant again, but that the baby's not mine, and it's also not hers…' Needless to say, that broke the ice quite nicely and helped set the tone for our first meeting."

Rich and Tommy are now the proud parents of two happy and lively boys. The couples I interviewed clearly relish being together and insist on enjoying life with each other, one day at a time.

One of the toughest tasks for me in putting this book together was having to choose which two dozen interviews from the original one hundred and two to include. Like being asked, "Which eight teeth are your favorite?" They're all quite wonderful, thank you. A different writer may have chosen to weave excerpts from all of the interviews into a single narrative, another perfectly valid approach. Personally, I love complete interviews and find them to be more satisfying to read than a patchwork of excerpts. Though I had initially planned to include forty interviews in the book, I changed course when one of my readers said, "It's too many. Go with twenty-five to thirty. Less is more." She was right, to my chagrin.

As much I would love to include all of the interviews, readers still need to be able to physically lift the book, so that idea was out. But choosing two dozen of the most representative pieces was really, really hard to do. I felt a bit like Sophie, having to choose which child to keep. I did the very best I could in choosing *la creme de la crème*, though there was an awful lot of *la creme* to choose from. Perhaps a volume two will be in order...

How to sequence the interviews in the book? It seemed to me that the most sensible approach was to group the interviews according to the number of years couples have been together. So Section One is comprised of pairs who have been together anywhere from ten to twenty years. Section Two features couples together between twenty and thirty years. Couples who have been together from thirty to forty years are in Section Three, followed by sections featuring couples together between forty to fifty, fifty to sixty, and sixty to seventy years. I strove to sequence the interviews within each section, as well, for maximum variety and diversity.

You will find included in *Love Together* interviews with both partners in only one couple, while the rest of the interviews feature only one of the partners in a given couple. Not surprisingly, each section has its own special feel and flavor. There was an additional good reason for sequencing the interviews according to number of years together: each section truly builds upon the preceding one and, generally speaking, the content of the interviews becomes deeper and richer the more years a couple has been together. All of these interviews, however, are superb.

How extraordinary it is to see the American landscape changing so rapidly these days for gay people and around issues like same-sex marriage. A tipping point has clearly been reached. Though gay people and gay couples have been around forever, it must seem to some as though there is a new human species suddenly on the scene. Virtually every other day, it seems that another state is joining the modern age and throwing out its antiquated marriage ban. It is all a bit dizzying, wonderfully so. Some of the interviewees in this book, who spoke about not being able to marry legally in their state, now can. Couples in Illinois who were domestic partners at the time of our interviews have since been grandfathered in as married partners. Although there is still much progress to be made, particularly in the stubborn South, those heel-dragging states will come around, too. It is only a matter of time. Love is winning out, as it always does.

These are truly exciting times to be living in, and I'm deeply grateful to the countless gay and lesbian pioneers who very selflessly laid the groundwork for the monumental social advances we are seeing today. Some of their stories appear in these pages. You will find a truly astonishing amount of long-term relationship experience among the interviewees in this volume. If one were to tally up the number of years each of these nearly two dozen interviewees have been together with their partner, that sum equates to an astounding seven hundred years—seven centuries—of collective experience sharing life and love with a companion. That's amazing.

To say that there is a vast amount of real-life wisdom present in these pages is an understatement. I hope you will find the interviews with all of these remarkable men to be as inspiring and educational as I have. They made the long journey of researching and writing *Love Together* a joyous one.

A READING SUGGESTION:

Because the interviews in this book are quite substantial pieces, readers may find it helpful to limit their reading to, say, three or four interviews per sitting, returning again on another occasion to take up another set. Methodically moving through the material in this manner will allow for adequate time to reflect upon the rich array of ideas and insights found throughout *Love Together*. If you are naturally geared toward speed-reading or simply enjoy your coffee extra strong and by the gallon, by all means sprint ahead, though you may miss some good things along the way!

THE INTERVIEW QUESTIONS

I knew up-front that if I wanted to get really good interviews, I would need to come up with a really good set of questions. After putting together the basic list, several friends offered valuable suggestions and clarifications. One or two additional questions were added later. For instance, after completing the first dozen or so interviews, I realized that including a question about how finances are handled would be a worthy addition, so that was added to the mix. An earlier question asking if interviewees regularly associate with other long-term couples was dropped. Many other additional questions arose spontaneously during the course of each interview as well.

I chose not to give any of the interviewees the questions prior to the time of our interview, as I wanted responses that would be as fresh and unrehearsed as possible. This turned out to be a good approach. The questions proved to be a good springboard for each interview to take off in refreshing directions and to take on its own unique shape and color. Virtually all the men I interviewed said afterwards that they found the questions to be thought-provoking and interesting, and the experience of doing the interview to be an enjoyable and worthwhile one. No one compared the questions or the interview experience to a root canal, which, of course, was a relief to me.

Here are the primary questions I asked each interviewee during the interviews:

1. How many years have you been together and what were your ages when you met?

2. What was going on for you at the time that you met and how did the two of you meet? Did you hit it off right away?

3. How long did it take for you to become sexual together?

4. Are you monogamous/sexually exclusive? If not, how do you incorporate sex with others into your relationship, and if so, do you have temptations to be with other men and how do you deal with those?

5. What is your definition of love, particularly as it pertains to your relationship?

6. Are you still sexual together? If so, how do you keep it from being routine? If not, why not?

7. In what ways are you affectionate with each other, and how do you express your love for one another?

8. Do you sleep together or separately?

9. In what ways do you try not to take your partner for granted and do you succeed at that?

10. Has your love deepened over time? How do you cultivate it?

11. How do you balance time and space together and apart? Do you ever feel crowded?

12. What has been your biggest communication hurdle?

13. How do you handle conflict and disagreement?

14. Have you ever sought counseling or therapy together?

15. Have you ever been close to ending the relationship and how did you get through it?

16. What is your spiritual path or religion, if any, and how does that impact your relationship?

17. Do you both have a prominent sense of humor and do you laugh often?

18. How often do you surprise each other?

19. How has being together helped you to grow as a person?

20. Would you marry if you could legally? Why or why not?

21. Have you ever considered becoming parents?

22. Do you pool funds or keep separate accounts? How are finances handled?

23. What do you see as being the key or keys to a healthy long-term relationship?

24. What keeps your relationship vital and growing?

25. What advice would you give to someone who aspires to be in a healthy long term relationship? This could be anything, such as how do you meet the right person, etc...

26. Do you feel that you were somehow destined to meet your partner, or that it was just luck and random chance?

THE INTERVIEWS

SECTION I:

COUPLES TOGETHER
TEN TO TWENTY YEARS

CHAPTER 1

KURT AND DEAN

"One of the advantages that Dean and I have is that we were both married to women, so we are both accustomed to having to compromise. We both had children so we understand that sometimes you sacrifice for the people you love and put yourself in second place. I think that's helped our relationship because we already had those skills in place when we became a couple."

* * * * *

Two fathers formerly married to women, Kurt and Dean met at a leather bar in Dallas. Dean was for many years a Baptist minister, while Kurt worked as a corporate executive. They fell in love with Costa Rica on a vacation stay and after building their dream home along the coast, have since retired there.

Kurt — (Dean)

When Dean and I met eleven years ago, I was fifty-three and he was forty-five. We had both been raised as good Southern Baptist boys, and what good Southern Baptist boys do is to grow up, go to college, get a good job, and then marry a good woman. Then you have children, and later you retire and enjoy your grandchildren. Anything that deviates from that path is suspect, and if you deviate *really* far from that, you run the risk of losing your family, your social standing, and your soul.

That's what we grew up with, and denial being the wonderful thing it is, I had convinced myself that my desires were just a phase and that I just needed to find a good woman and have kids, so I did that. When my kids were small I figured out, "OK, this is not going away, and this really is the problem..." The corollary to the Southern Baptist upbringing is that I was not raised to leave a woman with two small children, so I just decided to tough it out, which was very difficult. In the end what triggered the divorce was her alcoholism; she was and is an intractable alcoholic.

We separated in December of 2000, eleven months before our divorce was final. My divorce attorney at the time had told me, "Do not date. Do not go out. Do not play the gay card until the divorce is final..." I met Dean before the divorce was final. I had been sneaking out a bit, and there was a leather bar in Dallas that I was curious about but had never been to. Now bear in mind that at that time I had been living and working in a town of about eighty thousand in East Texas, deep in the Bible Belt, so I was VERY closeted.

A friend I had been seeing was supposed to come visit me on Memorial Day weekend, on May 25th, and called at the last minute to cancel. I was in a little, crappy apartment in the middle of the divorce, wondering if I was going to keep my job or if my kids would ever talk to me again, so I decided to go out, just to be with the tribe. I went to this leather bar dressed in a polo shirt and jeans and wearing some cologne, which was totally inappropriate for a leather bar. So here I am, first time in the leather bar and it was 8:30, obviously too early to be there, and there was nothing going on. There were a few guys there who weren't really attractive to me, so I'd just decided, "OK, I'm just going to finish this drink and go..."

Well, somehow Dean came in and got by me without my seeing him come in, but this very large, very hairy man in butt-less chaps walked by, and this voice to my left said, "There's something you don't see every day!"

I turned and looked and my first thought was, "Oh, my gosh, this guy's really cute. Quick, think of something cool to say..."

I was tongue-tied and couldn't talk and I just clammed up. But then after another minute, a cute guy walked by, and Dean said, "I saw you looking at that one, too," and then I was able to talk. We began to chat and then my drink ran out, and he bought me another drink. Then he said, "Do you want to come home with me?," and of course, all my instructions from my attorney and my own self-cautioning told me, "This is crazy! *Don't* do this!" But I did; I went home with him.

That was the Friday night of Memorial Day weekend, and we spent the whole night having sex and talking and having sex and talking. I really felt like Dean was a special person, but by Saturday morning my better judgment settled in and I was telling myself, "OK. You're in the middle of a divorce, your attorney told you not to do this, this could cost you a lot of money, this is really stupid, and you need to get of here..." So I left.

He gave me his phone number and said, "Will you come back? We can have dinner tonight...," and I said, "Yes, I will," though I wasn't sure I would. I went home to this little apartment, which was the first place I grabbed when I moved out of the house, when I left my ex-wife. It happened to be in a complex with a lot of East Indian people who cook with curry, so here I am on a Saturday afternoon in this apartment smelling of curry, feeling sorry for myself. I called Dean and said, "I'm coming back," and I went back and basically never left.

Then we went to church. He attended Cathedral of Hope in Dallas, which still may be the largest predominately gay and lesbian church in the country, and he asked me to go to church with him. I said I would, and I knew about Cathedral of Hope because my soon-to-be ex-wife's hairdresser went there, though I never thought I'd go there. So here I am walking into this church literally with one hand over my face, hoping no one recognized me, in the middle of a divorce —the nadir of my adult life—holding hands with this cute guy, and the greeter at the door shook my hand and said, "Welcome home." With that religious background, I started to cry and I think I cried throughout that whole service.

That was Sunday. By Monday morning, we'd spent another night together and we were just talking, and all of a sudden, it just got very quiet.

I asked Dean, "What are you thinking?"

He said, "I'm having a hard time not telling you I love you."

I said, "I'm having the same problem," and I had been, because I'd been feeling that. Yet the little voice in my head was saying, "This is stupid. Don't you dare say those words!" But that's how it happened, and it was pretty much love at first sight. I don't recommend that, as I don't think love at first sight makes sense for most people. It was lucky that in our case, it worked. So three months later, we moved in together and we've been together ever since.

I love Dean because I'm a better Kurt when I'm with him. I can't imagine not being with him, and I don't have any question in my mind that we're going to be together until one of us dies. I try always to remind myself about the ways that he balances my weaknesses and the great gifts that he brings to our relationship, which I really value; things like his optimism and his sociability and his patience. I try to notice those things every day and be grateful that I have someone in my life who's that way, because I can be a little melancholy, a little antisocial, and a little pessimistic.

I've certainly grown a lot because of this relationship. Dean expects me to get closer to my potential as a human being, and I love him so much I don't want to disappoint him in that! When he tells me I'm being pessimistic or I'm being too controlling or that I'm having much more anger than what the situation calls for, I tend to listen to him and to pay attention.

Eleven years into our relationship, sex can sometimes become routine, and we've struggled a bit with that. We look at a lot of videos together. We have negotiated a degree of openness in our relationship and we prefer to play together. Initially, I thought everything had to be sexually exclusive, and anything that wasn't, was not OK with me.

It took us several years to get to the negotiated point that we are at. Somewhere in there I read an interesting book called *The Second Skin*, which reads like a sociology text, and one of the things that the author says in it is that fewer gay male relationships are purely monogamous, and that most successful gay couples negotiate a point somewhere along that continuum between completely monogamous and completely open.

It took a while for me to get OK with that, but I am now. We are closer to the completely monogamous end of the spectrum than the completely open end. I do tend to think that monogamy is the exception and not the rule. I think that most men, given the hormonal environment we live in and what we deal with being males—and this is true whether you're gay or straight—most of us are not cut out to be monogamous.

A straight friend of mine once said to me, "I think all women want to have a home and a nest and children, and all men just want an endless stream of attractive sex partners." There's definitely some universal truth in that. It's one of the issues that I had to come to terms with, both for myself and in my relationship with Dean. Every gay couple negotiates a position somewhere along the monogamous/open spectrum, and I believe they have to do that if it's going to work long-term. How you deal with it depends upon what path your particular relationship takes.

Sex was great early on, and I know a lot of couples start out that way— we certainly did—and it's wonderful. But there are long periods of time during the day when you have to talk to the other person, and if you don't like them and you can't be happy and at peace in their presence when you're not having sex, then to me that would be a big warning sign. I've often said over the years that sex isn't everything, but it affects everything. So if the relationship is great but the sex is not, that would be another big red flag for me, because such a relationship is far less likely to succeed long-term.

One of the things we do is that we're very physically demonstrative with each other. We hug and touch a lot, Dean more than me probably. We tell each other many times a day, "I love you," or "I love to be with you." One of the things we made kind of a joke about in the wedding ceremony that we had is that we've always said to each other, "I love you more." "Oh, no, no. I love *you* more!" "I love you the *most*." We say that a lot, as well as things like, "You're my best friend. I love being with you." Or when we're apart, we will talk on the phone four or five times a day. I think that's important. We sleep together always and are big cuddlers. The only nights we've spent apart since we met were if one of us was gone on business or to visit family or something like that.

I'm the sort of person who's OK with being alone, and in fact some-times I find it soothing to be home alone with my own thoughts or reading something I'm interested in or playing with the dog. Dean likes to be together 24/7, but for me, I need a little time apart. We've never vacationed apart; we won't do that. We're apart some during the day, doing our different things, and always together at night.

We've always both been somewhat adventurous and we love to travel. We came to Costa Rica on vacation and fell in love. We love tropical climates and beaches and the ocean and we fell in love with the geography. The people are lovely, taxes are low, and the pace of life is slower. It just checked all the boxes on our list of places where we might retire, and over a six year period we found a building site and started planning a home and began moving towards that.

In 2007, I got a golden parachute from a major U.S. corporation as part of a hostile takeover play by another company, so we started building the house in 2008. It took a year and a half, and we've been here ever since. Where we live in Costa Rica has been a destination for gay Costa Ricans for sixty years, and it was discovered by Americans and Canadians in the 1980s. So there's a very large ex-pat community here, and we have a large group of friends.

You really have to be a little adventurous to do what we did, so all of our friends down here are quirky and adventurous and interesting. We spend a lot of time with friends and we have a lot more straight friends here than we had in Dallas. They're quirky and adventurous and interesting, too, so we get a lot of support and social nourishment from our friends here. The toughest part about moving here was that we had great friends in Dallas, and we still miss them. We work very hard to stay connected with about a dozen good friends there, all gay and lesbian couples. But as far as leaving the United States, particularly since 2008, when it's such a tense, depressing place, we don't miss that. When we go back there, nobody's happy and everyone's tense. Costa Rica twice has been named the happiest country on Earth, so we're at peace here, even though the highways and grocery stores are better in the states!

I don't think we've ever been close to ending the relationship. We've had some pretty strenuous arguments in previous years, which had to do with Dean's desire to be a little more sexually open that I was. We had some pretty big fights over that. We've had some pretty big fights over the years, but usually just over small things.

I've told him on a couple of occasions, "I've had enough of this. I don't like how we fight. I'm not going to live the rest of my life like this, and I'm leaving!" And he just says, "No, you're not. We're together forever. This is silly. Let's talk through it." But we've never really confronted the kind of a crisis that would cause us to think seriously about ending the relationship.

This may be characteristic of gay male relationships, especially if you've both been married to women before and you're both used to being husbands and daddies and fathers: it's natural for you both to want to take control. One thing we learned early on is that we can't both work on the same exact project, because we do things differently and then we fight over how we're doing it. It's really silly, but—for instance—if we work in the yard, one has to mow the grass and one has to trim the shrubs. We can't both work on the grass and on the shrubs. It just leads to fights, and when we fight we escalate and we yell at each other, which is hurtful.

One of the things we've struggled with is that after we do have a big fight, in five minutes Dean's ready to kiss and make up and everything's fine, where I'm like, "Wait a minute! You said all this stuff that's still going around in my head... I'm not ready for that." Just the difference in how we process fights has been a struggle. Usually I have to let it roll around in my head and then come to the realization that it was really ridiculous, it was nothing, and I love this person and I'm not going anywhere.

We've been in counseling together more than once. In the early years, it had to do with the monogamy versus non-monogamy question, but once that got resolved, it hasn't been an issue. We've been to counseling on two or three occasions. We have some friends who have been together sixteen years who unfortunately are going through a breakup because one of them insists, "Well, this is who I am and I'm not going to change. If you have a problem with it, it's your problem." We've never been that way.

Although our fights can be a little heated, we've always settled down afterwards and looked inside ourselves to see, "OK, how did I contribute to that and how can I not do that again?" It's hard to change. We still do some of the things that drive each other crazy that we've been doing for eleven years, but maybe less so than we used to. He'll say to me, "You're doing that thing again...," and I can say that to him, too, and that helps get us back on an even keel.

We laugh a lot. Dean makes me laugh all the time. We always look for the humor in everything, and humor is a great part of our lives. He has a very unique laugh, a very infectious laugh. One of the great things about Dean is that he's just a cheerful person. He wakes up happy. I can count on one hand the number of times in eleven years I've seen him down in the dumps or depressed, and it usually had to do with something his kids had done or said to him in the early years. He's a naturally upbeat person; he drives me crazy sometimes! I often tell friends, "He pulls me up out of the dumps, and I keep his feet on the ground so he doesn't just float away into the clouds."

Dean's also a big one for gifts and presents. It may just be a small thing, but he always has a surprise that way. One of the most fun things I can recall—we'd been together a couple of years then—I told him that I thought men in uniform were really hot. So one day I come home from work, and he had somehow gone to the Goodwill store and put together this complete admiral's uniform, and when I opened the door, there was this admiral standing there, and he started giving me orders... It was great. I loved it!

Barking the orders at me, and of course that led to some really great sex. Every Friday, he gives me a "Happy Friday" card. This has gone on for eleven and a half years. It's almost every Friday and typically it's a card with some hunky guy who's nude or almost nude, and he gets the ones that are blank so he can write his own message, and those usually have some-thing to do with what's going on in our life right now, and how much he loves me... I have shoe boxes full of these cards that I've saved. That's another way that he's spontaneous and he still does those. My husband reminds me all over again what a blessing he is to me and how much I love him.

The day after the 2004 election, when George Bush was elected for the first time, but it was his second term, I called in sick and stayed in bed all day. Afterwards, I just got up and told Dean, "You know what? Screw him. Let's have a big old gay wedding right here in Dallas, Texas!" So we did. We had a hundred and eighty-five people. The senior pastor at that time at Cathedral of Hope married us, and we had a religious ceremony. Dean's mother and her best friend, who's also a widow, walked Dean down the aisle. My son walked me down the aisle. It was at a point in things where our daughters chose not to attend. So we had a religious ceremony and then we went upstairs and had a sit-down dinner for one hundred eight-five people, with a bar and a seven-piece live band. The best party we've ever had!

We have both become suspicious of organized religion and very suspicious of the mainstream Christian church. I don't see much that pertains to the teachings of Christ in the mainstream Christian church in America these days. We remain very spiritual and we do go to Cathedral of Hope whenever we're in Dallas and we watch their services online many Sundays. We feel a deep connection to that church and that group of Christians. We talk about God a lot. Things will happen in our lives and we'll say, "That was a God thing."

Dean in particular has a big faith that everything will turn out OK, because God is watching out for us. There is no tolerant Christian church where we live, which is one of the things we miss, so we don't go to church here. We've both done a lot of reading about Christianity and homosexuality and have no doubts that it's the way we were made, and that it's part of the overall diversity of normal human experience. We don't think God hates us or that we're going to hell, and we've had discussions about whether there is a hell or not.

I have a Fundamentalist sister who told me she thought being gay is a weakness, much like alcoholism or drug addiction, and that it could be overcome with prayer, and that they would always love me. But should I ever find myself in a relationship, that person would never be welcome in their home. When she said that to me, she knew I was with Dean. I said, "Unfortunately that means I've been in your home for the last time, and that's sad." She said, "It makes me sad too." I've never been in her home again. They met Dean at my son's wedding, but they refused to meet him after that point. Their loss.

Dean and I really merged everything financially from the beginning. As far as monthly income and monthly expenses, we've had one checking account for years. When I got parachuted out, a lot of that went into a brokerage account, which is not a joint account. We went though a whole legal rigmarole to get things set up so that we can be protected. We have wills, we have advance directives, we have medical power of attorney for each other, we have legal, full power of attorney for each other. We have a document that gives each other the right to make decisions about disposal of remains after death. We spent probably five to eight thousand dollars to try to approximate the same protections Brittany Spears had when she was married for fifty-five hours! So when we die, it all goes into a trust, which the surviving partner is beneficiary of until he dies, and then it goes to the children.

One of the advantages Dean and I have is that we were both married to women, so we are both accustomed to having to compromise. We both had children, so we understand that sometimes you sacrifice for the people you love and put yourself in second place. I think that's helped our relationship because we already had those skills in place when we became a couple. One of the issues the friends I mentioned earlier who are breaking up have struggled with is that one of the partners was married and has children, while the other one was never married and doesn't have children. So when it comes time that the kids need some money or a little help with college tuition, they've had some knock-down, drag-out fights over that, because the one can't understand why you would give money to a kid who should have more sense and should manage better and should be more independent... We already had the skills to deal with those kinds of conflicts.

I don't think that everyone should necessarily have a partner. We have some single friends who just seem to struggle with being in a relationship. It seems that everyone has to decide what it is they want and what they're willing to give up to have that. I don't necessarily recommend that people do what Dean and I did, which was jump in too quickly. On one hand, I do believe in love at first sight, and we did have that, so I know it happens. On the other hand, it's probably the exception. I think if you're looking at getting into a relationship, you shouldn't commit permanently until you have been with that person a significant amount of time, a good six months at least. I also believe you shouldn't get into a relationship with someone until you have taken a two-week vacation with them, because when you travel, things are different. It gives you an opportunity to see "How does this person treat other people?" "What's this person like when he's not focused on his work?" And, "Can we be together 24/7 for two weeks without killing each other?"

What keeps our relationship growing is that we always look for the next adventure and the next dream. We've achieved our dream here in

Costa Rica pretty much. We have an incredible home. We have a great relationship, lots of friends, we love where we live. We're always exploring... What might be an interesting thing to do? What would be an interesting thing to see? What would be fun to learn about? What are we going to do when we're eighty-five? Will we still be in this house? Is there something we need to be doing to help other people? We've both been very generous over the years with charities and contributions to the church, so a sense of giving back has always been important to us, too.

CHAPTER 2

GARY AND DAN

"After I got back off the sub, I didn't share it right away because I didn't want him to overreact and think I was falling in love too quickly or anything, but at some point I said, "You know, I've never told anybody this, except for my mom, but I think I love you."

* * * * *

G ary and Dan Ross met in 2000 through a personal ad when Gary was a student at the Naval Academy and Dan was a full-time flight attendant. Gary was later promoted to the rank of lieutenant, and in 2011 he and Dan became the first same-sex military couple to legally marry in the United States. (They were married at Moose Meadow Lodge in Vermont; lodge owner Willie Docto's interview is also included in this book.) Since the time of these interviews, Gary has left the Navy and is working as an engineer in civilian life. He and Dan enjoy spending much more time together these days and are renovating their mid-century modern home in Northern California.

Gary Ross — (Dan Ross)

We've been together twelve years now. Dan was thirty-seven, and I was twenty-five when we met online in 2000. I had posted an ad on PlanetOut.com, saying that I was interested in a long-term relationship. I'm not even sure if PlanetOut is still around, but twelve years ago, it was certainly a place I felt safe posting an ad where my coworkers wouldn't see it, because of course that was before *Don't Ask, Don't Tell*. But Dan responded, and I presumed he was looking for the same thing. I think we only sent about three emails back and forth before we decided to meet, and really those emails were to figure out where to meet and what time. My intent was pretty much from the get-go that if someone responded to my ad—and I was very honest in my ad about what I was looking for and what I had to offer—then it was at least worth going out and meeting them in person.

I was a midshipman at the Naval Academy, so there were some fairly strict rules with how far we could go, what we have to wear when we're out, consumption of alcohol, and the times we're allowed to leave, so Dan and I actually decided to meet at the Nordstrom's in Annapolis on the third floor by the piano player, because again, it was all about finding a place where I didn't think anyone else from my school would be there. I was potentially risking my career by meeting someone of the same gender.

At the time, my emotions about meeting certainly would have been nervousness and anxiety: nervousness for what I was risking, anxiety for what I stood to gain, which was a partner to share my life with. That being said, I was definitely on guard as well, so I probably repressed most of my emotions and tackled everything like I tend to tackle everything now, which is just from a very engineer-type standpoint.

We had exchanged pictures before meeting. Of course, people always look a little different in person, but I knew that going in, so there was no shock or deception in the initial picture exchange either. I hoped Dan wasn't surprised by what he saw, and I wasn't surprised by what I saw. We went out for lunch at Macaroni Grill and had a nice lunch together, and I noticed some things about his mannerisms and his honesty at lunch. Then we followed it up with a movie. The movie itself was absolutely horrible: it was *Magnolia* with Tom Cruise. I think it's one of those films where you either love it or hate it, and I did not love it!

Like I said, I think I had repressed most of my emotions, and of course I couldn't act like I was excited or happy or giddy or anything at all because I was in uniform in Annapolis on a date with a guy, and it had to seem like I wasn't. So I leaned over and matter-of-factly said, "Well, you can pick the next movie…," because I think we both hated that movie—I did anyways—and that was sort if it. From that weekend on, we pretty much saw each other every weekend unless I was on a submarine or something, and went from there.

I really didn't realize how much I liked him or even that I loved him until about seven or eight months after we'd been seeing each other every single weekend and I got underway on a submarine for about a month or so. On a submarine, they shut the hatch, they go under water, and you lose contact with the world while you're under the water. I imagine it's slightly worse than prison because at least in prison you get phone calls, visitors, and mail. You get NOTHING on a sub.

Nowadays, I think you get email, but back then really you got nothing. So when you're locked away from the world, completely isolated, it gives you a chance to really appreciate what you had before you went under the water. After several weeks, I realized the only single thing on the entire planet that I missed, that I cared about, that I was excited to come back and see, was Dan. So it was at that moment when everything had been taken from me—of course, I volunteered to go on sub duty, so it's not a horrible story—but it was during that period where I had nothing that the only thing I wanted back was Dan.

Before then, I don't think I'd ever been in love with anybody— certainly lust, not love—and so it was at that point where I realized, "I've got something special here with Dan, because he's the one I want to go home to. He's the one I miss, the one I want to talk to, the one I want to share things with." So that was my "aha" moment.

After I got back off the sub, I didn't share it right away because I didn't want him to overreact and think I was falling in love too quickly or anything, but at some point, I said, "You know, I've never told anybody this, except for my mom, but I think I love you." And I explained why, and he thought it was the cutest thing ever.

After Dan and I met, it was probably about half a month until we actually had any sort of sexual contact. Being at the academy, you can only see each other on the weekends. Now I don't want to sound like a slut, but that would have been our second or maybe third date. Of course, the relationship built up online as well, but it would have been on about our third date in person. It wasn't that complicated to see each other on weekends. I was on what we called the YP Squadron, which is a fleet of training ships to teach us how to be Navy officers in Navy ships, and we used to get underway on these training ships three times a semester, or six times a year, for extended getaways.

Whenever we were underway, Dan was working as a flight attendant and he would plan his layovers in the same city that my training ships would be pulling into and spending the weekend. So for those it was just natural if we were in Boston for me to say, "Hey, guys, I'm going to go out in Boston and spend the night and I'll be back tomorrow," and no one asked any questions. On nights when I wasn't on what we call the "movement order," where the YP ships get underway for training, a lot of Naval Academy midshipmen have sponsors out in town, so for the weekend, they'll go to their sponsor's house, do their laundry, catch up on homework and sleep—basically spend time with a local family who wants to support a Navy midshipman. So to any of my coworkers, my fellow midshipmen, Dan was my sponsor.

When Dan and I got together on probably around our sixth date, sometime within the first month and a half to three months, we both thought it important to sit down and discuss what the limits should be on our relationship. Before we'd met each other, both of us had been with other people, and it was my belief that I thought our relationship would be stronger if we were monogamous and sexually exclusive with each other. Especially with Dan being a flight attendant and on different flights three times a day for five days a week, and me being in the Navy and pulling into different ports all over the place, both of us were in careers where if we had wanted to, we could have really had a lot of sexual contact. But because both of us were seeking a long-term relationship, our goal was really to do anything we could to try to help establish one.

We thought, "Yes, of course it's fun to have sex and yes, of course those desires exist in almost all people," but if we were to act on those desires, there was the worry that then we wouldn't be as happy with each other. So we wanted to share our sex only with each other and be sexually exclusive to strengthen our own relationship. That was the direction we laid out at the beginning. As far as how we deal with temptation, if we're together and a hot guy walks by, I imagine like any other couple—usually in a straight couple, the guy usually looks and gets slapped by the woman—

in our case we both look, and if one of us isn't looking, we point him out to the other, like, "Hey, look at him. He's cute!" And then that's the end of it.

Later we don't ask each other what we're thinking about when we're in bed—he says he usually fantasizes about me even when we're having sex, so that's great—but physically we only share ourselves with each other. Then if we're not together, I imagine it's still the exact same where, absolutely, I'm surrounded by very fit people in the military, and the average age is about twenty-one on just about any US military unit, so of course there are some very attractive people I work with. But because of my position, first of all, it's out of the question; an officer is never allowed to fraternize with the troops. So there's that, and there's the leadership responsibility that I have.

But even with those rules, there's still the commitment that I made to Dan, so absolutely I'm surrounded by beautiful people and that's a beautiful thing, but I think much like a doctor and keep it very professional at work and don't even let my mind go places where I don't want it to go.

Another factor has to do with the rate of STDs. Both of us were lucky— I think Dan more so because he's a little older—having gotten through our lives being somewhat sexually active before we met each other and not having gotten HIV or anything. For me, that definitely played into it, where it could make sense that if you're going to love someone maybe you shouldn't be exposing them to diseases that you could be getting out in town while you're having fun without them.

Dan is a lot better at keeping sex non-routine than I am. I definitely am the engineer-minded person, extremely vanilla. I mean, my gosh, if he hadn't ever asked for anything, I'd probably just do whatever position I'd tried first, and that would be all I'd ever do in my life. But he'll have different ideas, different positions, different things he wants to try. We haven't done any role-playing or anything and I don't think he's ever asked me to wear my uniform or whatnot.

One way sex stays non-routine is that we're separated for such long periods at a time that when we're together, maybe it's three days that we have every several months. Now that depends on my assignment, but that's certainly how it's going to be for the next several months until I'm back in

San Diego, and then hit or miss for the next year and a half. So if I'm not on shore duty—because right now I'm assigned to a ship—it's pretty impossible to get into a routine. Then on shore duty, Dan figures out what he wants to do, and I do my best to make him happy.

Affection is really important. A lot of people focus just on sex, and while that's gratifying, unfortunately even if you really take your time, you're lucky to last more than a couple hours! And then that leaves twenty-two other hours a day. Or if you have sex a few times a day, that still leaves the majority of the day—twenty hours a day or so—when you're not engaged in probably some form of foreplay. So every time I walk by, I brush his back or rub the back of his neck if he's sitting in his office chair and I'm walking to my office chair, which is after his. If I'm sitting on the couch, we'll be separated while we're eating our meals if we're watching TV, but then once we're done eating, I might lean over and cuddle up with him, or he might lean over and cuddle up with me.

In public, we limit the PDA (public display of affection), not because we're ashamed, which I believe is readily apparent when you see our interviews. I have no problem being public but I know that if I was holding his hand and someone made a comment that my initial reaction would be to go and get in a fight, and I honestly don't want to go to jail for severely hurting someone because they made a snide comment about my husband or me. So in public we don't do PDA, although I'll still say "I love you" quietly so he can hear it. Or I will stand next to him when we're shopping, but no hand-holding or kissing or anything like that, just because I'd rather not go and show someone that just because I'm gay doesn't mean I can't get into a good fight!

I find it interesting that here I am a military guy and I'm the command systems officer on my ship, so I'm in charge of all the guns, all the missiles, all the anti-terrorism, all the force protection—I mean, my job is to kill—and I love guns, but I'm gay, and that's OK. Of course, the stereotype is that if you're gay, you must be effeminate or want to dress up like a woman and all that. Certainly there is a cross-section of society that likes to do that, but just because I'm gay does not mean that I like to do so.

Regarding love, I think that love and lust are different and yet the same, so a relationship often starts with lust—that's usually what draws people together—but then it may eventually morph into love. We're all going to get old and we're all going to die eventually, so there has to be something more than the shell, the physical body, that attracts you. After you get to know someone, it's their personality, it's their quirks, it's what makes them happy, it's what puts a smile on their face or puts a spring in their step. It's when you feel comfortable disclosing who you are to someone else and you feel comfortable sharing a secret about yourself to that person, or when you're in trouble you know that that person will ALWAYS have your back.

While you'll find a lot of these traits in a best friend as well—which is why people may say, "This is my husband and he's my best friend,"—the love takes it a step further. So to me there are different levels of love, but I think that when you find someone sexually attractive at first, maybe because of the way they look, it's when you really know and connect with that person that the love happens.

Our love has definitely deepened over time. Time is a part of it, as are the many experiences we've shared. As far as what we do to cultivate it, Dan has some really amazing strengths in relationship building. He ensured and still ensures today that any time I have any time off he's planning some memorable experiences we can share together. Maybe it's a Mediterranean cruise or a cruise around Cuba or the Hawaiian Islands, a trip to Key West or Paris... Gosh, it seems like every time I turn around he's got a vacation planned for us, going somewhere.

I do love many aspects of my work, but it is a job, and if they stopped paying me, I would not be showing up for work. The great amount of time Dan and I spend apart is kind of bittersweet. I was just in New York City with Dan on Wednesday and then flew back to New Orleans. Leaving is *so* difficult. I described for you my comfort level with PDA, but at the airport I gave him a hug and told him I loved him quietly while I was hugging him and also how much I was going to miss him. So when you have to separate, it's just so sad and so depressing and it takes me a day or two to snap out of it sometimes.

But then both of us lead very busy, busy lives, so we're able to distract ourselves or immerse ourselves in our work environment, and then of course, there's the week or two building up to when you're going to get to see each other again, and that's very fun, wondering... *How's it going to be when I get off the airplane, and where's he going to be and what's he done to the apartment, and how has the apartment changed and what uniform should I wear when I pull in?* So I think that if you view it as small separations, it's a lot easier to cope with than just realizing that you're gone most of the time.

We exchange several emails a day, which aren't the most personal thing. On the ship, my Gmail is unreliable at best; if I'm able to get a connection, it takes a few minutes to download each message. Of course we're in port, and when we get underway, it gets that much worse. We have shipboard email, but when we're in port, I do my best to call every night if I can. Sometimes when we're underway, I'm able to get a telephone line off the ship, but bandwidth is so restricted that it's difficult to do that.

Some of our largest arguments are over the most benign stuff. In twelve years, I can only remember three, and it's about something like: *when we turn on this light switch, what light do we want to come on in the room?* We are just about perfectly aligned and very, very rarely do we do anything that the other person wouldn't have done anyway. Dan supports me in every single thing I want to do. In fact, for things that I want to do but don't want to spend the money on, he will actually usually buy it for me, because he knows that I'm very practical and I'll just think about something for years sometimes before actually wanting to buy it, and he'll get tired of listening to me debate every angle and aspect of it and say, "OK! We're going to get you that car you've been talking about for five months now." And likewise, anything he wants to do he just does, and that's accepted. He wanted a bicycle a couple weeks ago and went out and bought one, and I think it cost around five hundred dollars; not an expensive one and not a cheap one. It just works for us.

We certainly go through phases in our life where we think things are funny or things are more enjoyable. Lately, after our marriage, there's been a lot more public attention on us, so I'm not sure that we've actually gone out and just had a light night on the town. It seems that if we're going out, it's because we're wanting to have a quiet meal away from everything or because we're entertaining friends. I can't remember the last time we've done anything comical really.

Dan and I wanted to get married long before the repeal of *Don't Ask, Don't Tell*. I'm not sure exactly when we decided to but at one point, we did decide that we wanted to spend the rest of our lives together. So when the news of DADT getting repealed started to spread, we knew we would have otherwise been married long ago, so we might as well try to get married as soon as we possibly could now that the repeal was happening.

The beautiful thing about the repeal was that we knew the exact date it was actually going to happen, and so we were able to plan for our wedding to be as close to the date of the repeal as possible. Obviously, there are a set number of states which allow same-sex marriages, which limits it down, and since we already knew we wanted to be married as soon as we could, then we were looking at East Coast states. Because of the time zone difference, we'd be able to get married a couple of hours earlier that way. So it just sort of all fell into place.

We got married the second it was legal. Much like the ball dropping in Times Square, we had a countdown timer in the background at our ceremony and we asked the Justice of the Peace to time the ceremony as precisely as he could. He finished half a minute early—thirty-nine seconds or so—and said, "Normally at this point in the ceremony, I would pronounce you married, but by federal law I cannot do that for another thirty-nine seconds..." So everyone looked at the clock and we're just watching and watching and watching, and once the timer got to 0000, it changed to say IT'S FINALLY HERE!, and then at that point he said, "I now pronounce you married." So we were the first military couple to legally marry in the country.

I didn't think getting married would change things or me in all honesty, because the engineering side of me came up again and I thought, "It's a word. It's a ceremony. Nothing's really going to change..." But the truth of the matter is that it did change because every single day I've been in the military under DADT, I had more and more to lose. And then finally having all that weight lifted off my shoulders, when you're allowed to publicly say, "This is my husband," and when you no longer have to tell several lies a day at work, the weight that just falls off your shoulders is absolutely incredible.

Because the stress left me, Dan says that I pretty much was just like the day we met—happy, giddy, excited, willing to express my feelings more—so I think it was me being allowed to be myself again that really strengthened our relationship.

The support I've received since getting married and coming out has been really overwhelming. Of course, you're always going to have a few people here and there who want to cling to old traditions—although surprisingly, most of them eat shellfish, don't wear four-cornered shirts, and work on Sundays—but once you get past those few, the support is absolutely amazing. And the Navy, the military, has always been on the forefront of integration.

Often, I will contemplate things for a very long time before I take action, whether it's buying myself something or doing something. If I hadn't met Dan, I'd probably still not even have my first computer, my first laptop, probably wouldn't have my first car yet, would probably still be living on a ship or a barracks, even when I'm in home port. So he has forced me to realize that there's a lot more to life than just my military stuff. It will certainly be nice to retire from the military someday. In fact, that's been on my mind more and more as my level of responsibility goes up on the ship. Gosh, if I could retire today, I would, but I've got a few more years to push in on it. Once I'm able to retire, Dan and I will settle down somewhere in a state that recognizes our relationship and gives us every benefit that every other couple is entitled to. We'll settle down and probably open up a bed-and-breakfast. I think both of us are aligned on that thought.

In a healthy relationship, it's important to communicate and establish boundaries, and then make sure you both consent before either person breaks the boundaries. It's being open and honest with each other, trusting each other, which comes with the openness and honesty. Each person needs to do his part, which hopefully was established when the boundaries of the relationship were laid out.

From the get-go, Dan knew that I was a midshipman at the Academy and I had a career in the Navy as an officer, and he accepted that, and I haven't deviated from that course. I knew he was a flight attendant and I accepted that, but he got furloughed after 9-11 and laid off for a while. We talked about what he could do from there, and he chose to be a "home flipper," so we were buying homes and he was fixing them up, and then when we'd transfer, he'd sell them.

That didn't work out for us so well, so we sat down and talked and he decided that he was going to get a job in a health club now in California for various reasons. I think that's what it's about: you lay out a plan together and you both execute it as best as you can, and then if it doesn't pan out, you sit down and talk about it.

We move forward as a team. We've bought homes together and pets together and moved together, and we seem to be doing it pretty well without us disagreeing on the means to get to the ends. Now what works for Dan and me definitely won't work for everyone, and probably won't even work for most people, so I think a relationship is a very individual experience for everybody. But it's about finding somebody you feel comfortable with, and then once you feel really comfortable—where you can talk with them about anything—from there it's just about continuing to talk.

Dan had a silly rule that I didn't really appreciate for about the first eight years or so that we were together, which was never to go to bed angry at each other. Maybe we'd have a small disagreement or something, but we don't go to bed until we're not angry, So you don't let anything build up or fester, and it helps if you try to see it from the other person's side. Usually if both people understand the other person's perspective, it's a little easier to come to a conclusion.

Openness and honesty are really important in our relationship. A lot of it's the military lifestyle, because we move all the time; every year and a half or so since we've been together, we've been moving somewhere and starting a new life together. So there are a lot of new beginnings and new opportunities and new experiences, and we're the constant in each other's life and we support each other as we move around the country. So I think part of it is my job, which forces us to move around, and then part of it is

Dan always making sure that we maximize our time and experiences together. We find that we're happier together when we're not worried about material possessions, when we just go and do things. Maybe we go to France and we're just on our own together, exploring, not worried about anything material that we've accumulated.

Regarding finances, both of our names are on our accounts. Many people told me, "Well you should do a prenuptial agreement," or "Keep everything separate." "Nothing ever lasts." Well, statistically speaking, that's true. Most relationships don't last anymore, but I also think that if you go into a relationship ensuring your own protection from the get-go, that you're not all in, you're not completely devoted, and it's not going to be as strong a relationship if from the beginning you're already giving yourself an easy way out. So if you really want a long-term relationship, personally I think you need to be all in. And then it means something; it means you really have a life with someone.

CHAPTER 3
RYAN AND IAN

"My mother really wants more grandchildren and so she'll say,
"When are you and Ian going to have kids?" The running joke is
"We keep trying, Mom, but nothing's happening..."

* * * * *

Ryan Levy and Ian Eastveld met as college students at a Houston dance club. In the summer of 2000, they trained as chefs at the world famous Le Cordon Bleu cooking school in Paris. After running their own restaurant for several years, they turned their significant culinary talents to the art of winemaking, becoming certified sommeliers and wine educators. Today Ryan and Ian handcraft their own award-winning wines from a chef's perspective in both California and Argentina. Visit their online store at www.nicewines.com. They live in Houston.

Ryan Levy — (Ian Eastveld)

Ian and I have been together seventeen years. Like many gay couples, we have multiple anniversaries, because we're not yet afforded the privilege of being able to get married legally. We have an anniversary of the day we met, the anniversary of the day we got married in Canada, and the anniversary of our commitment ceremony in Houston, even though with all those days, it can be tough to remember them all!

We were both twenty-one when we met. I was between my junior and senior years of college at Rice University in Houston and went out one night with some friends to a now defunct dance club called Rich's. Ian was there with his friends also, and we spotted each other across the dance floor. We both slowly made our groups get closer and closer together until we were dancing back to back. I'm not sure who turned around first but we danced together and then we kissed. We ended up exchanging phone numbers and had our first date the next night.

When I first saw him, I thought he was gorgeous. I remember thinking, "Wow, I hope he's as interested in me as I am in him!" The funny thing is that before I gave him my number, I said, "So if I give you my number, will you call me?" He said, "I don't think so," and I said, "OK."

About ten minutes later he gave me his number and he said, "Call me." "OK..." This was before everyone had cell phones, so these were home phone numbers. I think Ian was nervous about calling, though I don't know who he thought he was going to have to talk to. Since he wasn't out yet, he might have been concerned that I would leave a "gay" message on his parent's answering machine. We were both very innocent and very new to the gay scene at the time.

It wasn't until the next night that we got to really talk at all. We met up at a coffee shop. What's really funny—and Ian will disavow this story—but we were to meet at this coffee shop, and I was thinking "It's a date!" So it's our first time going out for coffee, and he brought two of his friends to our date. Ian will tell you that he didn't think it was a date, but I think his friends were along to make sure I was worthy, and apparently I passed all the tests. I give him a lot of grief about it because it's fun, but it wasn't an issue at all having his friends there actually.

We spent every hour of the next week together because he was going to have to go back to school in Lubbock at Texas Tech, and I was going to school at Rice. So we had one week and we spent every waking hour together and really got to know each other. At one point, it started to rain just as we were going out on a motorboat on a lake, so we just stayed under the covered boat slip for three hours and talked in the rain. There was nothing to do except to get to know each other, which was great, and I think we both look back upon that moment as the point at which we started to fall in love with each other.

I'm pretty sure Ian spent the night with me every night that week. It was very romantic, and we actually waited a full three months before we had intercourse. When he would come to visit me in Houston and we stayed at my parent's house, my parents insisted that we sleep in separate rooms, which is really funny. I think my parents find that very humorous now. They have—amazingly—become my greatest allies and are fervent supporters of marriage equality and are very outspoken about it, which is why it's so funny to look back then because in the early days, I think they were uncomfortable with the whole idea. We joke together now. My mother really wants more grandchildren and so she'll say, "When are you and Ian going to have kids?" The running joke is "We keep trying, Mom, but nothing's happening..."

We broke up two times in the first year, which allowed us to go date and explore. We were apart for about three months and dated plenty of guys and we both came to the conclusion that there that was nothing better out there than what we already had. So that pulled us together and we've been exclusive and monogamous ever since.

I'm just getting too old to be interested in dealing with anyone else's baggage and problems anyway. Ian and I know the worst things about each other and we've tolerated each other for this long, so it's too much effort to do anything else! It's a lot less complicated anyway when it's just the two of you. We still enjoy sex together very much today. I never imagined that after this many years, I could continue to find someone so attractive and love him so much and still manage to find new and beautiful things about him. I guess I'm just lucky. And we spend all day with each other, too. It's not like I only see him in the evenings or that we have different schedules either.

We've always slept together. We both produce a fair amount of heat, so he sleeps on his side of the bed and I sleep on mine. We might cuddle for ten minutes and then we occupy our own side of the bed. We don't spend a whole lot of time in bed actually. Owning our own business, we're working a lot, and by the time we get home—whether it be from work or the gym or from seeing friends—we're pretty exhausted.

Ian and I started dating at a time when it was not terribly dangerous to be affectionate in public, though definitely there was some possible danger too. So I think we're a product of that environment and we're not—hopefully—overly affectionate in public. We're very thoughtful and caring for each other in private. I do see couples being very affectionate at a restaurant or at the store, but we're just used to using more restraint that way. It is still Texas after all.

I heard one of my favorite definitions of love in a movie, *Meet Joe Black*. In the film, Brad Pitt plays the Angel of Death and he doesn't understand love and wants to know what it is. One of the characters says, "Love is when the other person knows the absolute worst thing about you and it doesn't matter to them." That alone may not describe what love is, but it implies that the person knows you so well, all the good and all the bad, and they still accept and care about you and know that you are the one for them. That to me defines love, a "full-knowledge love."

We're really lucky that we met at such a young age because it's allowed us to really grow together, and we're continuing to grow and explore new things together. After graduating college, I moved to Austin to attend law school, and Ian moved there to be with me. He trained to become a chef, then was a teaching chef at the nation's largest vocational cooking school. We really got to know each other those three years because we lived in a 450-square-foot apartment together during that time. I joke with people that I don't know if it was the sheer lack of square footage that was difficult, or just the fact of two gay men sharing one tiny, tiny bathroom with one tiny, tiny vanity...

When I was graduating law school, Ian said, "I really want to take my culinary career to the next level," and I asked, "What does that mean?"

He said, "I want to go study at Le Cordon Bleu in Paris," and I said, "OK, I want to go too."

So I applied to Le Cordon Bleu—where Julia Child went to school—though I really didn't think I'd get accepted because my background was not as steeped in cuisine as Ian's. But I did get accepted, and we both went together to study at Le Cordon Bleu, where I was the only non-vocational chef in our class. It was beautifully romantic to be in Paris and to be going to school at Le Cordon Bleu and to live the French paradox: eat and drink and walk all over the city and not gain a pound. We graduated from Le Cordon Bleu, with Ian graduating with many more honors than I did. He's a much more talented chef than I am in the kitchen.

We moved to Dallas, where I started my career as a lawyer, and Ian started a catering company. After a couple years of running the catering company, he outgrew our apartment kitchen and needed a commercial one, and we ended up opening up a restaurant together. So I was lawyering by day and then helping Ian run the restaurant at night. We did that for a few years and then in 2005 we were very fortunate that an investor came along who wanted to buy the restaurant. It was perfect timing.

At the time, we sat down and said, "Where do we want to be ten years from now?" We'd sold the restaurant, and Ian had accepted a great job offer to be the director of culinary education for Viking Appliances and had just started doing that. So we looked ten years out and I could make partner at my law firm, and he could continue to run the cooking school, and it just wasn't what we wanted for each other. It wasn't where we imagined we would be so we thought, "What could we do that allows us to explore our hunger for travel, where we can spend time together and eat and drink and do everything we love to do?"

Ian had always wanted to take his education in wine further so we said, "Let's move out to California and we'll train to become sommeliers," and we trained under master sommelier David Glancey in California. During that process, we met a number of winemakers and people in the wine industry and were really bitten by the wine bug.

We started our first project out in Napa, which was to make a Stag District Cabernet Sauvignon. What was so appealing to us was the idea that we would make wine from the perspective of two chefs. I tell people that there are a lot of chemists who make wine, a lot of farmers, but there are not a lot of chefs who make wine from a chef's perspective. That was our goal, and our very first harvest was in 2007.

After we harvested the fruit and got it into barrels, we were like, "Now what?" Our mentor, who is another winemaker in Stag Leap, said, "Well, now you just wait."

The idea that we should just wait did not sit well with us; we wanted to keep busy. If you make wine in the Northern Hemisphere, you only harvest in October, but you can cheat the system and go to the Southern Hemisphere and harvest in March also. So that's what we did.

We went to Argentina and did what we call our "Argentinian Beauty Contest," where we literally spent two months going vineyard to vineyard looking for a grower—interviewing winemakers, interviewing growers, inspecting vineyards, tasting grapes, tasting juice—and finally stumbled upon a real hidden gem: a husband/wife team who are fifth-generation grape growers. Their family emigrated from Italy around 1898, and they're the kindest, nicest people you've ever met, and their fruit, their grapes, are amazing.

We told them about our passion, that we want to make wine from a chef's perspective and that we were interested in making wine from their grapes. We connected really well, and they loved our passion, as they are very passionate about the completely organic farming they do. So we started making wine in Argentina, too, and now suddenly, we could be busy year round. We can work during our spring down in Argentina and during fall in Napa, and it's a perfect combination that keeps us really busy. Our website is nicewines.com, where there are pictures and stories and blogs and all kinds of good stuff.

If relationships were easy, everybody would be in one. They require an unbelievable amount of compromise, humility, understanding, giving your partner the benefit of the doubt, anticipating needs, forgiving mistakes, apologizing, etc... It's really no different than any sort of partnership that people enter into. The reason there are so many divorces and dissolutions of partnerships is lack of communication, lack of compromise, lack of understanding.

One of the reasons Ian and I are lucky is that we both come from very communicative families, and I think we were both raised very similarly. There's nothing taboo at the dinner table, and you didn't come to the dinner table and not talk about what happened that day. Both our families are very blunt and forthright about things, which helps. It's very difficult to persist in a relationship or a partnership or any sort of arrangement where two people are meant to spend large amounts of time together and get along, if you can't be honest and upfront and talk about issues freely and openly.

We have a policy that we don't go to bed without discussing things, so things don't get a chance to fester. Let's say I forgot to take out the trash or do the laundry—whatever it is—the issue never persists for more than twenty-four hours because we address it. It always baffles me to see couples who won't tell each other when they're upset with one another, and they'll let something build up and say, "This has been on my mind and bothering me for six months." I don't understand such a mindset. This is the person ostensibly you're going to spend the rest of your life with and you can't tell them what frustrates you is that they don't put the seat down after going to the bathroom? I meet these people all the time and I just don't get it!

It's almost a cardinal rule to not take your partner for granted. Every once in a while, we have reality checks where we remind each other, "Hey, I've got a lot on my plate right now and I feel unappreciated." Ian and I are really good at telling each other when something like that happens, and the other will make a course correction and say, "I'm sorry. I'll be more thoughtful." I mean stuff like that happens often and it's healthy to communicate about it. If one of us is feeling neglected, we'll tell each other and address it. I feel very blessed to have that level of open communication in my life, that I can say whatever I want without fear that my partner's going to think less of me or think that I'm whining or insecure or whatever.

I come from a Jewish faith tradition. Ian does not come from a faith tradition, but he's been very active in the rituals and observances of Judaism in my family, mainly out of tradition, not because of any religious belief or observation. I think that the ritualistic aspect of Judaism binds and bonds families together and serves this connecting purpose. We just had Passover, and Ian always comes to Passover and he knows all the prayers and the readings and is a full participant at the Passover Seder. He's probably been to as many Bar Mitzvahs and Jewish weddings and funerals as most American Jews have.

Our commitment ceremony was performed by the cantor from the synagogue I grew up in. What was funny was that when I asked the cantor, who has known me all my life, if he would wed Ian and I, he said, "Absolutely." I looked at him, like, "Oh, it's not a problem?"

He said, "Did you think it was a problem because you are two men?," and I said, "Yeah."

He said, "The problem is that Ian's not Jewish, not that you're two men!"

So it was very wonderful and refreshing to know that my faith and the community I grew up in could be so embracing of our relationship.

We had a *ketubah*, an ancient document that has been used in Judaism for thousands of years. It's a beautiful, ornate Jewish wedding contract that was signed, in this case, by the groom and groom. We got married under a *chuppah* , the traditional four-post tent with a covering over the top which symbolizes a home. Then we ended our commitment ceremony with the traditional breaking of the glass. In a straight wedding, it is the man only who breaks the glass when he stomps on it. We each had a glass to break for ours. The entire experience was a heck of a lot of fun. We had been married in Canada already, so this was like the icing on the cake, and we had a great time with my friends and my family, celebrating together.

Ian is from Montreal, so we'd go to visit his family in Canada often. In June of 2003, Canada legalized same-sex marriage, and our next trip there was going to be the following year in August of 2004. We started planning the trip and I said to Ian, "You know, gay marriage is now legal in Canada," and he said, "Why don't we get married?" I said, "That's a good idea!" So we told his parents that we planned to get married while we were up there.

My parents, as well as Ian's sister and her husband, said they wanted to come, so all of us went up to Canada together. We got married at City Hall, and then afterwards we had a group-family honeymoon in the Niagara-on-the-Lake wine region near Toronto and went and did all the vineyard tours and enjoyed relaxing and eating and drinking. It was really amazing that my parents and Ian's parents could be there for that special occasion, and how fortunate we are that our parents were accepting enough to be there with us and embrace us, to have that support structure that so many young gay and lesbian people do not have.

I think it was a very big deal for our parents to be at the wedding. They treated us as spouses after that, and I believe it was after that point that my parents would introduce Ian as their son, and Ian's family would do the same with me, and I really think that was truly a by-product of our getting married. We'd already been together eight years at that time, but I think our marriage profoundly affected them especially.

I'd love to have kids and we talk about it, but right now the winery is our baby. It's taking up almost all of our time. Eventually we will have a kid, but it won't be this year. With our two dogs, we already have two children, and they require a lot of attention.

Speaking of our dogs, Ian and I enjoy humor and like to share funny things with each other and make jokes. I think we laugh at each other most of all. We will do stupid things and laugh at each other, whether it be falling down the stairs or whatever. One of my favorite moments was when Ian left a leg of lamb on the kitchen counter to cool after cooking. One of our dogs got to it and left little chew bites all around it. We were able to cut off all those parts and salvage it for dinner. What's even more funny is that night, after gorging herself on lamb, our dog Kylie was making this awful noise in the middle of the night, and Ian got up to go find out what the noise was. The dog had gotten sick of course from gorging on all this lamb. So Ian gets up and then I hear this other sound, which is his bare foot stepping in a pile of warm lamb vomit... We both realize what has happened, and as Ian said, "The worst part is not that we lost half the lamb or the fact that she pulled the lamb off the counter, but it's the fact that I'm stepping into this pile of fresh lamb vomit, and it's squishing through my toes..." So we laugh about the mistakes we make and the stupid things we sometimes do.

We don't do much in the way of surprises or gifts. We don't exchange gifts for Christmas. If I see something that I know he'll like or that we need I'll get it. I'm not going to get it and hide it for six months when he could have been using it for six months. Christmas and exchanging presents is really important to Ian's parents, so before Christmas, we'll go round up everything that we've bought each other over the last six months and wrap it up so we can have things to put underneath the tree at their house, so they don't think we're weird! But we buy things as we need them. Why wait?

After you've been with someone for seventeen years, you know what they like and you know what they don't like, so for me to go to the grocery store and buy something that I know he really likes and bring it home is just being thoughtful. Or if he goes shopping and buys a shirt for me that he thinks I'd like, it's thoughtful and sweet. Both of us are non-traditionalists in the sense that we don't need society to tell us when it's appropriate to get each other gifts. Like for Valentine's Day, we'll do an event at our winery and will host everyone and cook dinner for them or have a party or something. It's not a day that it's important for us to be alone by ourselves to do something forced and romantic.

Ian is a very thoughtful and compassionate person, and thankfully a lot of that has rubbed off on me and made me more thoughtful and compassionate too. I was probably more of a selfish person, where he's a very selfless person by nature. I am very driven and ambitious and I think that's rubbed off on him as well, so we've influenced each other in very good ways.

For a healthy relationship, communication about everything is essential. There's nothing more important. Allow your partner to have room to grow and take risks. Being able to encourage your partner to do that is so very, very critical. If you're interested in having a relationship, be the best person you can be. So many guys are looking for someone to complete them, and there is no one who can do that. They must come to the table complete, and then another person will find commonality with them and they'll make a bond together.

During these seventeen years together Ian and I have become extremely interdependent and we rely on each other for many things. I find that there's an amazing division of labor between us, that there are things that I rely on him to do, and things that he relies on me to do. But I believe we both came into the relationship not needing another person to complete us, but rather looking for another soul to complement our already complete self, someone to share life's experiences with. I feel blessed that we met each other and very, very lucky, too.

CHAPTER 4

MARTIN AND ROBERT

"At the beginning everything about one's lover is alarmingly attractive, persuasive, and seductive and histrionic—sort of alcoholic—just completely addictive. And then after a while I realize that those funny, hard toenails that I used to think were the sweetest things I'd ever seen in my life are now not so sweet. They're just those stupid, hard toenails that scrape against me at night in bed and I wish he would trim them. I can't believe that I used to find those alluring and attractive. But you have to, then, be large-spirited and remind yourself that you took this person as you wanted yourself to be taken, with the right to be less than perfect. Now I'm very morbid because I'm Irish and I know that one day those hard toenails are going to be in a coffin someplace either before I die or after I die, and I remind myself, with caritas, that I want to love this whole person, even the parts of him that occasionally annoy me and scrape against me."

* * * * *

Martin, a novelist, and Robert, a painter, met in 1998 at an artist colony in upstate New York. Their friendship developed into an intimacy which was a surprise to both of them, and gave birth to Robert's only adult love relationship with a man. Now married, they've adopted three children from overseas. The two busy fathers and their now-teenagers live in Massachusetts.

Martin — Robert

We've been together fifteen years. I was then forty-three, and Robert was forty-two when we met. At the time I was in the seventeenth year of a relationship with my former partner. He had taken a job ten thousand miles away in central Asia, and our intention was to stay together despite the long commute. So in the enforced separation that his work situation required, I was living alone in Massachusetts, and he would visit two or three times a year. At the same time, I was a self-employed writer and I went to an artist colony, where I had been a number of times before, in September of 1997 to work on a novel for adults. I met Robert there, who was working on a set of paintings for a New York opening. We met in early September, and it took about two and a half to three weeks to fall in love with each other.

Initially I was impressed with Robert's capacity to address a table of eighteen or twenty-two people who had just met each other, and take their measure and work out a fair, equitable system for how we would each contribute to the wine fund. Since I'm an organization person myself, I was terribly impressed with his efficiency, and the fact that nobody complained and everybody got with the program immediately. So that was my first impression of him. Robert was separated from his wife then but he was wearing a wedding ring and was not public about his separation. He talked about his wife, and every day she would ring and there would be a message on the bulletin board—which all residents saw as they walked past it—"Robert call Lori." So as I began to take the measure of different people in the colony, I noted that. I thought, "Of all the people here, he seems to have a very committed spouse, and he's married and he's straight, so it would be potentially less treacherous to befriend him..."

Now I befriended a lot of people, but if I thought there was any likelihood of my being seduced by the attractions of the environment or an individual, I generally tried not to put myself in the way of temptation. As the weeks went on and I found myself occasionally sitting next to him or we would gather at dinner and listen to one another speak, I was impressed with the breadth of his knowledge and his courtesy and also his work ethic, which I had in spades, too.

We began to go for strolls before the dinner hour, realizing that we had more and more in common. He had lived in England and so had I. Even though his background was in law, he had a deep regard for English literature, as I do. So we became friends and became close, under somewhat false pretenses as it were, because he didn't mention for some time that he and his wife were separated. After a couple of weeks it became clear to me that I was beginning to find him attractive and beginning to look forward to his company. It also seemed to me that he was warming up to me and becoming affectionate, which was somewhat of a surprise, given what I expected of him. We talked about a lot of things. I talked about being gay. I talked about my partner and really let my hair down about things that were going wrong in my own relationship, just because it was something to talk about as we went for those long walks.

There was usually a dance party toward the end of the third week in these month-long sessions, and Robert asked if I was going. I said, "Uh, I don't know. I have a limited amount of fun at dance parties because everybody here is straight. I don't mind dancing a little bit with straight people, but it's not as if it's the most fun thing in the world, so I may stop by for a little bit but not stay late."

He said, "Well, I'll dance with you if you come," and I said, "Oh, OK." So we danced together, and it struck me that he was profoundly uncomfortable, and I was proud of him for sticking it out and keeping his word. Now I realize that I misread his discomfort as being displeasure, but I think he was just going through a surprising and sudden life-shift. Within a couple of days when I approached him and said, "You know, I have the terrible feeling that I'm getting the wrong idea here...," he just said, "You're not. You're not..." That was the beginning of our relationship.

Robert was also self-employed and since his separation was spending a lot of time in colonies and going from colony to colony. When I went back to Massachusetts we were not certain whether this was going to be a one week hot and heavy romance or whether this would be something that would go forward into the future. He could see fairly clearly that he had fallen in love with me, and it was a life change he wanted to make. I was much more skeptical because I had made my commitment and my intentions known to my partner that we were in it for the long haul. So I went back to Massachusetts thinking this was just going to be a sad month and I was going to have to come to terms with the fact that I had a one-week affair, and it was not the way I'd prefer to have behaved, but it had happened.

Within just a couple weeks, Robert and I were in touch with each other and made plans to see each other in New York, just for an afternoon. I took the train down from Boston, and he drove up from D.C. and we had lunch together and hung out in the city for a couple of hours. When we parted, we made plans to spend more time together at the end of the month. My absent partner was coming back from Asia for a couple of weeks, but after that, I was going to go down and visit Robert at his family farm in Connecticut. That would be the first time we had time truly alone and we spent four or five days together. That was the beginning of the conversion for me, that maybe this was more than an accident of breaking my word and succumbing to temptation as it were. I was very concerned for my partner's health and well-being and I knew this was going to be a terrible surprise.

It took almost a year between the time I met Robert and when I finished formally severing my relationship with my former partner. I did it in stages and I did it in stages intentionally, in order that it not be too much of a shock to him.

One of the things that happened right away when I connected with Robert was a grave sense of both pleasure, delight, and surprise on the one hand, but also horror and self-doubt on the other. Horror at the fact that this was going to be a crushing and painful experience for my partner, but also for me because I had never been one to break up with anyone before. Other people had broken up with me, but I had not done the instigating of a break-up in any of my previous relationships, and, after all, my former partner and I had been together seventeen years. I loved and still do love my former partner, and the notion of hurting him—especially when he was living overseas—was very painful. And the notion of having betrayed him, and experiencing a sort of certain collapse of my own sense of character and of what it meant to give my word, was crushing. It was very upsetting; I cried a lot the first six months. I lost about twenty-five pounds from the anxiety and from not eating.

In March and April of that year Robert and I spent a number of sessions in artist colonies. I hadn't even known him for six months yet, so I didn't want to burn my bridges before I had crossed them. I also thought it was quite possible that Robert, who had never had a gay relationship before, might just be experiencing a shakeup and after a while might come to his senses and rub his eyes and say, "What was that all about...," and then go get married to a woman. So I didn't want to hurt my former partner any more than I absolutely needed to, in the event that I was Robert's one and only flash-in-the-pan gay experience. But Robert convinced me by steady protestation of affection and by his behavior that he was committed and he was excited and he was ready.

We later rented a house up in Vermont and spent six or seven weeks living together to make sure we wouldn't get bored with each other or realize we had to run screaming to the hills after two weeks. At the end of that, when we had to part, and I had to go to a conference in London, and Robert had to go back to D.C., the parting was just as painful as it had been for the previous nine months whenever we had to part, so that was the final confirmation for me about our relationship.

Robert and I first became sexual the day after dancing together. We've been monogamous all along, and any temptations to be with others have been minimal to non-existent. Since Robert had already interviewed before me and had alerted me that this question would come up, he said that you'd likely find us an extremely tedious pair of people to interview about this. But Robert and I are similarly made up in our regard for the admiration of constancy.

We have had in fifteen years and up until now and into the foreseeable future a capacity to continue to be stimulated by each other sexually and to supply one another's needs in sex and in love. I often make jokes with many of my straight friends that one of the real advantages of being a same-sex male couple—especially a male couple that's the same age and state of both vigor and decrepitude—is that your appetites are similarly calendared.

The first year we knew each other we had sex five or six times a day sometimes; we were similarly wired and excited. Then as it has tapered off and become more normalized as we've gotten older and also become more familiar, we've continued to stay very compatible. Our appetite is consistently matched, so now if we have sex two or three times a week, it's not one of us being interested and the other not. There are times when one or the other of us is too tired or falls asleep or something, but it's far more often where we're on the same page. After fifteen years there is a degree of routine to it. We both are rather fit for men of our age and we both admire each others' bodies and enjoy dressing in sexy underwear and going to bed wearing something sexy.

We usually hug each other once or twice a day. We're not cuddlers in terms of sitting on the sofa together, and when we watch TV we have separate chairs, though we use the same ottoman and our feet touch. We are rarely physically affectionate outside of the house. When my mother died six months ago, I grabbed Robert's hand as we were walking across the cemetery grass, which is something that—under normal circumstances—I wouldn't do because I know that would make him uncomfortable. But it was a moment in which I needed it, and he didn't shrink back. That's not to say that I wouldn't like it if he were a bit more affectionate in public, but it has not been a hard thing to accommodate myself to. We sleep together, except that I have a couple of mild health issues that often mean I have insomnia. So we always go to bed together, but I sometimes finish the night in a different room. About two-thirds of the time we wake up together, but maybe one-third of the time I have to go to another room.

In the deepest sense, the Latin word *caritas* is very often used to suggest charity, and by charity meaning large-spiritedness toward those you don't know; working for soup kitchens and caring about your enemy and all that Biblical stuff. But I think the practice of caritas, being large-spirited, toward your lover is equally important. So romance and sex and devotion is all built, for me, upon the struts of the bridge of caritas. Robert is a very giving person and he will happily make all the meals and do lots of stuff around the house. I'm aware of what he does and I'm also aware of what is not easy for him to do and I try very hard to fill in those gaps without being too obvious that I'm filling in. I'm better at making a mess in the kitchen and probably better at cleaning it up too. But I don't think I take him for granted.

Love deepens because it accrues history to it, so the longer we live together the more commonality we have in our experiences. Let's say we're both sixty. We're not quite, but let's say we are. We've known each other for fifteen years now, so now we have spent a quarter of our lives together.

That's twenty-five percent of shared history. When we met each other and when we were together for only a few months or the first couple of years, most of his history—for me—was sort of pre-history; his family, his friends and all. All of his friends and his family will always pre-date me, but the longer we go on together as an item, the more in proportion our love accrues a sort of totemic weight. So the history we share together is the foundation stone for increased love and affection.

The interesting thing is that when one is together there are occasionally wearinesses and eye-rolling moments and "Oh God, not this again..." He has his scar tissue, and I have mine. We're very good at avoiding the mire and muck and swamps of each other's danger zones, but every once in a while we go flailing and flapping into them. And at such times it is easier to get out because one has had the experience of it before. That doesn't mean there isn't occasionally a little gripiness, thinking, "Oh here we go again on this one... This sad little notion that I'll never get..." But back to that notion of caritas, that one wants to be large-spirited towards one's lover...

At the beginning, everything about one's lover is alarmingly attractive, persuasive, and seductive and histrionic—sort of alcoholic—just completely addictive. And then after a while you realize that those funny, hard toenails that I used to think were the sweetest things I'd ever seen in my life are now not so sweet. They're just those stupid, hard toenails that scrape against me at night in bed, and I wish he would trim them. I can't believe that I used to find those alluring and attractive. But you have to, then, be large-spirited and remind yourself that you took this person as you wanted yourself to be taken, with the right to be less than perfect. Now I'm very morbid because I'm Irish and I know that one day those hard toenails are going to be in a coffin someplace either before I die or after I die, and I remind myself, with caritas, that I want to love this whole person, even the parts of him that occasionally annoy me and scrape against me.

The only time I ever feel crowded has to do with our children. Robert and I do enjoy each others' company so much, and our children are wonderful, but they are children. By virtue of the species, they're needy, and there are many times where we have to put our appetite for each other's company on hold in order to take care of our parental responsibilities. Once in a while, because of the work that I do and the way that I do it, Robert will come home from his studio early because nothing much is going on for him that day in his head, and I will be at home just getting ready to get down to my work, which requires a fair amount of intense silence. And even though we have a large home, and he knows enough not to call up, I can just hear the garage door opening, and some little radio connection that I was tuning in on my subconscious in order to be able to work with it is severed simply by his being in the house, even if he's six rooms away with several doors closed. That's the only time I ever feel slightly crowded, but that has as much to do with the kind of work that I do. It's not like he's coming up and squeezing into my study and wanting to sit on my lap and distract me.

In the three or four years before meeting Robert, I had moved back from London and had discovered that the political climate in America had changed about men being able to adopt. Back in Boston, I was hearing various friends of mine saying, "Matt and Joe can't come for dinner tonight because they couldn't get a sitter..." I felt like I had stumbled into an alternative universe; between 1990 and 1994, the laws had changed in Massachusetts and I hadn't noticed it.

So almost immediately I began to push my former partner to consider adoption, and then he got that job in Central Asia. As mighty as I think my own capacities are, I didn't think I could be a single dad with a partner ten thousand miles away. It just wasn't practical for us to do it. But I had already begun to train myself into thinking that it might be possible to be a father, so when I met Robert and when it became clear that what we were experiencing was not just a thrilling "colony romance," as they call it, we began to joke right away about having a Chinese girl and being parents. That was part of the fantasy story we were telling ourselves in the first six months as a way of clueing each other in that we were contemplating what it might mean to be together a long time.

I had Robert come to a couple of adoption seminars and he was interested, but whenever we would talk about it he was clearly ambivalent about it. I was thinking, "His heart is in the right place but I can hear that he's not ready and may never be ready. Oh well." Then about nine months after we met each other, his mother died from cancer, right before we were going to start that summer in Vermont living together.

Literally forty-eight hours before she died, he turned to me and said, "I've changed my mind. I now see, as my mother is leaving this life, that what she did for me was the best thing she had done with her life, and I want to be able to do the best thing I might do with my life too." At which point I reached into the back seat and pulled out the clipboard on which the forms were all filled out and ready for his signature. He signed them and we got them notarized and we applied to adopt our first child when we had only known each other nine months. Nine months after that we had our first child at home, and today we have three kids.

In the beginning I was the more natural parent because I have a background in education and I have six brothers and sisters, all of them very fecund. I've always enjoyed children and have spent many dinner parties playing around with a two-year-old rather than sitting down on the couch with the old professor, trying to crack his brain about what he knew and didn't know. So I had said, a little cavalierly, that all Robert needed to do was everything that I couldn't do, but I would do an awful lot of it. And that was true; I had a lot more confidence at the beginning. But Robert really grew into the role, especially by the time we got our second child, and as the kids have become teenagers Robert is proving in many ways to be better at it. So we began as unequal partners, and Robert came up to speed within about a year. The kids get along exactly, precisely as well as three kids who are fourteen, twelve, and eleven might be expected to get along, No better and no worse.

I tend to speak in metaphors because that's just how I think. Robert, as a former lawyer, tends to speak in quantifiable terms. We've only had about three fights in fifteen years, and one of them was during Bush versus Gore, before the Supreme Court settled that particular argument. I asked Robert how he thought the popular vote in Florida went. He said he didn't know because the votes weren't counted. When I asked him what his guess or his instinct was, he just couldn't reply. He said, "Since the votes haven't been counted I don't have an opinion. I don't know."

I thought he was being bullheaded not to have an opinion. I had an opinion and an instinct and I hadn't personally counted the votes either, and I could not get him to offer an opinion about it. I found that bizarre, and it has never happened again in quite so stark terms, but that's a good example about how occasionally he and I differ. I think I'm more intuitive and more instinctive and because of my training as a novelist. As part of my professional apparatus, I look at what seem to be simple situations and try to estimate the complexity underneath the apparent simplicity. That's my job and that's what makes human nature interesting to me, and I rely on that for writing fiction. I think that makes me in many ways a better judge of character and a better judge of the social moment, and Robert relies on me for this. He much more cut and dry and often doesn't trust his own instincts. But he trusts my apprehension of the human mystery.

I am Roman Catholic by birth and by choice, although it is not easy these days. Robert was a convert to Catholicism in his first marriage, which was one of the things that was appealing to me about him when we met, that we had this in common. My former partner was a cultural Muslim, if occasionally an apostate. So while I wouldn't choose my partner on the basis of religion and I didn't, the fact that Robert happened to be Catholic was appealing to me, especially if we were going to possibly raise children together, because we would not have to fight about what the rubrics of the universe seemed to be, at least as demonstrated to children in the growing up years.

Indeed, our first date, besides the walking that we did, was to go to Mass. We were the only two people at the arts colony who wanted to go to church on Sunday mornings, so we drove fifteen miles there and fifteen miles back, and druing those long trips I told Robert about some of my early love affairs and what their effect has been on me over the years. So all of that being said, we have a slightly different apprehension of what it means to be a Catholic these days. I have very much a belief and an experience that the church is built from the ground up like a democracy, and that the good priest and the devoted nun who teach and heal and work in hospitals and all are just as much the church as the Pope and the bishops.

That being said, the sadness and the brutality of the hierarchy of the church in the last ten years has been so extreme that even I, who champion the grassroots rights of people to belong to a faith community, have been worn down. We're still Catholics and still go to church and contribute and raise our kids as Catholics, but it is with a little more jaundiced view than I wish I had had to experience in my own life. I do know that Robert is a deeply feeling and deeply spiritual person.

We've been married for seven years. I had wanted to do it since I learned that it was possible but I had not ever expected it would be possible and was quite surprised about it when it came to pass. It did not change the way that we were together. We'd had a private ceremony where we pledged to be faithful on a mountaintop in the Adirondacks, near where we met some years earlier. The main thing is that the marriage did do something, both political and psychological.

It was transformative to have a public event with Robert's hard-nosed Republican father sitting in the front row, and my staunch and progressive but still old-fashioned Irish mother sitting in the front row... To have them both there acknowledging the public nature of our commitment, and to have our children there giving us away and walking us to the aisle and then walking away with us at the end. To have all of our friends there and almost all our siblings there; that was important for our children to see, that our marriage was endorsed by the larger community of family and friends.

The other important thing is that all people have their limitations and weaknesses, and I have the capacity to be suspicious and to worry, to wonder if my partner might be cheating on me or is suppressing the true nature of an affection he might be feeling for somebody else. Part of this paranoia actually increased after meeting Robert because I could see more directly how it could happen; it had happened to me! I thought, "If this could happen to even me, who is so old-fashioned and so reliable, it could certainly happen to anyone."

But when your partner is wearing a wedding ring and when they have pledged to you in front of other people, including your own children, one is loaned a sense of security that helps shore up one during those weird moments of insecurity and doubt. We are married. We both have rings on. We have said this in the eyes of God and humanity and yes, that doesn't mean that someone can't stray. But here's my ring to prove that he's promised not to. That has really helped me psychologically. I don't think Robert suffers the same doubts that I occasionally do, so I don't know that he'd say it's a similar benefit. But that's certainly how I feel.

Robert has a different skill-set when it comes to dealing with setbacks. He was an oldest son of secular Jewish and Protestant parents and was beloved; he was quite possibly the Messiah to his parents and grandparents. I was the middle child of a much larger, less prosperous Irish-Catholic family, and on the occasion of my birth my first mother died, so I was the occasion of great sadness and distress for my father and my older three siblings. I wasn't a pariah but I certainly grew up with an undue share of guilt and responsibility. Being with Robert, who does not think that every plate is going to crash and every piece of uncooked chicken is going to cause fatal botulism, has really helped me in some very basic ways of trusting the universe. It hasn't changed me but it has helped me because when I fumble in a certain amount of fear about the danger of the world I know that Robert has an equally irrational trust in the world. So that kind of balances us out.

I am more likely to be funny from the podium, and Robert is more likely to be funny when it's just the two of us. He becomes a bit more poker-faced when there are more people around. He's very sexy and funny and quick in private, but in public, he's more formal. We do make each other laugh regularly and we both like to use words in an amusing and unsettling way and like getting the belly-laugh of having been able to plant a luscious verbal surprise in the middle of a boring sentence. That's one of the things we give to each other. We both love language and we love to use it in clever and unexpected ways.

Money-wise, we kept separate accounts in the beginning because Robert had some lingering obligations to his estranged and then divorced wife. I had some unwritten but heartfelt obligations to the partner I was leaving. I bought out his share of the house and effectively gave him the full value of the house as it now stood, because I knew that he had not chosen this unexpected turn of events. At the beginning when we met, Robert was quite a bit more prosperous than I, by a factor of about two to one. Then in the first four or five years that we knew each other my career went into high gear and I began to have more cash on hand than I'd expected. I had some work to do to persuade Robert that there was no need for us each to pay fifty percent of every bill if my resources had accidently outstripped his.

That was hard for him but he took it under advisement, and over a couple of years he's yielded little by little.

Now he's accepted the fact that I came to the table with a certain portfolio of resources and they grew unexpectedly. We have bought two more pieces of property since we met, and both of them are in both our names, regardless of who has put which amount of money into them. I'm also in the process of setting up a charitable foundation, so that when I die—say I die before he does—he and the children will have the obligation to give away the extra money that we don't need, rather than deed it to our children, thereby, we think, poisoning their lives and ruining their need to work for themselves.

Lasting relationships take patience and humor. I think both partners are obliged to keep growing, and that sometimes means goading the other into not standing still. Luckily we are both intellectually oriented, so intellectual stimulation is something we share, which is richly rewarding. It's one of the most obvious ways to keep developing. We're both also in fiendishly good health, but of course that's not going to stay the same forever. We've done the necessary legal things to prepare for that but we have not really begun to explore what it would be like if one of us were to become incapacitated and what that would mean for the other emotionally, experientially, organizationally, etc... I suppose that's something people learn on the fly.

Our culture promotes such unrealistic expectations of love. I believe that self-loathing is a by-product of the Madison Avenue-Hollywood-Entertainment-Industrial complex, and by that I mean the perfect forms and figures of beautiful young men are perfect forms and figures that a) we likely never had and never will, and b) we are unlikely ever to meet. And reality-based expectations are hard to come by when you're young, and it probably is the biggest challenge to a younger person who is not in a committed relationship to know and accept yourself for who you are.

That doesn't mean you can't lose ten pounds or go to the gym, but it does mean that you're not ever going to be Matt Damon at twenty-four if you weren't actually Matt Damon in 1986. I think I had a fairly hefty portion of self-confidence and am well practiced at ego management—perhaps more than most—but I suffered like everybody else for the fact that

I was small-boned and wispy and was never going to be a he-man or deserve a spread in GQ or have a certain kind of chin. It's superficial but it does affect your sense of self. So I would say be good to yourself, be kind to yourself, work at yourself, but be realistic.

I have had only two long-term relationships, and then have dated guys anywhere from a week to four or five months. I never met anybody in a bar. I only met people in places where I would not be ashamed to be seen by anybody else in my life, and by that I mean parents, siblings, pastors, etc... I met boyfriends in church groups and in choirs. I met one in a gay and lesbian awareness group at the Cambridge Center for Adult Education. Arts education courses. Experiences that were going to build me up anyway, whether I met anybody or not. I do think that's one of the advantages of going to places that are going to nourish you anyway, as you never come away empty-handed.

You've always at least had the chance to sing or listen to music or to look at attractive people, even if there was no one you got hooked up with. You've had the chance to learn something about art or listen to interesting life stories. It has built you up and given you something and you're not empty-handed, even if you didn't get someone to bring home for a cup of tea.

CHAPTER 5

PATRICK AND FRASER

"That whole period of courting each other in all aspects of our relationship—intellectually, emotionally, romantically, sexually— was really important, and those were not things I'd experienced before. I had an instinct that I wanted to play it more slowly, and looking back on things now after having been with him for ten years, I'm quite pleased that I did it that way. It just permitted a lot of healthy flourishing together."

* * * * *

Patrick and Fraser met a decade ago in Canada after a mutual acquaintance recommended they should. Now married, the two create and publish their own line of gay erotic comics through their business, Class Comics, www.classcomics.com. Fraser manages the business and does some of the writing, while Patrick does the majority of the artwork. His evocative illustrations have earned him the title, "the Stan Lee (Marvel Comics) of gay erotic comics." The couple lives in Vancouver, British Columbia.

Patrick — (Fraser)

We've been together ten years as of March 16th, which is also the day we later got married on; reasoning that it would be one less date to have to remember. I was twenty-nine when we met, and Fraser was thirty. I'm vaguely related to the person who introduced us, through my brother's wife. Fraser was working with her relative Steve at the time, and they were good friends. Steve went up to Fraser and said, "I know somebody who I think you might really like. You guys seem to have a lot of things in common.

Would you like to get in touch with him?" He pretty much ran the same sales pitch by me, and I wasn't in the very best place at the time. My grandmother had just passed away and I had just gone through a series of "dud" boyfriends, so I said, "If he wants to phone, great, but I'm not calling." I was playing hard to get, I suppose. When Steve asked Fraser if he wanted to call, Fraser likes to say he was being all bold and said, "Yes, I'll call him," but apparently he was actually quite nervous about doing so. Fraser did finally phone me, and we found that we connected really well.

What was somewhat ironic was that he phoned initially, left a message, and I phoned him back, but it was during an episode of *Buffy the Vampire Slayer*. *Buffy the Vampire Slayer* was a show we both really liked watching, though I had no idea about this. It turned out that the day that I phoned him, it was a repeat episode, but he hadn't seen it yet and was watching it. He said, "Do you mind if I call you back after *Buffy*?" and then he apparently immediately thought, "Oh, my God... What have I just done? What kind of moron says that to a potential date?" But it endeared him to me because I thought, "Oh, my God. He likes *Buffy*!"

I said, "Yes, absolutely. Call me back after *Buffy*." So that was a really good icebreaker for us.

From that point on, we met and had lunch and just found that we really, really got on together. It was great. When we met at lunch, Fraser basically snuck up on me. He was really nervous about coming to lunch apparently, and I remember I got there first and was sitting and waiting, and I felt nervous, too. I didn't actually see him come in, and he somehow snuck up around me—he was lucky that he picked out the right guy—and he just plopped in the chair in front of me and said, "OK, I'm here. This is me. This is who I am..."

I thought, "Wow, he's as neurotic as I am on first dates. This is great!" Fraser was good at breaking the ice, and I thought he was really cute and really sweet and not pretentious or pushy; just really quite easygoing, despite his nerves. I just found that all really charming and appealing, so there was that magical first impression. Just the way he sat in front of me; it was like, "Oh, my God. OK, you're here and you're cute and you're nice!" It just sort of snowballed.

Fraser had been out in Vancouver for a few years and had moved from Ontario to British Columbia with a couple of his friends. I'd been in Vancouver for several years by that point and was trying to make a go of my art and trying to figure out exactly where I wanted to be in life. And I think that when I met Fraser, he and I immediately got on on a personal and intimate level, but we also realized that we had a great deal in common in terms of a potential business venture. So we focused on the art I was doing and with Fraser's assistance, we got some exposure for my work that I hadn't had before, which really propelled us to form Class Comics, the publishing company we now run together.

I can say that it didn't take me long to realize that I would be with him until I croak. Why I say that is because I am not a particularly easy person to get on with. I'm quite critical sometimes, and while I don't go out of my way to be difficult, I'm an artist, and artists tend to have that temperament where we can be a bit fiery. And what I really love about Fraser is all of the wonderful qualities that make him up. I find him calming and soothing, and he accepts me for the quirkiness of my artistic side, and doesn't judge or look down on it or anything. I think we were definitely meant to be together because we complement each other extremely well, and it's not just the fact that we love each other, but we're truly like the proverbial puzzle pieces that fit together.

We didn't jump into sex right away, and I remember that rather fondly. With previous boyfriends, I had always told myself, "I'm not going to just jump into bed," and then inevitably I would, only to realize later down the road, "Wow, was that a mistake..." So I was determined to get to know Fraser and just enjoy that phase of flirting with each other—the courting, if you will. I don't recall exactly how long it took us to become intimate, but we didn't rush into things and when we did become intimate, it was really great. I already knew at that point that I loved him, though I didn't say so then. That just tends to scare people. You say, "I love you," and they're like, "OK, well. See you later!" I thought, "I'll wait and keep it to myself." But being together just felt really right.

We are sexually exclusive and have been from the get-go. One of the things we really connected on from the beginning was that we were both looking for that in another partner. I had dated someone a couple of years before Fraser who I was really growing to like a great deal. He was somebody who worked really quickly and he'd just blurted out at one point that he loved me, though I wasn't quite there yet. But things were going well, and I thought, "I'll see where this leads..." One day he just blindsided me and said, "You can't call me or come over this weekend because I've got a play friend who's in town and I'm going to be spending time having lots of sex with him."

Now to each his own, and I don't judge people who have open relationships. If it works for them, great, but I know that it doesn't work for me. I told him, "You know what? I adore you. You're really sweet, but clearly this is not going to work for you and me." So I knew because of that particular experience, I definitely wanted to be with someone who was like-minded and who wouldn't look for something outside the relationship. And I'm pleased to say that, knock on wood, we have not looked outside of our relationship. After ten years of being together, we're still having a lot of fun, which is pretty cool. We're still discovering some sexual aspects to each other after a decade together. We enjoy coming up with new and different things to try and we definitely have the same kinds of buttons that we like to push in each other, too.

With our business, Class Comics, we produce erotic comics. I write and draw a lot of the stuff we do, and Fraser also writes and has other artists illustrate his work. It's unabashed and very hardcore, completely a celebration of the full spectrum of gay sex. It's somewhat funny because we have some friends who are always saying, "How do you do it? A) How can you focus on this stuff and not get so turned on that you want to ditch the work and then go fool around?" and B) How do you have the energy to still fool around after you focus all that time and sexual energy into this work?"

It's interesting, because through our work we've discovered, "Hey, this could be fun to try..." We push the sexual envelope in our work and as well in our personal life together. We're not shy about trying different things. How many people can say that their work is sometimes a bit of an aphrodisiac? We're very good at reading each other, too. If I'm really focusing on work, but he's feeling up for fooling around, he knows to wait and he won't come and knock, and I'll do the same thing if I know he's really working solidly on something. But there are times where we say, "Hey! Want to play hooky this afternoon?" It's pretty cool, and we still have that kind of fun.

We're very affectionate in our own home. We hug and kiss all the time. We're not big hand-holders in public because we both come from small towns where if you stand out that way, you're dead. It's just the way we grew up. I certainly won't walk on the other side of the street from him when we're out in public of course. The other day we were at the mall shopping, and this woman pitching a product at a booth stopped us and said, "So how do you guys know each other?" I held up my hand with my wedding band and said, "We're married." So I have no problem openly saying that, but in terms of physical contact, we're really not the type to hold each other in public.

I'm actually quite conservative honestly and I don't particularly enjoy watching couples making out in the middle of a park. But at home, we're very playful and we have a lot of fun together. When we watch TV, we'll cuddle or in bed we'll cuddle. Then when it's time to sleep we prefer to just roll over to our own sides of the bed because Fraser generates so much heat that I literally can't sleep holding him. He's just way too warm! I also tend to be a light sleeper, where he could sleep through World War Three. But we both realized long ago that it was no slight to our relationship to each have our own side of the bed and to sleep that way.

Love is a complicity, a certain teamwork, almost being able to read each other without even saying anything. It's an acceptance of who the other is without judgment, without trying to change them. When we're in business together or when we're out with friends we can usually gauge each other's thoughts just by looking at each other. That doesn't always work, but for the most part we do have a good complicity. There's just a really great, natural fit and an easy honing in on the others waves and moods.

I'm a person who is generally quite detached. I tend to be very logical and focused on what I'm doing in the moment, the work I'm doing and the work that Fraser and I are doing as well as all the various projects in our personal life. I come from a family which is very loving but not very demonstrative and open about saying "I love you," even though I knew that they did. I'm someone who is also very logical about my feelings about love. A friend of mine once asked me once why I didn't call them all the time, and I said, "It's because I'm confident in our friendship and the love that we share." There's not this constant need for reassurance. It's funny with Fraser, I know that I love him when he's around. But it's when he's away that I really, really start missing him and I experience all these little, sweet moments and find myself looking forward to his coming home. When it really comes down to it, the love is always there, but it's when he's not right next to me that I realize, "Holy crap, I really love this guy!" I consciously realize it then.

It took us about a year to move in together. I have an apartment that I was living in by myself, and Fraser had actually purchased a condo, and his then-best friend, an ordained minister, was living with him until she received her appointment from the church. She and I didn't get on super well, but once she left, I started going to his place more often. Until that point, he was coming to my place most of the time. Moving in together wasn't a quick process and we both wanted to be really sure. Finally I moved into Fraser's place. But it was nice to both be at a point in our lives where it really made sense to take it slow on all fronts.

That whole period of courting each other in all aspects of our relationship—intellectually, emotionally, romantically, sexually—was really important, and those were not things I'd experienced before. I had an instinct that I wanted to play it more slowly, and looking back on things now after having been with him for ten years, I'm quite pleased that I did it that way. It just permitted a lot healthy flourishing together.

We work from home so we're literally together ninety-eight percent of the time, which is also something that stuns people a little bit. We live together and we work together, so we're virtually always together. When we work, we have very different ways of working, and we really respect and understand each other's methods, if you will. So during the day I don't actually see him that much and vice versa. I call it "going under," because I draw with headphones and music on and I'm intensely centered and focused on what I'm doing, and and as a result, if he knows I'm drawing—even if a call or whatever has come in for me—he won't even come and knock at the door. He just lets me do my thing, and I appreciate that because being pulled out of that flow of creative energy makes it really difficult to get back into it. So he just lets me do my thing, and I let him do his.

Fraser does a lot of the business side of our work together, so if his door is closed, I don't disturb him. I figure he's crunching numbers or writing scripts, so I'm just leaving him to his thing. But we've developed methods of communicating with each other in those moments which aren't intrusive, and we have Google Chat on our computers. A lot of times, a little message might pop up on the screen which says, "Are you hungry for lunch?" It's not a knock at the door or somebody coming in and rousing you from what you're doing and interrupting the flow. It's just a little window, and if you happen to see it, great. If not, the other person just goes and makes his own lunch and that's that.

We each have our own office and very different work styles and moods, and we don't necessarily keep regular hours either. I tend to like working late into the evenings and am not a morning person; I detest mornings. I can be up fairly early but won't necessarily dive into work right away, whereas Fraser likes to get up, check email, and then get to it basically. So we each go with our natural flow, and we're lucky in the sense that since we're self-employed, we can do it whenever we please throughout the day, as long as the work gets done.

As far as living together, we don't particularly find that we ever get to the point where we feel like we're stepping on each other's heads, if you will. Being more moody than he is, I'm more likely to sometimes need a change of scenery. Fraser is more even-tempered and he'll often understand this before I will and he'll say, "You know what, Honey? You should maybe just go out and get some fresh air and take a drive to the comic shop or do something outside the house for a while." It's like knowing when you need a walk, and often I'll be like, "Oh, yeah, I am feeling a bit of cabin fever. Good idea!" Being at home most of the time, it's good because he reminds me that there is an outside world and it's OK if I go and have fun. I'm not chained to my desk after all, and it's good to go out for a bit and come back refreshed. Maybe it's sickeningly sweet but we're just really in tune with one another!

Fraser tries to protect me a lot from things, which, God bless him, is adorable and sweet, but it's sometimes to his detriment. What I mean by that is being self-employed, sometimes we have really good months and sometimes we don't. If he's stressed about something financially, he may not let on just how stressed he is, and I do not want him carrying those burdens all by himself. He does the business aspect of Class Comics and oversees most of our personal finances and accounts too, where my primary focus is different. Sometimes I'll tell him, "You've got to tell me this stuff. You need to share this with me because otherwise you're carrying it alone and that's not fair." I don't like it because it's impacting him negatively. But he's improved over time and become more open in this area, and it makes him feel better and lighter about it, and better able to go tackle things.

We laugh a lot together. I once heard a grandfather say, "You know, I may be seventy-five years of age, but inside I'm still twenty." He's still young at heart. It's funny because I've always collected comics and I collect toys—Fraser's the same way—and we really have a very youthful appreciation for those kinds of things. We use silly little voices sometimes when we're goofing around, and it totally cracks the other one up because it's just so ludicrous. It's just fun, and we have a good time. We're extremely silly together and we laugh very easily. Neither of us take ourselves personally very seriously either, so it gives us the ability to laugh with each other at each other about one another. We both have a good sense of humor and I always tend to be the clown when I'm with groups of people. My dad is very funny, and I would like to think that I've inherited a little bit of that from him. I tend to have no problem being the butt of jokes and making fun of myself for the benefit of others, and Fraser is very much that way too.

Fraser's a total coffee addict. Often if I'm out, I'll come home with a coffee from Starbucks out of the blue and have that for him, and he loves that. He does the same for me. We don't do flowers and we don't attach an awful lot of importance to those, shall we say, pseudo-traditional acts of gift giving. We will do Valentine's Day dinner out and of course chocolates because we both love chocolate, but more due to our fondness for chocolates than because it's expected because it's Valentine's Day. We like to get cards for each other, and there are so many beautiful, nicely designed cards out there, so when we see one that makes us think of the other person, we'll grab it immediately.

Regarding marriage, Fraser wanted to marry, but it was not as important to me, initially. I think weddings in general are often just so overblown; extremely expensive, over the top, psychotic shows of doves flying and pooping everywhere, and bridesmaids and huge floral displays... To me it's a *Gong Show*, and I say that because almost every wedding I've ever been to has either not worked out in the end or has just been a complete, overblown, colossal expenditure. To do what? To basically say how much you love this person? I don't think you need to spend billions of dollars to show other people that you love a person.

In our case, Fraser and I have purchased a number of properties together, and to me, that was a big commitment, like, "Wow, I love you this much that I feel like doing this with you..." It's a big commitment. So until then, I hadn't really considered, "Well, do I need a wedding? Do I need that official ceremony, that official paper?" Fraser knew that I thought weddings were pretty stupid and he started bringing the topic up slowly and gradually, and eventually I thought, "If we have a wedding, we would have one that suited us, not one that's tailored to what other people think our wedding should be. And that was tough because whenever you tell someone you're getting married, they will give you a hundred suggestions and recommendations, including, "You need fire-dancing Hawaiian jugglers!," a suggestion that actually came up from a friend.

We're not complicated guys, and we just wanted something very simple. So our ceremony was really lovely and was essentially just Fraser, myself, two of our best friends witnessing, and the minister. Our parents were extremely understanding and very respectful of what we wanted, and the following summer we all got together and our sets of parents met each other for the first time. So we were able to celebrate part two of our wedding with them, and they got on beautifully, and the six of us had a wonderful time together. But it's all about your own definition of what a wedding is, and once I realized that I didn't have to the whole Hollywood or TV wedding, it was easier for me.

Up until the time of the wedding, I was nervous but thought, "This makes sense. It's logical because I love him and we've been together this long and I plan to be with him for the rest of my life. So this makes sense." But when I got to the wedding, I was giddy and just really immersed in the emotion of being there. I'm not a teary kind of guy and I won't cry in front of you unless I've got a gun to my head basically, and I didn't cry at the wedding but I got misty, which for me is a big deal. It was such a perfect moment. I didn't realize that it could be quite like that until I was in it, thinking, "Wow, this is awesome..."

It didn't necessarily alter our bond in that we were always so strongly connected, but in truth, for the first few months after the wedding, there was a certain euphoria that comes from knowing that you're bound in the eyes of the law and in the eyes of God, if those are your beliefs. There's a really amazing feeling to knowing that you belong to him and he belongs to you. I thought, "Wow, this is really cool..." I think that getting married made me more aware of how deeply I love Fraser.

I grew up Catholic and have long since left the Catholic church behind. One thing I didn't leave behind is my belief in God. I don't sit at the foot of my bed on my knees every night and pray but I do talk to God a lot. I see God in nature and in the good things that people do for one another. What I pray for mostly is for the wellness of people and for things to go generally well. It's hard for me to express that in front of others, and it isn't a shame thing or anything like that. I'm very private when it comes to this and I'd rather just appreciate it quietly. Fraser knows that's where I'm at, and I don't think he'd say he believes or disbelieves in God necessarily, but he just tends to approach things in a different manner. He's totally respectful of my really deep belief in God and in something greater than all of us, and I appreciate that and never feel judged or anything when I express it.

Being with Fraser has helped me not to judge myself quite as much anymore. For much of my life, I've been very hard on myself, and sometimes, Fraser is able to say, "You know what? You need to chill the hell out because you're just blowing this out of proportion..." Now from anyone else I wouldn't take that, but from him, I can really just take those words in and apply them, which is pretty monumental for me. I think I'm more grown up about things now, though being almost forty years old probably has a lot to do with it, too. But meeting someone in my late twenties who is so kind and so level-headed and who is just a really well-rounded, great person couldn't help but impact me and how I've continued to develop. Whether it's through a certain amount of osmosis or just like-mindedness, you awaken things in each other. Fraser has definitely helped me grow as a person, and I'd like to think I've done the same for him.

For a relationship to work, there has to be respect, communication, understanding, and trust. There are other factors, but those four are pretty essential. I need someone who can communicate respectfully and who can talk like an adult without a lot of screaming or drama. And trust—if you don't trust the person you're with fully, that's a problem. I've been in relationships in the past where I didn't know if I could trust the person, and that leads to angst and to paranoia, which is sometimes quite justified. And that's the worst thing, when you've got that little nagging voice in your head saying, "You know, you don't want to look at this and maybe you should..." That's a problem, and that's not a little voice I want to hear in my relationship, and I never have with Fraser. I know absolutely where he stands and where I stand.

What's funny is that we're both flirtatious in a playful way when we're with other people, and gay men as a rule are very flirtatious. And it's all healthy and it makes you feel good, and it's not flirtatious in a way that is pushing to lead to anything. We've been on several gay cruises together, and what I like is—because Fraser is really cute—a lot of guys will come up to him and chat him up, and he can be perfectly pleasant. I'm not ever concerned that I will find him in our stateroom with somebody else, and vice versa. We're both very grateful that we can be together and that we can feel one hundred percent confident, sexually and emotionally, with each other. There's no worry about, "What's he bringing home to me?"

We have a couple friends who got flirtatious to the point where they wouldn't have said no if we had said, "OK, let's all have fun together." And we talk openly about that, about would we want to do that? The honest truth is that it's always fun to think that somebody finds you sexy and attractive, but I think for me—and for Fraser, too—that's kind of where it ends.

Because at the end of the day it's like yes, the flirting is fun, but I wouldn't commit to going beyond that with someone else just because I don't have a need to.

I'm very, very sexually satisfied with Fraser. I have a lot of fun with him. Sometimes we're very playful and we like to experiment and push the envelope with one another a bit. I love that about him, that we're very much in tune, so I don't really see what sex with two other people—short of experiencing a foursome—would really bring. We're very flattered though for sure! Exclusivity makes things a whole lot simpler for us.

We keep nurturing that fun side of our relationship. We have a good time and we laugh with each other. We still surprise each other once in a while in terms of learning something new about the other. I always marvel at that and love that I don't know everything about him still after ten years together. We're very family oriented in that we both are very close to our parents. Our families are very important to us, and you don't want to get Fraser's mom and me on the phone because we're on for hours!

But Fraser and I just really appreciate each other. The realization that you're with somebody you love so much and that you have such a good time with, that even when times are really hard and you're stressed out from whatever external factors are there, you can comfort and respect and understand each other through whatever's going on. So those things definitely keep the relationship going strong. I think if that ever stopped being the case we'd have to seriously look at why it did and would have to look at either rekindling things or going to that next logical point.

Sometimes I find people want to fit with the person they're with so badly that they will overlook things or they'll actively ignore stuff that just isn't working. Having done it myself in previous relationships I can confidently say that that's a huge mistake. What ends up happening is that one morning you wake up and go, "Holy crap, I don't even know what I'm doing here now..." For a long-term relationship to work, you have to know that you're in the right place with the person you're in the relationship with. That is all encompassing too, and includes the things you have in common, the things you don't have in common, the love you feel for them, as well as realistically gauging the level of that love. Is it puppy love or is it I-want-to-be-in-love-so-I'm-making-myself-be-in-love?

It needs to be genuine, and that leads to trusting the person you're with and trusting yourself with that person, too. Those are really important things. Are you compatible as people? Sometimes you can love a person deeply but not really like them. Personally, when I realized that I used to acquiesce to these things and that doing so wasn't working for me, that's when I was able to let that all go. When I look around at the couples who are really strong and working out well, I see that they have an honesty with each other and with themselves about where they are in their relationship and about how they fit together. Of course there's no perfect recipe and there are no perfect people or relationships, and I'm not saying that Fraser and I don't have arguments. We're both very passionate individuals and when we get a point that we feel is worth arguing we will certainly do that.

Regarding sexual monogamy versus open relationships, I have friends who have been in open relationships and who said, "I really care for this person and he wants an open relationship, so I'll agree to that." If one person really doesn't genuinely want an open relationship, it's not going to work. If you want to be monogamous but the person with you doesn't, no amount of saying to yourself, "Maybe I can make this work…" is going to make it work. There seem to almost be two different types of wiring in men, and one kind is not necessarily better than the other. But if you are wired for exclusivity, you have to respect that about yourself, and also understand that you need to find a like-minded partner to make it work long-term.

Kindness is really important in relationships, too. We certainly all have our tempers and our days. We have friends who are married and who talk to each other like they are the mangiest dogs on the street. I don't understand that. There is no reason to communicate with one another that way. Sure, you're upset. OK, I get it. You're angry because you feel slighted or whatever, but swearing at and tearing down someone who is supposed to be your partner, your teammate in life, doesn't work and doesn't help the situation. I wish people could see that. Kindness is huge, and we all want to be treated with consideration and respect.

CHAPTER 6

JASON AND DEMARCO

"He was acting very nervous that whole evening, though I didn't really think about it too much, and at the end of dinner he just snuck a ring up on the table in a box and scooted it over to me. I said, "What's this?," and I popped it open, and deMarco said, "Will you marry me?" I was like, "Really?" I was shocked. I think I said "Really?" three times before I actually said "Yes."

* * * * *

Singer-songwriters Jason Warner and deMarco DeCiccio met in Hollywood in 2001. The pop duo's first single climbed the Billboard charts while their second single won Music Video of the Year 2006 on MTV's *LOGO*. The couple was featured on the cover of *Advocate Magazine* ("Gay Christian Lovers") and were also the subject of a full-length, feature documentary film titled *We're All Angels.* More recently, Jason and deMarco became the proud fathers of their two sons, who resemble the singers to an uncanny degree. Jason has published a book about their experience, titled *The Journey of Same Sex Surrogacy,* which is available on Amazon and through their website, www.jasonanddemarco.com. The family now makes their home in Tennessee.

Jason Warner — (deMarco DeCiccio)

We've been together eleven years. When we met I was twenty-six, and deMatrco was twenty-five. I had previously been in a three-year relationship and had just moved to L.A. in February of 2001. I was really not looking for a relationship at all. Being single in L.A. sounded like a good plan to me, but that changed pretty quickly when I met deMarco at a restaurant in June. I had met the owner of the restaurant on a previous visit, and he knew that I was a singer and he told me, "There's a guy here who works for me who sings. The next time you come in, I'll have to introduce you."

So the next time I went in, the owner said, "Hey, it's good to see you again. That guy I told you about is here. Do you want me to introduce you?"

I was actually on a date, so I was kind of like, "Sure." So he introduced my date and me to deMarco. There weren't any instant stars or anything, and since I was on a date, I was trying to be respectful of my date. My date actually flirted with him more than I did!

After meeting deMarco that first time, he ended up serving me one of the following times I went in. We started talking about music and songwriting and just started connecting more and more. We also had a mutual friend, and I was in discussions with our mutual friend's manager about managing me at the time. So we moved in similar circles, and I was with a group of friends that night and I said, "Well, why don't we get together for lunch one day and we can talk," really not setting it up as a date; just saying, "Hey, let's get together..."

Little did we know that when we got together, I'd pretty much tell him my whole life story, and then he'd tell me, "I think I'm bi..." It was a real turn-off, because having just gotten out of this relationship, I thought, "I really want the next guy I date to be someone who's out, who knows who he is, someone I don't have to go through this whole coming-out process with again."

So when deMarco said he thought he was bi—he was dating a girl at the time, actually—I thought, "OK, this is NOT what I'm looking for." When I dropped him off that day, he said, "Hold on a second," and he ran in and got a CD of his, an Italian CD he had recorded. When I put it in the stereo as I drove away, I really thought that would be the last time I'd see him or I just thought we'd be friends, and then I heard the CD, and as soon as the CD started, I thought, "Oh shit..." As soon as I heard him singing, there was some connection I felt. Ironically enough, it's in Italian, so it's not like I even understood the words, but there was just some energy there. I also didn't know that prior to meeting me, the owner of the restaurant used to play my CD late at night at the place when they were cleaning up and closing. So deMarco had been hearing me sing for months and had asked, "Who is that guy?" That's when the owner told him, "The next time he's here, I'll make sure I introduce him."

I didn't know any of that backstory, so when I met deMarco the first time while I was on a date. I really didn't pay a lot of attention to him. He always jokes and says he basically felt ignored. He had a moment where he said, "I hate him. I must have him!"

I was at the bar late one night and my friends had left, so I stayed and asked deMarco if he wanted me to wait for him to get off work. He said, "Yes." I don't know what made me stay that night and offer to wait until he got off work, but he went and paid one of the bartenders to close for him, and then we went and jumped into my car. It just so happened that I was new to L.A. so I wasn't really familiar with the freeways, but at one point, we got to a sign that said Marina Del Ray.

My landlord had a sailboat there, and I had been out with my landlord several times on his boat, so I knew where we were when I saw that sign, and we ended up at my landlord's boat. It was a really beautiful experience. That's the place where we really connected and that was the first moment where both of us let our walls down, and deMarco was finally himself. I saw who he was, and we had a beautiful night on the boat, and then woke up together the next morning and never separated. That was it. We moved in together like a month later.

Once we started really hanging out, the making out just went further and further, so I don't remember if I gave him oral sex on the fifth day or what. We probably waited a couple months before we had intercourse, but it all happened really naturally, and the intimacy grew the longer we were together. Looking back, I think it's because I had been in a bad relationship beforehand, and deMarco was new to this that we were slow and didn't rush things. I believe it was easier for both of us to go slower because of that, and honestly, because I was his first, he didn't really know what he liked sexually. I'm pretty versatile so I basically gave him time to figure out what he enjoyed. I knew I was his first so I didn't want to just plunge right in!

My previous boyfriend had been married to a woman when I met him, so I knew what it was like being with someone who was coming out. I knew that no matter how much they said "I love you and I want to be with you," there's always the coming out process of wanting to experience things. So in the beginning of our relationship, I pretty much gave deMarco the freedom to do what he wanted to do and I think that because I gave him that freedom, it actually made him want it less. I think it helped.

But deMarco's and my rule was always that if anything did happen, we would just be honest about it. It's not a matter of "Is it going to break us up?" It's a matter of "How are we going to work through it?" So that's just always been our agreement, and in the early part of our relationship, we did go through some times where things did happen outside of the relationship. But we quickly made the choice that that's not what we wanted going forward. A lot of guys coming out later feel that they missed an adolescence almost, and so they need to go out and sow a few oats. My thing with him was "Just please don't lie to me," and I think because of that approach, we were able to stay together.

We've had many conversations about all of this over the course of eleven years. Neither of us have ever wanted to go outside of our relationship. I mean it's never been OK for me to say, "OK, I can go have sex and you can go have sex." We've talked about "How do we feel about bringing someone in to our relationship?" and concluded "Why open the door for something that could cause issues?" We know it works for some people, but it just wouldn't for us.

The other thing is that because of who we are and what we do, we do have a sense that we're seen somewhat as role models also, so that factors into things, too. Is the desire there at times? Of course. Over eleven years, there have been many times and there have been many opportunities, but I think it always comes back to—and it's not that it's right or wrong—it's that we have something of a responsibility to who we are and what we stand for, and regardless of what we believe, there are a lot of people who could potentially be disappointed or let down if they were to find out such things about us. So I think for us it's easier not to have to worry about all of that or to cross those bridges.

I would never be in a relationship that isn't sexual, though I know some guys can be, and we know couples who aren't sexual. I'm too sexual of a person to be in a relationship that isn't. It's different than it was early on. There are some months where we'll go and have sex two or three times a week and then there are other months where we could go three weeks and not have sex. Of course, having babies pretty much changed everything those months, because you get so exhausted you don't want to do anything but sleep! But now a year into it, I feel like we're back on track relationship-wise, as we were before the babies came along. So we're definitely sexually active; it just varies as far as the frequency. We cuddle. We kiss. We enjoy lying down together watching TV or a movie. We'll hold hands in the car, not all the time, but there are moments where we do. I think that's something we both consciously try to work on, remembering to pay attention to the other.

We have a joke of sorts that when we feel like we're being ignored, we say, "Notice me!" to the other. One time at a church, we were singing and there was a little girl there who kept saying to her mom, "Notice me! Notice me!" We thought that was so cute, because she was just being so honest, like, "Hello! Notice me..." So that's our little inside phrase to each other when one of us feels overlooked, like, "Helloooo!," and we say, "Notice me...," and it pulls us back in to give each other a hug or a kiss and just have that moment of acknowledgment.

We try to check in with each other periodically: "How are you feeling about everything? Are things good? Do you think we could be working on this or that?" I do think those check-ins are good for us. They bring us back to center, and how are we feeling and is everything good and are you happy? Those kinds of questions really help.

We just had a date night the other night, and on the way home we checked in, and it was good. Some good stuff came up. It just brings us both back to knowing what the other is thinking and feeling. We try and have a date night once a week, usually on Fridays. We've been in business together for ten years and have been together for eleven. Even before we were dads, date nights could very easily turn into business, where we'd end up talking about this or that aspect. Now after the babies, we're both involved in new businesses as well as our music, so I think it's a little easier today because it's not all about the music and our music career. There are more facets to our life now.

You have to work toward love being unconditional. I don't think love is really love unless it is unconditional, and unconditional love is hard to find! I think it's hard to find within oneself—for oneself—and for others and for our partner. But you need to get to a place of not trying to change someone and just loving them for who they are and what they bring to life. And hopefully those areas where they are strong benefit you and vice versa.

The reason deMarco and I work is because we're so different. When I look at my past relationships, the reason they didn't was because we were too alike. deMarco and I really fill up the empty spots for each other, and I think that's why it's worked. With a lot of our couple-friends too, they're very different, but that's why their relationships work. And yet you also have to have enough commonality so that you enjoy one another. It's been unique for me to find someone who's so different and yet we share enough similarities, too, that it all just somehow fits.

When you first meet someone, you have the passion and the excitement, and then you move into new phases. And of course, having children brought a whole new realm of love to deMarco and me. Then you not only love your partner as your partner, but as the father of your children, so there's a whole other type of love that I experience toward deMarco, seeing him with the boys and experiencing the boys with him. So this is a new phase for us.

Two years ago, he went into his own business, and just watching him grow in that; there's a part of me that really loves who he's becoming and who he's become in this new venture and this new role. So since we're always changing and evolving, our love is always changing and evolving, too. It's definitely deepening. When you're with someone so long, it either deepens or it just becomes routine. By no means do we have a perfect relationship, but our love for each other continues to deepen as we grow older.

Five years into our relationship, we started talking about having kids. I had always wanted children and I always joke and say that when I was a kid

I wanted kids. I looked forward to growing up, getting married, and having kids. Later on, when I realized I was gay, the biggest heartache was thinking I was never going to have children. So when deMarco and I had been together five years, we started talking about kids.

I've always just had a heart for kids, and one of the things we've done a lot with our music is sharing with our fans and audiences about teenage suicide and homeless and runaway kids. So I've always had a passion for youth and young adults, and initially I always thought that we would adopt or maybe have a foster kid. deMarco and I initially talked about fostering or adopting, and I started looking up some agencies and doing some research.

deMarco was open to it, but he had moved from his native Canada to Los Angeles to pursue his career, and his career had always been really important to him, so bringing kids into the picture was a really big step for him. For me, it was more natural, where for him it was more of a choice. When we first started talking about it I could definitely sense that it wasn't the time yet, but after a few more years passed, we were suddenly getting all these neon signs... We have friends in New Jersey who are this straight couple, whom we told that we were thinking about adopting. We'd heard about surrogacy but also heard that it was outrageously expensive, too.

The wife of our straight couple basically said, "If you ever want to have your biological kids, I'll do it for you." We were like, "Really?"

And, "You'd better check with your husband..." He was there, of course, and they kind of laughed. Not too long after that, they said, "If you guys are really serious about this, we want you to know that we're serious too, if this is an avenue you'd want to try." They were so serious that after her last pregnancy, since they didn't want any more kids, he got a vasectomy so that she would be able to do this if she wanted to.

Shortly thereafter, we performed at a banquet-type event, and when we sat down at a table, on my right was—ironically—a fertility doctor from Boston, and on my left was a fertility lawyer from L.A., and that night I basically asked every question I could think of. When we left, I just said to deMarco, "God, I just feel like we're getting neon signs that we're supposed to do this..." This happened right after the couple in Jersey had offered to help us. Talking with the doctor and the lawyer was very educational, and I left there feeling like, "My God, I could actually have a biological child!" I'd never even really considered it as an option before, and by that point, we already knew we had an egg donor and possibly surrogate who was willing to do this. So we started exploring that path.

Our egg donor unfortunately had some complications prior to us moving forward, which made her unable to carry for us, but she was still able to be our donor. So we went through that process back in 2007 and we ended up with twelve embryos. We had twelve eggs, and six of them fertilized with my sample, and six of them with deMarco's sample. So we ended up with twelve embryos and we froze them back in 2007, because we knew we weren't yet ready.

2006 and 2007 were kind of the height of things happening for us. We had a music video that was Video of the Year on *LOGO*. We had a documentary that was coming out on *Showtime*. We just had a lot of big things happening and we knew it wasn't the time to have a baby. We actually ended up using the doctor from Boston we'd sat next to, who told us that you can freeze embryos successfully for up to ten years, and we knew we'd want to be parents within ten years for sure.

We felt that either when we were financially in a position to find a surrogate with an agency or when a surrogate would come to us, then we'd know it would be time to move forward. And that's really how it happened. We moved to Houston from L.A. in 2008 because our producer lived here and we were recording a new album at that time. At the same time, an area church offered us a part-time job, and the youth director there and I became extremely good friends; she really became like a sister to me. She knew we were in this process and she offered to be the surrogate for us. We decided to move forward with that in 2010, and they thawed my embryos and deMarco's embryos, and one of each survived, so they transferred both of them and both "took." So we got pregnant the first try, and it was fraternal twins—same egg donor, so they had the same biological mother—but one is my biological son and one is deMarco's biological son. They're twin boys and they were born on May 23rd, 2011.

It's crazy how much the boys look like deMarco and me. They're basically mini "us's." Mason has brown, curly hair, and Noah has straight, blond hair. People think we had ourselves cloned! It's pretty uncanny. Even our doctor has said she's never seen anything like it. The kids are awesome. Once we got through the first year, there was just a moment of "Oh, my God, we made it!" The first six months were the hardest by far, and then once they hit nine months, it just got more and more fun. And now we're having a ball with them. We're both really fortunate that we both pretty much work from home and have our own schedules so we've been able to be here mostly full-time, and then my parents relocated here after the kids were born, so they're here helping as well.

Our biggest communication hurdle has been that deMarco usually doesn't go into depth about anything, so if I ask how his day was, he'll say, "Great." If he asks me how my day was, I will start with how I brushed my teeth and go through the day in detail. So there are times where I would like him to elaborate about this or that.

His biggest thing with me is probably my listening. I'm not the world's best listener, and usually as someone is talking, I'm thinking of what I'm going to say... The first few years of our relationship, there were some things that happened, and my grandmother—who's very grounded and very spiritual—was a good mediator for us. She'd interpret what we were each trying to say, because we weren't really hearing each other. So that's the only time we've had someone step in to help us.

Other than that we've been fortunate that we haven't really needed counseling or therapy. The other night on date night we went to the movies, and this couple was sitting next to us and she was calling him an asshole and he was calling her a bitch... It's funny that I heard them but didn't say anything, and on the way home, deMarco said, "God, I just can't imagine having a relationship like the couple sitting next to us. Why be with someone if you're going to be like that with each other?" I thought it was funny because listening to the two of them I was thinking, "I'm so glad that we're in a healthy relationship!"

My previous relationship had been pretty volatile, but I think that as you evolve as a person and as you grow and learn to love yourself, that's what you attract to you. I was then at a point where I didn't love or appreciate myself and I read a book called *In the Meantime*, by Ilyana

Vinzent, which was really an amazing book. After I read that book and got to a point of really feeling like I didn't need someone to complete me, that's when I met deMarco. So maybe that's why it's all worked. I didn't really feel like I needed him. I was OK on my own and complete on my own, and anyone else was a nice addition.

Spirituality has played a huge part in our lives. When I met deMarco, I had started exploring a new spiritual path. I'd been raised very Evangelical Christian and then was Pentacostal, so I had a lot of dogma and doctrine that I carried along with me. deMarco was raised Catholic and didn't really have any baggage, having gone to church mostly on holidays. He wasn't a devout Catholic so he was pretty open, and when I met him I was reading Marianne Williamson and Deepak Chopra and was really starting to expand my Christianity more to New Thought Christianity. And that's really where our path has continued, and I just basically brought him along with me, because he was very open and receptive.

The church that hired us in Houston was a Unity Church, which is a New Thought Church. I love Unity and its message, though I think we're more contemporary in certain ways too. So it's kind of hard because we don't really fit in. There are a lot of things about Contemporary Christianity that we like and we still love praise and worship, but we differ with a lot of the theology. So it's been an interesting dilemma for us because not only do we have to worry about the gay/Christian thing, but now we have to worry about the spiritual/Christian thing...

A lot of churches have issues with the metaphysical approach, so even if they're OK with you being gay, if they find out you're metaphysical, they're not crazy about that! It's been a really interesting journey for us. Musically where we fit in is the fundamentalist mega-churches, because our music is more contemporary Christian. But we're really paving our own way, and we've always had to, not only relationship-wise but career-wise. There's not a place for us in the Christian contemporary market, so we started singing in gay-friendly churches and then New Thought churches, which tend to be gay-friendly.

Then we did pop, so we've had some success in the pop world, too. Yet even in the pop world, somehow the spirituality comes along with the music. Even with a song that isn't spiritual—I don't know if it's an energy or what—but people get that there's something spiritual to us. There's a song of ours called *Trying to Get to You* that went onto the Billboard charts and was a dance remix, and people were writing and saying, "That song really ministered to me..." And we're just cracking up because it's a completely non-religious song, but for them they interpreted it otherwise. So it's interesting. The *Advocate* did a cover story back in 2004 on us, and the title was Gay Christian Lovers, which kind of really put a stamp on us. That wasn't a bad thing per se, but there are a lot of assumptions that come along with that word Christian that we're not. So people are often quite surprised when they find out who we really are spiritually, because it's very outside of what they may have expected. Hopefully that will continue evolving as well, because we always want to be growing spiritually. But we've always kept God or love or the Divine at the center of our relationship.

deMarco and I have an amazing companionship, and that's a really beautiful thing to have, when you know you're not on the journey alone. Beginning with that night on the sailboat, we really connected and felt like we knew each other on a soul level. It just felt so natural for both of us. When we met each other, we were in our mid-twenties and were really sort of beginning life. I'd only been graduated from college for four or five years at that time, so I feel like we've really grown up together. I was a pretty innocent, traditional church boy when he and I met, and I'm probably more grounded now. I'm better at compromising in a relationship now and better at loving unconditionally than I was before.

You really have to love yourself unconditionally first and allow yourself to experience what you experience without judgment, and you have to do that with your partner. And to realize that just as much as you're on your spiritual path, they're on their spiritual path, and you have to honor that, even if it means that there are things about it you don't like or agree with. When you get to that point, that's really when magic can happen.

We laugh a lot. In the beginning of our relationship, we both just laughed so much, and that's been key for us. We still make each other laugh. As far as romance, I'm more the romantic one. For years, I surprised him with things, but things don't mean the same to him. Eventually I realized I was actually doing for him what I wanted him to be doing for me. Knowing that I like things like that, deMarco tries to make a special effort every now and then to do something that way. For him, my doing the dishes or the laundry is romantic; he feels that I love him through my doing those things. For me, I feel loved when he gives me things. There's even a book about the variety of "love languages," and his has to do with me doing, and mine has to do with him giving. So we try to conscious about that.

There was a running joke because I kept saying, "When is he going to ask me to marry him?" It was just assumed that deMarco would ask me. He said, "When it's legal, we'll do it." So when they made it legal in L.A., which was around our seventh anniversary, I thought he was taking me out for our anniversary, but he actually took me out to propose. We hadn't moved back to Houston yet, but we were here, and he took me out to a gay-owned restaurant. He was acting very nervous that whole evening, though I didn't really think about it too much, and at the end of dinner, he just snuck a ring up on the table in a box and scooted it over to me.

I said, "What's this?," and I popped it open, and deMarco said, "Will you marry me?"

I was like, "Really?" I was shocked. I think I said "Really?" three times before I actually said "Yes."

That was a total surprise. I really had no idea he was proposing, and the ring was really beautiful. It was a French antique, and I could tell he really put a lot of thought into getting something unique. That was on July 1st, a few days before our anniversary. We ended up getting married on August 22nd in L.A., before Prop 8 happened in November. Other than our boys being born, the experience of our wedding, which came later, was one of the most magical days of our life.

It really was a fairy tale wedding, having all our friends and family together in this absolutely beautiful location, a little white chapel out in the hill country outside of Houston. There's a plaza outside that makes it seem like you're in Italy somewhere. Even though we'd legally married in L.A., we both felt that we really wanted to wait to have a wedding until our families could all be there, too. The timing was beautiful, and it was really a magical experience.

With the boys, we were very close with our surrogate, so we were there for every ultrasound and we were there for the deliveries. The day they were born was by far the most amazing day of my life. I was just in another world, watching these two little beings—who you know are going to change your life forever—come into our life. We'd been waiting for nine months and dreaming about having kids for years, and then they just suddenly appeared. It was just totally amazing. I felt so much love for our surrogate and for her being willing to do what she did. That was a day I can say I think I felt the most pure, authentic love that I've ever felt, which is why it's the most amazing day of my life. And that's what we're all striving to feel every day.

Honesty and unconditional love and generosity and willingness are all important in a healthy relationship. You have to be willing to work through whatever comes along. Anything is possible in life. You have to have faith and you have to have hope. If you want a loving relationship, visualize it, and then you also have to take action. You can wait all day for someone to come into your life, but if you're not putting yourself out there to meet that person, you're handicapping yourself. Anything is possible, and if you really want it badly enough you can create it. deMarco and I are creating a life together, and life continues to inspire and engage us and excite us. You have to be excited about your life together as it is today as well as about all the good things still to come.

Section II:

Couples Together
Twenty to Thirty Years

CHAPTER 7

MATT AND SCOTT

"It's great that there's a freedom there for gay people just to say, "Hey, we already have an unconventional relationship in the first place, so why not just be open to finding out how that relationship can best suit the two of us—in whatever form that may take—and not be constrained by society's norms?" So we've been open to that, to discovering what works best for us."

* * * * *

Matt and Scott first oogled each other across a crowded San Francisco cafe over twenty years ago. Their first brief conversation led to a love relationship about which Matt says, "It's kind of wild that after all these years we still enjoy each other's company on an almost unlimited basis." Scott is a freelance artist, while Matt works as an international trade executive. Now married, they continue to live in the Bay area with Diego, their Golden Lab.

Matt — (Scott)

Scott and I will be together twenty-three years in December. When we met at the Cafe Flore here in San Francisco, Scott was twenty-four, and I was twenty-eight. I was there with a friend, and he was there with a friend, and we just happened to catch each other's eye across the cafe, and were oogling each other across the room. At one point, my friend got up to use the restroom, and Scott took the opportunity to come over and introduce himself and say, "I think we're being a little bit rude to our friends... Since we're obviously interested in each other, I thought I'd introduce myself and give you my phone number. Maybe we can get together sometime after the holidays."

That was December 22nd, right before Christmas. During that brief conversation, he told me that he had just come back from a year and a half in Europe and that he worked at a Banana Republic store in town. He said he had grown up in San Francisco and had studied theater at N.Y.U.

Afterwards, I thought, "I can't wait to see this guy again until after Christmas," so I just happened to go Christmas shopping the next day and casually dropped into his store and surprised him. Scott was very happy to see me and was able to take a break, and we went and had a cup of coffee together. That was our first little date-let.

We just hit it off right away, and if it wasn't love at first sight, it was at least lust at first sight. There was definitely a very strong connection between us, and I think we both sensed that this might be something special. Scott specifically talked about his wish to get to know each other a bit before we had sex, that if it was going to be something special between us he wanted to hold off a bit on that. I believe it was New Year's Eve when we finally hit the sack, about eight days later, which for gay men is a lifetime, of course. We had several dates together leading up to it.

He lived a couple of miles away from me, and we just spent a lot of time together. One of his roommates at the time knew that the two of us were talking about eventually moving in together and he kind of forced the issue at one point by saying, "I actually found somebody else I'm interested in rooming with, so if you guys decide to move in together, this wouldn't be a bad time..." So along about the first of October we moved in together, and though we went out and looked for a new place together, Scott just ended up moving in with me and making my place his home. That was about nine months into our relationship, and the timing seemed right.

Interestingly, about two months later, I was called into my boss's boss's office and was told, "We have good news for you. We're giving you a promotion to Tampa, Florida!"

I said, "Oh, do I have to interview for it or anything?," and they said, "Oh, no. We want you for the position and we're very excited to offer it to you."

Of course in the back of my mind, I'm thinking, "Holy shit! What does this mean for my relationship with Scott?" I came home that night and had a very tearful conversation with him, saying "Oh, my God, what are we going to do?" Luckily, Scott was in a situation where he wasn't that established in San Francisco and fortunately, he thought it would be kind of a neat adventure and he agreed: "Yeah, I'll move to Florida with you."

As it turned out, the move was a really good thing for our relationship because in San Francisco, we each had our own sets of friends and our own lifestyle. Moving to a new place where neither of us had ever been before forced us to really develop a bond and to develop friendships and a connection to a new place. It brought us closer together.

With the housing market so comparatively cheap there, it made more sense to buy than to rent so we bought a house together, too. That was another hugely bonding experience for us. We had belonged to a gay and lesbian running club called the Front Runners in San Francisco, and eventually, we started a Front Runners chapter in Tampa. There was a real need for something like that there, as Tampa didn't have a very developed gay community. That was a great experience for us, and it became wildly successful, too; within two years, I think we had three hundred members. It was crazy! We developed so many friendships from that, and it turned out to be a really, really good experience overall.

Initially, we were completely monogamous, and quite honestly, when we were in Tampa, I had a little fling with somebody. It was a night where I was off on a company picnic and had been drinking and my guard was a bit down and I just happened to stop at a rest stop outside of Orlando on the way home. Some guy next to me was totally cruising me there, and it was the first time I'd ever experienced anything like that. I ended up doing something with him and another guy and shared that with Scott when I got home, and it nearly ended our relationship. That was really, really hard. I basically had to beg and plead with him to stay and not to leave me, and fortunately he did, and we got past it.

My job was such that I was on this management track where every few years, they were going to move me up and around, and actually the next move would probably have been to Venezuela. Of course, a gay couple doesn't have any status in a foreign country—let alone our own country— so we just decided we wanted to move back to California where we would both get jobs and basically root ourselves in the Bay area and make that our permanent home. We both were missing California, and we also had a cabin up in the mountains there that we had enjoyed getting to on weekends and were missing, too, so we made the decision jointly to uproot ourselves again and head back to San Francisco, where I would change careers. And it's worked out for us.

Shortly after we moved back to California, Scott had a little fling with somebody, and I thought, "OK, I guess we're even now." But then I realized, "You know, if we have a strong enough emotional connection with one another, then that sort of thing should not destroy our relationship." We came to realize that our bond can withstand that kind of thing, and we are men—not that that's an excuse—and that we do have sexual desires for not just each other but for other people, and we need to somehow deal with that. So we've tried to be as open as possible about all of that and we really have been mostly monogamous all along.

A few years ago, we experimented with the idea of opening up our relationship to non-monogamy, and it ended up not working too well for us. Scott ended up getting emotionally attached to a guy he had met and actually started having these fantasies about running off with him. The guy also had a partner, and fortunately for our relationship, it wasn't a mutual thing where this guy wanted to run off with Scott too, otherwise it could have had a very different outcome.

The lesson for us was that that's the risk we take when we open up our relationship. When we open ourselves to having sex outside the relationship, there is that possibility that we may develop an emotional connection to one of these people, or that they might develop an emotional connection with one of us that is not mutual, which could hurt them. We potentially put ourselves in the position of hurting other people or ourselves when we go there, so about two years ago, we closed things up again and have gone back to monogamy.

So it's been a journey. We recognize that for gay men in a gay relationship there really aren't the role models out there, and we are creating these relationships that have never been sanctioned by society. A "normal" way of being in a gay relationship hasn't been developed by our society, so we really just create the relationship as it works out best for us as we go along. It's great that there's a freedom there for gay people just to say, "Hey, we already have an unconventional relationship in the first place, so why not just be open to finding out how that relationship can best suit the two of us—in whatever form that may take—and not be constrained by society's norms?" So we've been open to that, to discovering what works best for us.

At first, we decided that monogamy was the way we wanted to go, and eventually that changed, and now we are back to monogamy and feeling like that's the best thing for us. Our particular path may not be best for another gay relationship, and we try not to judge other's relationships, but this is the journey that we have taken. We have friends who are extremely monogamous and they would never even want to try non-monogamy, and we know other relationships that are just the opposite and they would never even want to try monogamy. But for us, it's been mostly monogamy.

Scott and I sleep together and are very affectionate with each other. We cuddle and spoon and definitely like to touch a lot. When he's not around— he's been staying with his ailing mom for the last several weeks—and I've been home by myself I don't sleep as well or go to bed as early because I don't like getting into bed by myself so much. Luckily, I've got the dog that I can encourage to jump up on the bed and hang out with me for a little bit! But Scott and I very much like to sleep together and hold hands and be affectionate and spoon or various things over the course of the night. Those things are important to us, and physical contact is a really important human need.

I consciously have this goal of trying to surprise him with romantic gestures, like giving him flowers or surprising him with dinner at such and such a restaurant or giving him a hug or a kiss out of the blue or initiate sex. But it is a challenge not to just get caught up in our own day-to-day life and just to remind each other that "You're special. I love you and I'm not taking you for granted." It's challenging!

Love to me means expressing my devotion and caring for Scott, and it's also having a deep inner caring and compassion as well. I recognize my love for him oftentimes when he's not around, when I'm at work or he's away or I'm away. There's a longing there to be with him and spend time together. I strive not to take him for granted and just allow him to be his own self and not try to mold him into what I would like him to be in terms of what I would consider the ideal mate to be like. I want him to have the freedom to blossom and be himself and have the space to just express himself fully.

There are times when, especially when you have disagreements or arguments or we get upset with one another, that I want to say, "I wish you were more like this or more like that..." Those are times where I have to just really step back and recognize that Scott is different from me and that I'm different from him, and sometimes those differences are going to grate on each of us. Those differences can also be good and productive. We can help each other to grow in certain areas where the other may have some deficit or feel they'd like to improve. I may have qualities that Scott admires, and he has qualities I admire, and it's good that we allow ourselves to have those differences and commit to working together through those times of friction.

For me, the situation where I almost lost Scott made me realize very clearly just how important he was and is to me. I think that sometimes happens when you lose something or are about to, you get this sudden clarity about how important it really is. I knew I'd done a very hurtful thing and I couldn't imagine losing him; it would have just crushed me. I literally pleaded with him to stay and to forgive me and to give me another chance, and fortunately, he did. I really dodged a bullet, and it taught me a huge life lesson. Luckily, we've been able to resolve our conflicts in a civil manner and have never gotten verbally or physically abusive with each other.

I probably tend to yell a bit more than he does, and it grates me that he can be very clear in his points without raising his voice. I want to say, "Why don't you just yell or something!" But fortunately we've been able to have a process for airing things out and talking about them and being able to see each other's point of view and then getting past the conflict. That's a real blessing, that we can do so without attacking each other and saying things in anger we'd later regret. It's just not necessary or helpful to say cutting and biting words to each other, or to anyone else for that matter.

It's interesting to ponder what provides the glue to keep a relationship together. I often think, "What is it that attracts me to Scott and keeps me attracted to him?" There's no doubt that there's definitely a chemical attraction between us. There always has been and there still is to this day. There was that physical attraction from the beginning, and that's what drew us to each other as we saw each other across the cafe—"That guy's cute!"—and I can safely say that it's still there to this day.

We've both changed, we've aged a little bit, but I can still look at him and think, "He's that handsome guy that I met twenty-three years ago." With men especially, that physical attraction is important. It's the initial glue of a relationship, and then you get to know each other and you realize that there are a lot of other neat qualities and characteristics there that attract you to the person as well.

The sex is good and has always been pretty strong for us, even after all these years. It can sometimes be a bit more mundane, I suppose, but at the same time, there's that sexual energy and attraction we still share, which is important. A big part of sex is communication, and for me, talking about sexual issues has been challenging. Scott is much better about it and he's helped open up the conversation about sex and about our desires and longings, about what he likes and needs in sex. We've always talked about the fact that we're attracted to other men as well and have a longing for other men outside of our relationship.

That's an important topic, which is a difficult thing for gay men to broach, and at some point, you have to feel comfortable and trust one another to admit that "Hey, I'm a man. I look at other men and think, "Boy, wouldn't it be hot to hop in the sack with him!" We talk about those things.

A big key to a successful relationship is really having an open line of communication. Scott is really, really good at very open, effective communication. I've learned a lot from him and try to just be as open about communicating with him as I possibly can. I don't know if it has to do with coming from a big family as I did, but sometimes I feel like I learned to subvert my own personal needs for the needs of the collective. I've had to learn how to express what my needs in the relationship are to Scott, and realize that it's important for me to express that, and then to negotiate my needs versus his needs, and at least put it out there to make myself feel that I'm being heard, that I'm not letting myself become subverted in the relationship. To fall into thinking that the other person's needs should have a priority over my own needs is not a recipe for long-term success.

We've individually gone to therapy, but haven't jointly. I went through a period where I was really struggling with my work and my career and had gotten into a very stressful, no-win situation there, so I sought out career counseling and personal psychotherapy as well and made some good, positive changes. Scott went to a therapist when he went through the period where he got emotionally attached to that other guy he'd met. Although we're both very open to therapy and have experienced its value, we've never felt the need to go to couples counseling. We're not against it, and would seek it out if we felt that need for it someday.

We typically assume that we're going to spend our non-work time together. If not we just talk about "I've got a work event," or "I'd like to get together with so-and-so," or I'll run on my own or take a bike ride. We negotiate doing our own thing as well. Our work schedules align in the summer, but not during the rest of the year, when I have Saturdays to run errands or get my hair cut or go out on a bike ride with friends, which he doesn't necessarily like to do.

On Mondays, it's pretty much Scott's own time to himself. But otherwise, the assumption is that we spend much of our free time together and jointly get together with friends or go out to dinner with people. The great thing is that we both just like spending time together. It's kind of wild that after all these years, we just still enjoy each other's company on an almost unlimited basis. I almost marvel at it sometimes that we don't get sick of each other! But for whatever reason—maybe that's part of the glue that keeps us together—we really enjoy spending time with each other and jointly spending time with other friends and family members.

Scott and I travel well together, and actually I think that traveling well together is a good indicator of what is going to be a successful relationship. It's a test, and I know that we passed that test early on. We love road trips and we've traveled through Europe and South America and all over the world together. We get on each other's nerves from time to time and recognize that maybe we need to take a little time away from one another during the trip but otherwise we just really enjoy each other's company.

Scott and I have very similar spiritual paths, though neither of us is religious. I grew up Catholic and have since moved away from that and from organized religion as a whole. Actually right before I came out I was a born-again Christian, which was my last attempt to cure myself of being gay, and after that experience I pretty much discarded religion as a whole.

Both Scott and I have a real spiritual journey we are on. I think we have a holistic approach to life and we understand that we need to attend to our physical, emotional, mental and spiritual needs, and that those are connected. We're both advocates of meditation and looking inside ourselves and tapping into our intuition and our connectedness with one another and with the people around us and the greater universe. It's really important to maintain a mindfulness in life. I'm somewhat agnostic in that I believe in a higher power though I'm not sure if I believe in a God. I do know that life has a meaning and that we're all interconnected, and that having such an outlook definitely helps you get through the difficulties of the day-to-day.

We each have a different type of sense of humor but we do laugh a lot. That's actually sometimes an area of contention too because I tend to take things more literally, and Scott can have a bitchy or biting or ironic sense of humor. In this era of Facebook, where I've seen things he's posted or said to other people, I realize, "He's really funny and smart and clever!" I've really come to appreciate Scott's wit and intelligence a lot more.

Over the years, he's somewhat censored directing that humor at me because he knows that I have this tendency to get my feelings hurt. My humor tends to be more dorky I guess, but we absolutely do a lot of laughing together, and it's certainly also great for releasing tension. My dad is a real jokester and he's at least taught me the value of having a good sense of humor and how it lends a more lighthearted atmosphere to things. Since I can get overly serious I often need to lighten up a bit!

We're married. Back in 2004, our mayor illegally allowed marriages at San Francisco City Hall. I was pretty plugged in to the political scene here and had gotten advance word that the mayor was going to do this. It was two days before Valentine's Day, February 12th, the day that traditionally, at least in California, gay couples would go down to the County Clerk's office and apply for marriage certificates and get turned down and then have a little protest and go back home. This was that particular day in 2004, and it turns out that our mayor had been to Washington and just had witnessed Bush reiterate his opposition to same-sex marriage in his State of the Union address, and our mayor was so offended by that position that when he came back to San Francisco he said, "I want to do something that counters that notion." So he decided to take advantage of this opportunity on the 12th, when he knew that gay couples would be doing their annual thing at City Hall. He talked to the City Attorney and other officials and asked, "Can we somehow go ahead and issue legal marriage licenses to same-sex couples?" He decided that they were going to do it and that it would be legal.

So Scott and I happened to be there that day and got in line at the County Clerk's office, expecting we'd get turned down as usual. But it turned out that they told us they were going to issue marriage licenses and then asked us the question, "So are you ready to get married today?"

Scott and I looked at each other and said, "I think they're serious... OK. Yeah!" It turns out the city officials had also notified the press that some-thing significant would be happening and that they really should be there. So CNN and Fox News and all these big network channels came as well, and we were literally couple number seven in line and got our marriage certificate and then went over to the Assessor's Office and were married, and CNN actually videotaped our wedding ceremony and put us on the news that night.

We had friends from all over the world, from Germany and Israel and even Tanzania, emailing us and saying, "Wow, we saw you guys get married today!" It was crazy. Scott and I had been together fourteen years at that point and we knew we'd probably get married when it became legal, and we realized when we had the actual ceremony just how powerful declaring your love and commitment to one another publicly really was and is. Even though we'd been together many years and considered ourselves a loving, committed couple, it just took things to a much deeper level. It was unbelievably powerful. I became such a strong advocate for marriage equality after that, where I'd been much more lukewarm about it before.

It's funny, but I often tell people that I think I had more girlfriends over the course of my life than all three of my straight brothers combined, and I'm not proud of the fact that I had lots of girlfriends back then, but what that said to me is that I was always relationship-oriented and that I really wanted a long-term relationship. I had bought into the idea of getting married and having kids, a white picket fence—the whole nine yards—so when I realized I was gay that really stayed with me, though now I wanted a long-term relationship with a man.

Long-term relationships aren't for everyone. I have a lot of friends, and sometimes I will think to myself about a particular friend, "Why are you single? You're just such a catch..." I think some guys want to be in a relationship, but maybe they're just not willing to really accommodate another person into their life to that extent. There are definitely also guys who just really prefer one-night stands or short-term hookups and who get stimulated by the sex and the variety. There are straight people like that, too, of course.

Chemistry is really important in a relationship and good chemistry can make for a healthy and lasting bond. Communication is absolutely key; you have to have the most open and honest communication possible while being loving and constructive with each other. Commitment is another key ingredient. It's saying, "I'm going to consciously commit myself to this person, knowing that we're going to have some difficult times and some struggles which we're going to have to get through." I have to be willing to say, "I know these bumps in the road are going to occur and I'm willing to put in the work to get through them and to get to the other side, and it's going to make us better people for having gone through them, and will make our relationship even stronger."

Conscious is another important "C"; to be conscious in your relation-ship, and realistic in understanding that neither you or the other person are perfect, but together you can help each other improve in certain areas. It's also important to allow and encourage your partner to be their own person, their own unique and independent self. Even if you'd rather they be different in some ways or more this or more that, try to let go of that. Say "I love you for the person you are and I want to encourage the person you are." Surprise each other and love each other and be careful about the words that you choose in speaking. Try to avoid thoughtlessly saying things you could regret later on.

Scott and I have talked about this and we agree that relationships are not unconditional, that love is conditional. Conditional meaning that you can't just say or do anything you want and still expect that person to continue to love you and continue to be committed to you in the relationship. You have to be conscious that the relationship is conditional and be thoughtful in choosing your words and actions. Do your best to try and communicate and support, and be mindful of how you behave toward one another. Sometimes it's best to just not say or do something and some words are best left unsaid.

Having an intimate relationship can really be an opportunity to learn a lot about yourself. I continue to learn so much from Scott about myself and about the world, and apparently the same is true for him with me. Relationships can be a great opportunity to become a better, more loving person. Sometimes we project onto our partner or say things that in reality we don't mean because we're feeling a bit insecure or whatever. I might think, "Why is he saying that to me?," and then realize, "Oh, he's just feeling a bit vulnerable or insecure at the moment and this might be a situation where, rather than get upset with him, I just need to love him instead and encourage him and realize that he needs some love right now." Any type of relationship can provide an opportunity to become a better person, but an intimate relationship, because of the closeness and the intensity, offers an even greater opportunity for you to grow and change.

CHAPTER 8

STEVE AND MARK

"What a comfort it is to know that through difficult times, through health issues, through whatever you're faced with in life and in relationship that there's someone there who has your best interests at heart and is there to be a loving support. It means the world, because we all go through challenges and difficult times, and sometimes it's difficult to get through them, but when you have the love and understanding of a life partner who wants to be there to help you work and grow through those issues, it's a beautiful thing."

* * * * *

It was love at first sight when Steve Habgood and Mark Sadlek met through a Dallas business organization twenty-five years ago, though it took them several months to become lovers. Their "Ceremony of Affirmation" In 1993 prompted *Life Magazine* to contact them about possibly being included in an article on the then-unheard of topic of gay marriage. The forward-thinking couple was featured in the terrific, stereotype-breaking article in the November 1996 edition. Still active today in helping advance the cause of equality, Steve works in real estate, while Mark is employed as an executive coach. They make their home in Dallas.

Steve Habgood — (Mark Sadlek)

We've been together twenty-four years. I was twenty-eight when we started out, and Mark was thirty. At that point, we were still in a career-building stage, still young and energetic and outgoing and the like. I had gotten a bit tired of the bars, where there didn't seem to be a lot of opportunities to meet other people of like minds and interests. It wasn't that I didn't have fun at the bars, but I wasn't really interacting with people who I thought would be inspiring and challenging and fulfilling.

A friend of mine mentioned that he was wanting to start a male networking group and asked if I would be interested in being part of the founding board, and I said, "Yeah, that sounds really interesting." The group was kind of a precursor to a gay and lesbian Chamber of Commerce of sorts. This would have been in 1988, and there wasn't anything like it around in Dallas at the time. So we started this organization called ARETE—a Greek word for excellence—a men's networking organization, and I served on the board and also coincidentally was asked if I would be the speaker chairman, my role being to find a speaker for every meeting.

A mutual friend of ours knew that I was involved in the organization and knew that Mark loved public speaking, so he said, "I'd like to introduce you to a friend of mine..." We were at an ARETE function in a ballroom here at the Melrose Hotel here in Dallas, and he brought Mark around a column—I can remember it like it was yesterday—and introduced us. It's hard to describe in words, but there was just an instant, electric, magical feeling that took place right at that moment. I didn't know inherently that he was going to be my life partner, but I did know that this individual was going to play a really important role in my life—and I knew it instantly.

At the time, I was in a relationship that was not doing well, and we'd been having issues and troubles. But I met Mark, and he said, "I understand you're the speaker chairman and I'm really involved in public speaking and really like to do that. Would you need anyone to help on your committee?"

I said, "Absolutely. I'd love the help."

So he volunteered to become a committee member, and we basically just became friends over the next three months while my then-relationship was continuing to deteriorate. We would do things socially, and in fact my ex and Mark and I would go out for dinner and hang out sometimes. I finally had to take my ex to lunch one day and say, "For the betterment of both of us, this relationship is not healthy. It's not going anywhere. I want to still respect you and be your friend, and if we continue down this path, I don't think that's going to be possible. So I think in both of our best interests we need to end this." He agreed, and Mark—jokingly—says that I drove to the nearest 7-11 and called him from a pay phone, because back then we didn't have cell phones, and asked him if he'd like to go see a movie. That's not actually how it happened. I actually did drive all the way home, but in all honesty, the first thing I did was pick up the phone and call Mark and ask him if he wanted to see a movie, and he said, "Sure, that would be fun." We went to see a movie that night and we've been together ever since.

During those first three months we knew each other, he was giving me my space and I was giving him his, because I wasn't going to compromise my relationship by doing something with someone while I was in it, and he wasn't going to compromise mine by attempting to do anything. So we kept a friendly distance, but I could just feel in my heart that there was something very special about Mark. He didn't really let on to me during that time that he had the exact same feelings. And then once we didn't have a relationship standing in between us any more, it was just an immediate connection.

It's funny that Mark and I had both lived in Dallas for three years, and we have a large, dynamic, interactive, very social gay community here, but in those three years, our paths had never crossed. I don't think our mutual friend was in any way thinking matchmaking either; he just said, "You guys need to know each other." But the energy that was there between us when we met is really hard to adequately describe. It was just there immediately.

Once we were free to be together, we were intimate pretty quickly. Mark and I have been monogamous since day one, which was something that was important to both of us. I'd had a rather energetic youth and played around quite a bit and enjoyed what I did when I did it, but by the time I had met Mark I was ready to put that wildness behind me and really find someone to settle down with. We've continued to be sexually exclusive throughout these twenty-four years, and certainly here and there, I interact with other individuals who are handsome and dynamic and exciting, but I just respect them for who they are as people and enjoy the time that I get to spend with them.

For Mark and me sexually, always wanting to come home to your partner, your lover, has always worked for the both of us. We are still sexual though certainly not at the pace that we were at in the early years of our relationship. But there still is that draw, that intimacy, that shared love, that is so special with someone who touches your heart in a way that no one else does. We've had individuals approach us over the years and ask to be a part of, and it's a little uncomfortable, but we've said no. Monogamy is just what the foundation of our relationship is built on.

More than lust, more than passion, and in some cases even more than love, one of the things that I think is really an integral part of a relationship is that your partner is a best friend, a companion, someone you really look forward to spending time with, even if it's doing mundane tasks or chores together. The fact that you enjoy spending time with each other, doing whatever it may be, is integral to any long-term relationship, and we have that. So twenty-four years into it and hopefully twenty-four more years into it, as we continue to look back, having each other as a best friend, as a true companion, remains a central part of the foundation of our relationship.

Love, to me, is an intimacy, a respect, a shared level of trust, a companionship. So it's a combination of things, but when you have that level of respect for each other as individuals and that level of trust, that this person is there for you through thick and thin, in good health and bad—whatever the circumstances may be—you have someone who allows you to grow as an individual. If you don't allow for growth, and you're striving for or looking to build upon a long-term relationship, you're going to run into some real challenges along the way. Everyone grows as an individual over time, and if you're not open to that growth, then it will create conflict.

We are cuddlers. We used to have a queen-size bed and we moved to a king-size, and I will say that a queen-size bed is SO much better if you're cuddlers. A king-size bed is really big and allows you your own space, but queen-size is just more conducive to cuddling. Mark and I like to cuddle a lot and we show affection to each other routinely. We'll walk arm in arm in different places. We were just in Maui and we were walking into the hotel after parking the car, arm in arm around each other, and I think we caught a stare or two. But it's who we are, and it's something to be shared and not hidden.

I have to try at it to keep from taking Mark for granted. I succeed at it most of the time, but being human, there are times where I don't fully appreciate everything that he is and has done for me. So I try to make a conscious effort about always understanding that even the little things that he does all mean a lot, and they're done out of love and compassion, and I always try to reach out and be reciprocal as much as possible.

Communication is integral to any successful endeavor or relationship, and there certainly have been times for us where communication has broken down. Rather than being open to discussing issues, we've pulled back into our shells and not been as communicative as we needed to be. Over twenty-four years we've had multiple instances of that, and I think it just takes time working through that withdrawn time or that hurt time— whatever the feelings may have been—and getting to a point of comfort and of safety, of being able to sit down and talk through the issues, and listen to what the other individual has to say, and to understand the other's perspective. And that's not always easy! There's no question about that. There are times when it breaks down, and we just have to work through it and get to a point of comfort and of opening back up to each other.

Once we did couples therapy for probably twelve or fourteen months. It was very helpful and healthy. It wasn't an impasse we were at exactly, but when you're together that amount of time you're going to go through phases and challenges—and again, getting back to allowing people to grow—I've been through a couple of different career changes. Mark's been through them as well, but when you make a change that makes a big impact on how you share time with each other, it can be a huge issue.

Going into residential real estate, I went from a Monday to Friday 8-to-5 situation, where we had our weekends together and sharing and cooking and travel and friends, into this new career which is essentially 24/7, where weekends and our usual time together went out the window... That was a difficult period for us to come to understand and to respect where each other was coming from, and of allowing each other to grow. It doesn't mean that it happens instantly; you have to work through it.

Fortunately for us, there has been a strong enough foundation there for the couple of different times in our relationship where we've had to work through those issues. I'm still in residential real estate, and Mark has come to be an incredibly supportive partner in that. It's not easy for the other half, because when you say, "I'm going to be home at 7," and you don't get home until 7:45 or 8:15 because of a client demand, and if that continues to happen time after time, it can wear anyone out. But he's come to understand it, and I try my best to define parameters of when I am available to give away my time for my clients and when that's over, I want to then carve out all the rest of that days time for my partner and our life and our personal joy. Again, it's not always easy, but you just have to work at it and make it happen. So having enough time for each other remains an ongoing challenge.

One of the beautiful aspects of Mark is his ability to bring levity, to bring a sense of humor to the table. He makes me smile and makes me laugh like no one else that I know. He's witty and he's charming and he does fun, quirky things that cause me to ask, "Where does *that* come from?!" But at the end of the day, I don't really care because it's so enjoyable and it brings that smile to my face. Because I can get a little too focused, a little too serious, about whatever it is that we're dealing with at the time, Mark's ability to bring levity and laughter to our relationship is another important keystone in our foundation. We'll be somewhere with other people, and he will just pull a statement out of thin air, and we'll all just look at each other and say, "Where did THAT come from?" But he has that uncanny ability, and it almost always makes me smile or laugh.

We do like to surprise each other, though there's no schedule to it. It is so nice to know that he thought of something special to do, whether it was a card on my pillow or finding fresh flowers when I get home for the day. I tend to be our trip planner, so I'm our organizer and plan all of our trips and make arrangements and call the hotels and so forth, and I've taken him on a couple different surprise trips where I'll say, "Hey, are you available Friday through Monday of this particular weekend?"

He'll say, "Yes, what are we going to do?," and I'll say, "We're gonna do something fun." He won't even know where we're going—literally—

until we're at the airport and getting to the gate. He also did the same thing one time for me and planned an intricate trip and put a lot of thought and organization into it. Unfortunately, I got called into jury duty for a murder trial and the days kept ticking by, and we found the gentleman guilty three hours after we were supposed to take off... So we had to cancel the trip, but just the fact that Mark had taken the initiative to organize the trip meant the world to me.

I don't have a religion and I'd say I'm even light on the spirituality. I do have a spirituality about me and I do know that there is a greater being and a higher power. Do I fully understand or embrace it? Maybe not. Mark probably does much more so. But that hasn't in itself created a challenge or a schism for us.

We had long conversations many years ago about possibly becoming parents. I was driving those discussions a little harder as I was more passionate about it than he. I love spending time with kids and my nieces and nephews and Mark's nieces and nephews. The inner child really comes out in me along with the playfulness and I just love spending time with kids. So we talked about it for many years and explored different options and surrogacy and adoptions... After talking about it for several years, it became clear that we both weren't on board one hundred percent, and if you're going to make a decision that important in your life and in your relationship, in my opinion you both need to be on board one hundred percent. We had a long conversation on a drive back from Arizona to Albuquerque and we talked through everything at great length and came to terms that we were not going to move forward with becoming parents. Once we made that decision, we haven't looked back and have just been blessed with the relationship that we have with each other.

Being with Mark has made me more open, more accepting, more understanding of other people and other relationships. It's strengthened me as an individual substantially, and I attribute that all to Mark's character, his compassion, and his love. Though we're not legally married, we had a ceremony back in 1993. Back then there really weren't a whole lot of ceremonies of that nature going on, and there wasn't really a guidebook. We called ours a Ceremony of Affirmation. We were affirming our love for each other in front of our friends and family, and we had about eighty people together. Mark was somewhat pushing for it or encouraging it, where I was a bit more *"que sera"* about it.

It turned out to be the most powerful, emotional, loving day of my life. I will always look back on that experience and what it was like for these individuals to come together to share in our love, back in a time when that really wasn't happening a whole lot publicly. I'll always cherish that experience, and now we're looking to come up to our twenty-fifth anniversary, and we're hoping to get legally married, unfortunately in another state. Texas is one of the thirty-one that has Constitutional amendments against it, but I think it's important for us to reaffirm that element of our life and at least have a legal marriage in a state that does respect it. Hopefully the laws of our land will change...

For us it's always been all for one and one for all in our finances. That's always been my philosophy, and it didn't matter if he had X number of dollars or I had X number of dollars; whatever we had we had together, and it was for each other's use, betterment, and enjoyment. We've been through periods of substantially different incomes, and it doesn't ever come up and is never a question. We've just always shared everything as one.

Mark had a mild heart attack recently. It was one of the scariest moments in my life, to think that out of the blue—in a split second—life could change instantly and dramatically. He had shared with me several days earlier that something was not right and that he was going to see his doctor. He said, "I've been having these episodes where I run out of energy and I've been having chest pains...." I was like, "You've been having WHAT?" So he scheduled an appointment with his doctor on a Thursday and had an EKG and a series of blood tests taken, and there were enough indications from that visit that the doctor scheduled a stress test for Mark the following Monday. Sunday night he was a little bit quieter than usual but I didn't think much of it, and when we got home from dinner he said, "You know, I'm going to have some tea and read in the front room."

I said, "I'm going to have some tea, too, but I think I'm going to get in bed and just fall off to sleep." About thirty or forty minutes later, he got in bed and tossed and turned a couple different times, and I thought he was trying to get comfortable. He reached over and grabbed my arm and said, "Honey, I think you need to call 9-1-1." He was having all the telltale signs of a heart attack, and I said, "I'm going to get you to the hospital," because we live about two minutes away from there.

I raced him to the hospital and got him into the emergency room. They admitted him, and he had an angioplasty. It worked out for the best, but it was the scariest moment of my life, thinking that his life might be passing. It was the longest two-minute drive of my life! The blessing of it was that it was found and treated.

Mark had a ninety-five percent blockage in one of his primary arteries, and he had a stint put in and the stint brought back blood flow to that artery that had not been getting blood for years. He is stronger and better and healthier today by far than he was just ten days ago. Experiences like this are always especially eye-opening.

I had another medical scare a couple years ago when I was hit by a flying snowboarder from twenty-five feet up coming off a jump and broke five of my ribs and punctured a lung and was in the ICU for several days. So we've both had medical scares, where in an instant everything could change. But through the grace of God or greater beings, we were both able to make it through them, and are stronger people as a result. Those experiences make you realize the preciousness of every moment of life, because we don't ever really know when that's going to be taken away from us.

We just moved into a new house three weeks ago, and the whole purpose of the move was to downsize and simplify our lives. We used to have a lot bigger house and a lot more land and we said, "If we make decisions today so that when we want or need to make decisions tomorrow about our future and our retirement, those will be easy, snap decisions, instead of "How are we going to get there?" decisions. So we're beginning to simplify our lives and our surroundings and our needs, even though we're really just beginning to talk about retirement and our future.

Life Magazine did an article on us back in 1996, which was an amazing experience. We talked at length about it even before we decided to say yes, because they interviewed multiple couples across the country for possible inclusion. We had dialogues about "If they select us, is this something we really want to do?" and "What are the implications of it?" and "Will we get hate mail and hate phone calls?" and "Do we need to consider changing our number?" We walked through all of those issues. "What is the impact on our family? How are they going to deal with this?" Because this was making a really public statement, we ultimately decided that if, in whatever small way, we could help others see that there are healthy, loving, same-sex relationships that are not just about sexuality, but are about life and love and companionship and encouragement, that it would be great to have even a small role in that.

Ultimately the article ended up featuring just Mark and me, and of course, we didn't know how everything would unfold until the magazine hit the stands... The phone calls and the letters that we got—obviously from people we'd never heard of or met—touched our lives so much. When you have the opportunity to talk with a fourteen-year-old from Oklahoma who lived in the middle of the country and didn't really even know that there were other gay people out there, and he was calling to ask if we were real, and if this was true, that there was love in relationships... It was those types of experiences resulting from that article which changed us, because in a small way what we had hoped for was coming to pass, about showing others that there are these kinds of relationships, and for people who didn't understand homosexuality and relationships of two same-sex individuals, that maybe we could open their minds just a little bit to see something different.

I think that's what *Life*'s objective was. They really reached out to middle America, which was their primary audience, with this piece. I'll never forget the very first phone call I got, and I didn't even know the magazine had hit the stands. All I knew was that it was coming out.

I was on the phone back home, and a call waiting tone came in and I said, "Do you mind holding on for a second?," and the person on the other end said, "Sure."

So I said, "Hello..."

There was a bit of a pause and a woman said, "Is this Mark or Steve?"

I said, "This is Steve..."

She said, "Is this Steve...Habgood?"

I said, "Yeah," and she said, "The Steve Habgood who was in *Life Magazine*?"

At that point, my heart just dropped to the floor. I was so prepared—or maybe ill-prepared—for the onslaught of venom and anger and hatred that was just going to potentially spew out of this individual... And it was the exact opposite. She said, "Steve, I just have to tell you... I'm a straight woman, married with kids, from Carrolton, Texas, and I just needed to call and thank you and Mark for who and what you are. You've helped me to see a different side of people that I wasn't able to see before." And it was those types of experiences that resulted from the article I will cherish forever and ever. We got many positive phone calls and positive letters.

The *Life* reporter and the photographer lived in our home with us for a week and took something like fourteen hundred photographs. After the article was published, we had gotten back together and were having a conversation, and I said, "We haven't had any negative, hateful things come our way at all," and the reporter, a woman, said, "The magazine did. A lot of stuff got sent in to the editors and publishers."

I asked, "Can we see those?"

She replied, "Steve, do you really want to?"

I said, "Yeah, I think I do."

She said, "Think about it. You just shared with me that your experience was nothing but supportive and positive and encouraging. Do you want to add that meanness to it?"

I had to stop and think and I thanked her. I said, "My perspective on life is the more information the better, but you've just helped me understand that no, I do not need to see that." So we never did.

Lasting relationships take trust, respect, and being best friends with each other. If you don't trust each other and respect each other as individuals and don't look forward to spending time together, even just doing the simplest things, then it's probably not going to stand the test of time. Those elements are pretty essential. It's being there for each other. I support Mark in areas that he needs at different times of his life, and he's there to support me in different things that I need. What a comfort it is to know that through difficult times, through health issues, through whatever you're faced with in life and in relationship, that there's someone there who has your best interests at heart and is there to be a loving support. It means the world, because we all go through challenges and difficult times, and sometimes it's difficult to get through them, but when you have the love and understanding of a life partner who wants to be there to help you work and grow through those issues, it's a beautiful thing.

Each relationship is going to be unique, and what works for one doesn't necessarily work for another, but when we are asked from time to time what makes it work for us I just go back to those foundational elements; love, trust, and respect. If you have those three elements in your life, you are at least laying the groundwork for the opportunity for a wonderful, loving, long-term relationship to happen.

CHAPTER 9

ROB AND STEVE

"In those moments when you want to say something to the other person but you're just so afraid... Throw yourself off the edge. Do it. If I had not done that, we would not be where we are now. If I had shut down, if I had done everything I had done in every relationship with men and women beforehand with him, it would not have worked. That's the difference, and I was like, "This is worth trying. This is worth exposing myself. If he thinks I'm insane, this is worth everything because I need to know if this is what I think it is."

* * * * *

Rob Dorgan and Steve Bolia met twenty-five years ago at a popular restaurant in downtown Cincinnati. Over a number of months their friendship blossomed into love. Students of the famous late astrologer Linda Goodman, they teach yoga and lead weekend workshops on reflexology, healthy living, astrology, and meditation. Rob and Steve are certified massage therapists and personal trainers and also perform non-traditional weddings. For more info visit www.robandsteveyoga.com. They live in Kentucky.

Rob Dorgan — (Steve Bolia)

We've been together twenty-six years as of September 3rd. At the time, I was twenty-five and Steve was twenty-seven. I was in graduate school in Cincinnati and had gone to Europe for the first time, for four months, which changed my life. When I got back, I started my PhD program and became very disgruntled with the whole thing. Something wasn't right, and I was just over being in school, and the Europe trip just made me realize that there's so much more to life than just being in school all the time. So I basically resigned, thinking it was only going to be temporary, and decided I wanted to do something totally mindless and I took a job as a server in a little gay-friendly restaurant downtown. It was really hard getting anyone to hire me because I was working on a PhD and had no experience, but this place did, and though I thought it would be a low-key job, of course serving isn't necessarily all that low-key...

Steve had actually worked there and now he was living upstairs from the restaurant in this really cool apartment, so all the customers and everybody knew him. He had just left to go work in a fine dining restaurant, but he still hung out there with his girlfriend. The staff people introduced us. One of the cooks and a bartender, both women, said, "You guys should meet. We hang out and party together after work," and with his apartment being right upstairs, it was very easy to just go upstairs and hang out. I knew pretty much from the first time I met him, "Whoa! Something's really different..." But of course, he was still dating women, and though I didn't know it at the time, he had experimented a bit with men, too. We became friends, and that was in March of 1986.

Then I got a job as a flight attendant and ended up moving to New York in April, and Steve and I stayed in touch. I was somewhat mentoring him a little bit because I had dated women too not that long beforehand and I was just trying to be very supportive. Coming out is a hard process; not only do you have to admit it to yourself but also to your family, and he was really afraid of alienating his family. So we kept up a friendship mostly through letters, and I still have all the letters we've ever written to each other. He came up and visited, and then when I'd go home, we would hang out.

In September, I came home for Labor Day weekend and was going to go to a Kenny Loggins concert with friends, and Steve and I were going to meet up later. We had just spent so much time together and had built up such an emotional bond as friends that one thing led to another and that weekend we really... got together. So that's our anniversary, and we've been together ever since. I moved back to Ohio in October then because I knew a long-distance relationship wasn't going to work and that this was something special. So I moved home.

We had really talked openly and clearly with each other about our experiences for quite some time before then, and I really think that building the whole friendship thing before we had sex in September was something that really cemented it for us. We both knew that we liked each other, that we were very similar, and that we were becoming really good friends, so the next step was a little bit easier. Sometimes you have to wade through the sexual tension part of a new relationship with somebody before finding out what the reality of the relationship is. I was very attracted to him at first but at the same time I didn't think anything was going to happen because I thought he was so confused and so caught in the middle between this woman he was engaged to, and men, that there was no hidden agenda. I was just offering a friendship. I did do some shallow things though, like, "Let's work out at the gym together!" just so we could shower together. Men, you know how that goes. It was harmless.

Every couple is different and the partners have to figure out what works for them. What we get a lot from other male couples is, "Do you guys still have sex?" We still have a lot of sex. Though we're primarily exclusive with each other, we have had some encounters together. But our communication can handle that, and it's not for everybody. It's not a daily or weekly thing. There for a while it might have been like once a year or a couple times a year, so it's not very frequent. But it's always together. It's usually someone we have an emotional connection with, and then something like that will just kind of happen.

We're both really sensual and sexual people and even in the early years, we were open enough to kid around about our attractions. Another advantage is that Steve and I are so in synch in so many ways—sometimes people think we're brothers, probably from being together so long—but we actually have very similar taste in men. We are also both very versatile. People always tell us we look so much alike; we're the same weight, the same height, we share clothes...

Over the last twenty-six years, especially if there's been someone about whom one of us feels "Oh, my God, I've got such a crush on that one," we're really talking it through. But the underlying thing with us is that there's nobody who could replace Steve. Nobody! It doesn't matter how sexually attracted I might be to somebody; it's just not an option.

We've been emotionally attached actually to two young men in the last couple years, which was something of a new phase in our relationship. One is fifteen years younger than us, and we had a period of time where we hung out. At one point, he said, "I can't keep doing this because you guys have what I want, and I can't get that while I'm with you guys. And it's not a negative thing, but it's obvious that it's the two of you and then me..." He wanted the intimacy with one other person that we share.

Shortly after that he did meet someone, and we're really good friends with him and his partner now. He'll say, "You know, I give you guys such credit because I got to experience your relationship from the inside out." He's very thankful for that, and even his boyfriend will say, "You guys were such a huge influence on Stephen, and I don't know if we could have the same relationship we have if he hadn't seen that with you two, because he didn't have any gay role models for relationships."

Steve and I experiment with things and we talk about fantasies and we role play, and also of course have great intimate moments where we are ourselves, and those are always the most incredible. We have done a series of the Body Electric workshops and have done four or five different weekends of theirs and even went to one of their workshops in Hawaii. We're now licensed massage therapists and we massage each other regularly, so those kinds of activities help to keep a lot of passion there. It's good to keep things interesting. We've always been very affectionate with each other too.

We know when one of us is out of whack, especially me. Sometimes my "Capricorn cold wall" goes up. It's this emotional wall that goes up whenever Capricorns are trying to protect ourselves from whatever. To get over this, it takes just really letting go and taking some chances, and that's really hard until you find the right person. Really that's what happened with me and Steve. Early into it I was like, "I can't let this wall get between us..."

I remember the one night I woke up and we'd had a little spat and it was going on, and I thought, "This is usually when I check out and I move on from people." So I woke him up and I took the chance of telling him how intense and tied up emotionally I was inside. And Steve has been part of that entire process for me. Even the first weekend we went to Body Electric, I knew it would be good for me but I knew it would challenge me to the nth degree, and it did. But I remember well the night that I made the decision that I had to take some chances and open up to him or I would lose him. So I opened up.

Being with Steve has taught me the real meaning of unconditional love, and I have since then tried to move it outward from this central place of what we have together and offer it to other people, whether they know it or not. It's loving without judgment, loving people and letting them grow, allowing people to be where they are in the moment. Because I'm evolving, why wouldn't someone else be, too? Also trying not to pigeonhole people or put them in a place that's static, because nothing is static! So practicing that with each other has helped us, even with this new experience of massage school where they taught us: "The more you can go into each room with no judgment and with unconditional love, you don't have to worry about what happens because you will help the person." And it is so true.

In your relationships with people, one-on-one especially, when you just open your heart, it's amazing what can take place. But it's not easy to do, because we're so guarded and we judge everything and every person that we have a hard time letting the wall down when we don't need it, and there are a lot of times when we don't need it with people.

Steve and I have quality time together every day. For instance, coming off this school program, we had to be there at 9 a.m. so we would get up at 6 and each do our separate meditation or yoga, and then we'd still have a good two hours together to chat, talk about dreams... Sometimes we'll pick a Tarot card—on the new moon every month, we have a ceremony where we pick one of the Zen Tarot cards, which gives us a focus for the month—and we chat about what we'd like to do individually or as a couple. That all is part of our love for each other, and it takes that commitment. Even when we were working our corporate jobs before we quit last year, we got up early.

People would say, "How can you be late for work? You guys get up at 6 a.m.!"

We'd respond, "Well it's much more interesting hanging out and talking to each other than it is coming to work..." We'd get distracted.

Our love together has deepened to a level that I didn't even think I was capable of. So I'm excited for the future because who knows how much deeper it's going to get? It sounds so cliché, but we'll sit there sometimes and say, "Oh, my God, what is this?" Or we'll just act like little kids and go, "Oh, my God! We are so fortunate to have found each other!" I would like everybody to have this experience, because it's such a great thing in my life. It's been the thing in this lifetime that has taken my soul to another level, definitely. Steve and I are true kindred spirits.

In twenty-six years, we've worked together almost the entire time. We went on that journey with the well-known astrology author Linda Goodman together early on and we were in the mountains of Colorado for a year with her. We helped her with her last book, titled *Goobers*. There was virtually no one else in that little town, and that year really made us know how bonded we were. As we waited for galley pages to be sent back from the publisher to her, we would hang out 24/7 and we learned astrology from her.

We lived right next door. Early on, that really bonded us together because we went on a spiritual quest. When we came back from Colorado, we went to Europe for four months, so there again we were together. Then we opened a small business, a little store. We even ran another company together. So we've had the opportunity to work together and we have only been apart less than two weeks—ten nights—in the last twenty-six years, and that's not for everybody. Sometimes there's not that kind of compatibility, and there are other people who need more space, and long-distance relationships can work. But it's possible to find somebody with whom you're so compatible that everything just clicks.

I don't really want to be away from him 9 to 5. Then you end up spending more time with your co-workers than your partner. So we've really worked at trying to always do something that we can do together. Of course, we both have our issues and maybe things we don't want to talk about but we do eventually, and a lot of it can just be emotions. Sometimes when it does come up that one of us wants to do something that the other one's not really into, it takes a discussion to work it out. We do have separate projects too so we talk about it and how best to support each other in that.

I'm a Capricorn, and Steve's a Virgo. Of course, working with Linda, we both know the ins and outs of our charts, and they're really compatible, with a lot of past lives together. She told us some specifics that really made a lot of sense. So every once in a while, we have a little past-life karma come up, especially so in our early years.

We are very committed to certain things together. We work out almost always together. We exercise together. We're both into yoga so we take classes together and we also teach together. Our spiritual path is pretty eclectic. I grew up Catholic, and he grew up with no religion. I had some of that old Catholic stuff to get rid of and was really searching for a different spirituality.

I stumbled onto Linda Goodman, and that was really kind of the first thing for us. We went and sought her out and worked for her and through that experience realized that the whole guru thing was not for us and still isn't. We're organized-religion-shy, whatever the form, but have developed a really deep sense of spirit about God and the universe. It's part of our everyday life, the way we look at what happens to us in the day, between us, and everyday events and what lesson is there in those... Seeing everything as a learning experience. The yoga and doing no harm and living a gentle life and being peaceful to the planet, the insects, the animals, to each other, just seems to really make sense to us.

We're both ordained ministers in the Universal Light Church and we do weddings. I'll do the ceremony part, and Steve will help with the planning. We do these really cool weddings for people who want something really different. But for ourselves, getting married isn't something we feel is a necessity at this point. We want marriage to be legal, absolutely, but I don't really need the government to approve our relationship. I might possibly do it if it was going to help us financially.

We were both in credit card debt when we first met, and that was one of the first things we worked on together. We said, "If we're going to move forward, we need to be debt-free, so how can we do this?" In the first year and a half or so we were together, we paid off both of our bills. We pooled our monies pretty early and after two years, we didn't have any separate accounts any more. Friends tried to advise me against that and I told them, "This is different." Anyway, obviously it's worked out.

We laugh all the time. Even sometimes when we're arguing, if one of us can make a joke and get the other one laughing, it just takes all the intensity out of it. Our sense of humor is very similar and we're always right there, ready to laugh. We still surprise each other too, and it's funny; we'll say, "God, I can't believe that after twenty-six years, I'm still surprised at something that you're doing or saying..."

I especially will say, "Let's do blah, blah, blah,...," and he'll be like, "Where's that coming from?" I'll say, "I don't know. We just need to do something different today." And Steve will go, "Alright."

This relationship has been the biggest growth thing for me because I'm really experiencing unconditional love from someone. Again going back to astrology, Capricorns are very insecure that way, never thinking that they're quite lovable enough, that they're never going to find anyone who can love them for all their foibles, so they stay really guarded and build this big castle around themselves emotionally because they feel like nobody's going to understand or they're not going to find anybody. And that's not the case. I still have a little tiny wall sometimes, but that has probably been the biggest thing, being able to get through that—what I would call my personal limitations—through Steve's love and acceptance of me. Because sometime's it's come down to the point of "Why does he love me so much? I'm such an asshole!" Or feeling like I'm so fucked up because I'm very intense.

Between the two of us, I'm definitely the more driven and intense. And he doesn't care. He's such a great support with my own growth. It's like now my abandonment issues are almost gone, and I've had those all of my life, always feeling that men especially were going to leave me, because of a childhood thing with my dad. Steve has helped me to heal that to the point where I was even calling my dad a couple times a year before he died, and I went to see him... Steve really helped me with that part of it, the male bonding, and knowing he wasn't going to leave and he was going to stick with me, and actually likes my eccentricities, which I didn't think anyone did.

Total communication is so important in a relationship. You really can't have secrets. We all have our heart of hearts where there just are things we think we can't communicate to somebody else because they are either too dark or too sad or too whatever. And when we have a communication level with another human being where we can share that, that's a real opening up, a real switch in our incarnation, a real push forward. So open communication is really important. In those moments when you want to say something to the other person but you're just so afraid...

Throw yourself off the edge. Do it. If I had not done that, we would not be where we are now. If I had shut down, if I had done everything I had done in every relationship with men and women beforehand with him, it would not have worked. That's the difference, and I was like, "This is worth trying. This is worth exposing myself. If he thinks I'm insane, this is worth everything because I need to know if this is what I think it is, which was a sense of fate or destiny with him. That there was a choice at one point on my part early on where I had to communicate with him about everything— the intense negative stuff as well as what I was thinking about other people sexually—because I had never been really faithful to anybody before Steve either.

That was another thing. I realized, "That's always screwed this up," basically my own fragile ego needing to be stroked. So facing a lot of your own shadows within your relationship is so important, as it was for me. You've got to take some risk with yourself first, then risk putting it out there for the other person, and I think that's what makes the relationship richer and all the more worthwhile. Also important is a sense of spirituality, having similar beliefs in something greater that us. I don't want to get too much into the God thing, but there's a commonality between all human beings as well as between the two of us, so I think a sense of spirituality is really important. Yoga and meditation have both been really important for us in that regard.

Our sense of spirit together is really strong as is our playfulness, both in normal humor and also the playfulness that we keep within the relationship sexually. We enjoy the sensuality we have with ourselves and even with our friends, and it's fun trying new and different things.

Don't tap into any of the age stuff, all the lies and false assumptions people make about age and aging. It's totally bogus! I'm not sure why we do that to each other and I don't know why gay men do that, especially to our elders. We don't seem to respect as a group the older generation within our circles. For some reason, the gay culture is so into youth and beauty, and we have to move out of that. So many of us are aging, and there's going to be a huge population of us, and now we're going to have our own nursing homes and retirement communities.

How do we cultivate loving the elders? Between us, we are trying really hard not to tap into the typical aging process stuff. We're not trying to escape aging but trying to focus on learning and on what we've learned. What has maturity brought you? I think that's a really important question as you grow up—as Steve and I like to say—and we're still loving each other each step of the way. It's the cycle of Nature and we have to embrace it, instead of fearing it and running away from it our whole lives until they're over.

To increase your chances of meeting the right person, try to be non-judgmental about where you're meeting someone. Online dating was not a possibility for us, but I've had friends who met that way. So that might be the way to do it. Any situation that you go into, just try to be open. It could happen anywhere, from a fleeting glance across the room and you taking the chance to go over and say, "I don't know why but I feel like we've known each other before..." You have no idea. And since life is short, why not have some fun with it?

A lot of times, we've strangled our lives so much that we don't have any romance anymore, and it's up to us, even when we're alone and away from our partners, to make life as romantic as possible. If you're single, take some chances on how to meet people. Don't necessarily think that you have to meet them professionally or you can't meet them online. Be open, because you just never know when someone else is out there doing the exact same thing you are.

CHAPTER 10

WILLIE AND GREG

"It took him three years to ask me to live with him. Greg had roommates, and one day when we were flying to Florida to visit some friends he leaned over and said, "My roommates are moving out. Would you like to move in?" This is after three years of dating, and I looked at him and said, "Do you want me to move in with you or do you want the rent?" He said, "Both."

Willie Docto and Greg Trulson met over two decades ago when they were both weekend guests at a gay owned B&B in West Virginia. Today they are the innkeepers/owners of Moose Meadow Lodge—www.moosemeadowlodge.com— Central Vermont's only luxury log home B&B. Willie concertizes as a freelance classical violinist, while Greg is a popular Justice of the Peace and an accomplished woodworker. They are the featured couple in the central photo on the cover of this book.

Willie Docto — (Greg Trulson)

Greg and I have been together for over twenty years. I was thirty when we met, and Greg was thirty-eight. In September of 1992, we overlapped at a gay-owned log home bed-and-breakfast in the mountains of West Virginia. We now own a log home B&B in the mountains of Vermont, so we've come full circle! Greg and I were both guests at the B&B in West Virginia. Actually I had rented the entire facility, which was three different buildings, and had a whole bunch of friends who were supposed to come out and we were all going to meet up there.

Two weeks before our arrival date, everyone started to call me and say, "I need to cancel..." "I have conflicts and I can't go..." So I called the owner up and said, "Bob, I only need two rooms. Four of us are going to be in one room, and one couple will be in the other room."

He said, "Don't worry about it. I'll sell the rooms."

It just so happened that he had a waiting list, and Greg was on that waiting list, so Greg booked a room with a friend who was visiting from Atlanta. He and I met at breakfast.

I thought he was very cute, very attractive, and unusual in a lot of ways. He was very fun, and there was a Midwestern innocence about him I liked. Greg's from Minnesota and he had a really good, positive energy. We all met up for breakfast and then a bunch of us that day made plans to get together for dinner. At that time, there were no restaurants in the B&B or nearby, so we had to drive forty-five minutes and we all carpooled and met up at this restaurant. Greg sat next to me at the restaurant.

Afterwards we came back to the B&B and a group of us started playing a card game called *Pit*, which is based on the commodities exchange. Greg brought the game, which I had never played before, and it's a very loud game. In fact, the innkeeper asked us to go to the basement to play because we were really loud and keeping him up. We actually played *Enya* on the boom-box just to keep ourselves calm!

Both Greg and I scored very high and we found ourselves being very competitive with each other in this game, and that's what initially connected us. It wasn't so much during the dinner, but afterward during the card game when we really connected.

Before we checked out of the B&B, I invited Greg to join my friends and me for a weekly happy hour we used to do every Tuesday in a down-town hotel in Washington D.C. He showed up. At the happy hour, I asked him if he would be interested in going biking that following weekend, and he said that he would, except he had plans to go to a gay rodeo. He asked me to go to the rodeo, which was on Saturday, and I said, "Sure." So we went to the rodeo on Saturday and then went biking on Sunday. After that, we ended up spending most every weekend together for a very long time, though we did start out platonically. Greg was living in Alexandria, and I was living in D.C.

The gay rodeo was great. A gay rodeo is very similar to a traditional rodeo and features the same events, plus they have some fun, campy events, and the big square dancing tent where people two-step and square dance. But we found ourselves really enjoying the rodeo and talking and talking and talking... All of a sudden we looked around, and the rodeo had finished and everyone had left the stands except the two of us! Before we left the rodeo, Greg said, "Why don't you just spend the night at my place?"

I said, "I kind of have this unofficial rule of not sleeping with someone on the first date...," though I just made it up.

He said, "Well we don't have to *do* anything . There's nothing expected. It'll just be more convenient, and we can just wake up and go biking from there tomorrow."

I said, "Well, OK...," and I always joke that at the stroke of midnight is when we consummated our relationship, so I didn't break my rule. The morning after is OK, isn't it?

It took him three years to ask me to live with him. Greg had roommates, and one day when we were flying to Florida to visit some friends, he leaned over and said, "My roommates are moving out. Would you like to move in?" That was after three years of dating, and I looked at him and said, "Do you want me to move in with you or do you want the rent?"

He said, "Both."

That was in August of '95, and then that November, he got a job offer to move to Vermont. So we didn't live together very long before the move to Vermont occurred. Greg came home one night and said, "I got a job in Vermont. Do you want to move with me?"

I said, "No! I have a nice life here..."

After I calmed down, I told him, "If you want me to leave my job, my career, my network, and everything I've built up here in fifteen years, then let's do something I can get into. Like a lot of people we've always fantasized about owning a B&B, so let's buy a house that we can turn into a B&B... "

We thought we'd be doing that much later in life—in our retirement—but we ended up starting one when we were in our thirties, which was a great opportunity. We started looking for a house we could turn into a B&B, and that's what we did. We opened the B&B two years after we moved here. The first two years we got used to the house and made some major renovations, got our permits, and then opened up. We've been here sixteen years already now.

Love is multi-layered and complicated and constantly evolving. It's definitely something that develops and gets better over time if you really love somebody. It gets better and makes you stronger and more complete. Love is about decisions we make together—simple decisions and major decisions.

For instance, the decision to move to Vermont, and the fact that I left my career, my network, my friends, and my family to start a whole new life here, was major and it brought us closer together. Remodeling a house and turning it into a bed-and-breakfast was like giving birth to a child for us. Creating a business together and supporting each other's interests and activities have all contributed to building and enhancing our relationship.

I used to work for the National Association of Home Builders in Washington D.C. so I met and talked and worked with a lot of builders. Many of them often said that building or remodeling a house often made couples divorce, and it had the total opposite effect with Greg and me. It was like having a child we both loved and nurtured from the beginning. We conceived it, we gave birth to it, and now it's maturing and we're watching it take shape and create its own identity.

Our B&B has really brought Greg and me together, and the two of us are very intertwined with our business. When our guests go to local businesses, to shops and restaurants, they're often asked where they're staying, and instead of saying they're staying at Moose Meadow Lodge, they'll say, "We're staying with Willie and Greg." People will frequently say our names before they'll say our business name.

We live and work together so we are constantly together. Greg and I are very intimate and close with each other and have no secrets between us. We get along so well that we never really fight. It sounds weird, but we do not have screaming or shouting matches of any sort.

Sometimes I'll get mad at him, and he'll just look at me and say, "Why are you screaming?"

I'll go, "I'm sorry, Honey, I didn't mean to scream..."

But we're pretty boring in the sense that there isn't a lot of drama in our lives. Greg and I are definitely committed to each other. We're a very loving and supportive couple and we have a very secure relationship. Of course, when you first start out, sex is initially a very important and exciting part of the relationship. Now that we're in our fifties, as the human body changes and as the relationship continues to mature, sex has become a less significant part of things overall. But we have a very healthy relationship.

Greg and I always sleep together. I can't sleep until he's in bed. He works late at night a lot, even though he's only two rooms away. I have to physically put a pillow behind my back so I feel like he's there before I can fall asleep. I'm like a little puppy with a hot water bottle wrapped in a towel! We are definitely spooners, too. I spoon him more than he spoons me, but that's OK.

I constantly remind myself not to take Greg for granted, and I don't think he takes me for granted, either. We try to show appreciation for all the big things, as well as the little things each of us does. Just saying thank you is important. I plan events and concerts, and Greg does a lot of things for me and is always very helpful. I can always count on him so I make sure I show him my appreciation.

I think being spontaneous is important, too. I'll say, "Let's go out to lunch," or "Let's go grab a bite to eat." A lot of our day is already posted on the calendar because we're so busy, so sometimes it's nice to just be spontaneous. But neither of us takes the other for granted nor do we feel that the other is taking us for granted.

We live and work together and are feet away from each other almost 24/7, and I never find myself feeling crowded. Greg and I give each other freedom. If one of us decides, "I'm going to do this or that," the other says, "OK." We each have different aspirations and interests and we support each other in those interests. I'm a violinist and I play concerts and sometimes travel for my music. Greg is a hunter and he's very focused on hunting during hunting season. We just had venison stew tonight made from a deer he caught three days ago.

I'm not sure how other people do it, but we do not pool our funds. We have separate personal accounts. Our business account is shared of course, because the business is an entity in itself that we both co-own. As far as our personal finances go, we're independent, which in a way is good because we allow ourselves the freedom to do what we like and to invest in what we like. So it's not an issue if one person decides they're going to go out and buy a $15,000 violin, because the other person's not paying for that. On the other hand, if he wants to buy a $1,000 moose head, I'm not necessarily going to say, "Uh, what are you doing?"

Greg is a Justice of the Peace, or actually what I call a "celebrity Justice of the Peace." He's hired a lot by different resorts and different couples around the state and he's constantly on television on the news about something—as I am—because of our involvement with the Vermont Gay Tourism Association.

Greg is a character. I'm sort of the straight man in the relationship, where's he's very humorous and funny and the life of the party. Even with little kids. When my nieces and nephews were young, they would flock around him, because he's always full of fun and tricks. In fact, when my nieces were young they would call here, and I would answer the phone and they'd say, "Hi, Uncle Willie. Where's Uncle Greg?"

And I'd say, "Wait a minute. Don't you want to talk to Uncle Willie?," and they'd go, "Oh, OK, Uncle Willie. Uh... Uh... What's Uncle Greg doing?"

Greg's a very popular Justice of the Peace. He officiated the first gay marriage in Vermont at our place. In 2000, Vermont became the first state to have civil unions. We'd been in operation for a couple of years then and I was redoing our website so it would address gay weddings. So when civil unions became available, the media started calling us and interviewing us and all of a sudden, AP picked it up, and we were all over the news about how we were preparing to welcome gay couples to be civil-unioned, and we were subsequently very successful in doing that for many years.

In 2009, Vermont became the first state to pass gay marriage legislatively; all the other states have had gay marriage because of court ruling. The media started calling again looking for a couple to photograph on the first day, September 1st, and we didn't have a couple. Out of the blue, this couple called soon after from upstate New York—just a couple of hours away—who wanted to get married as soon as it became legal here.

We said, "Sure, and why don't you come on August 31st so that you can be the first couple in Vermont to get married, and if you don't mind, we'll invite the media..." They were thrilled and excited, so that's what we did. At the stroke of midnight, they got married, and we had all the local affiliates of the major networks here: ABC, NBC, CBS and Fox.

Greg and I are both married and civil-unioned. When we had the civil union in 2001, we just invited friends and didn't involve our family. We regret that because the experience was so significant for us and we both love our families. Well, we got our wish when Vermont made gay marriage available in 2009. Two of Greg's brothers and their wives were here, and my mom and my aunt were here as well. It was really meaningful for me to have my staunch Catholic mom there, and she's very supportive. Greg and I are totally out, and Vermont is a small state where everyone knows each other. A lot of people call Vermont a small town, because we only have 620,000 residents in the entire state. We are both extremely involved in the community.

We never seriously considered having kids. I would have loved to have kids because I'm very paternal and domestic and am the housekeeper and the cook. Greg's a lot of fun and he attracts children because he knows how to communicate with them. He thinks like a child and jokes around like a child and he's so good with children. He's a good disciplinarian and a good entertainer, but he's never wanted to have kids. So when he said, "I'm not interested," I just never pursued it. I didn't want it enough to fight for it. But we do have plenty of nieces and nephews between us.

We were both raised in religious families. Greg and I both believe in God and we're both very spiritual people, but we don't observe the practices we were raised with. We don't really talk about religion. We talk a lot more about politics.

We laugh a lot. Greg keeps me laughing every day, even after twenty years. He genuinely makes me laugh. I watch him interact with our guests and tell stories and I laugh along with them like it's my first time hearing his little stories.

Between the two of us I'm more the "surpriser." I'm a professional event planner so I know how to put surprises on and I've done surprises for him for many years, and he's always surprised and he loves it. For his fiftieth birthday, I rented the Barre Opera House and pretended he was going there to marry two lesbians, one of whom was an opera singer who wanted to get married in an opera house. So he came thinking he was going to officiate a wedding, and the house manager asked him to sit down in the empty auditorium. The lights went off and then the curtains opened up, and there were seventy of Greg's friends there onstage wishing him a surprise happy birthday. That's the kind of surprise I like to put together.

I believe that Greg and I were destined to be where we are now. We have definitely found a niche for ourselves and created our identity around our life here in Vermont. We've created something we feel is very special with our B&B here, and a lot of people who have experienced it can understand what I'm talking about. Until you come here and get your own experience of the lodge and us and our interactions, it's hard to explain. So I don't know if Greg and I were destined to meet, but we were definitely destined to do what we're doing now. I could be doing this with another partner but I found the very best partner to do it with!

I've grown a lot due to Greg's support, his encouragement, and the honest feedback he gives me. I'm a very serious person and sometimes I obsess too much and worry, and Greg's lightheartedness and sense of humor is a good counterbalance for me. We're opposites in many ways but we very much complement each other. Raising our child—our business— keeps our relationship growing. Doing things together, communicating well, but also pursuing our individual interests are all important to us. We would never want to hold each other back. That's really important. I don't ever want to feel stifled or not able to be creative and pursue my dreams and hopes.

You need laughter for a relationship to thrive. Trust has to be there, as well as respect. Respect is very important, both for yourself and for your partner. You always want to show your partner's best side and best face in public, and don't want to ever embarrass them in public. We have a couple of friends who will fight at the dinner table in a restaurant. We don't ever fight but if we ever got short-tempered with each other we would never do so in public. We'd wait until we got in the car! It's also important to never let your partner feel alienated or alone or ignored in a group. You should be proud of that person, especially when you're out together.

If you want a healthy relationship, be patient, Give it time and let it grow organically. Do things to help it grow. Feed it. It's a lot of work. Relationships are work and they're not easy. Love is not easy, and I think if people understand that, their relationships will be even stronger. If you're in a relationship it's important to act like you're in a relationship. Don't make important decisions on your own without consulting your partner. I would never say, "Oh, by the way I'm leaving town next week because I want to play a concert down in D.C." I would give Greg proper advance notice and say, "I'd really like to go down and play a concert in D.C in three months. Will that be OK?" You have to answer to your partner, and if you give him respect, he'll give you respect in return.

CHAPTER 11

CRAIG AND PAUL

"Most likely in any long-term relationship you do become somewhat codependent—it's probably just part of the deal—so there's always that balance/struggle where, if my partner's depressed or angry or whatever, how much do I have to participate in that? Can I just step back from it and care for him and see that he has to work through some of the stuff, or how much do I have to get in there and fix things or make things better for him?"

Craig and Paul met a quarter of a century ago through a gay men's chorus they both sang in. Craig works as a clinical social worker, while Paul is employed as a teacher. Married now for a number of years, they make their home on a farm in Connecticut with a wide array of birds and mammals.

Craig — (Paul)

We've been together twenty-three years. I'm now sixty-one, and Paul's fifty-seven, so I was thirty-eight at the time we met. We were both in a gay men's chorus and probably just briefly said hello to each other there initially. Sometime later the chorus went to a bar for a dance night. Since he was tall and I needed a dance partner, I asked Paul to dance. We enjoyed dancing together, so I just started asking him questions and learned that he was a father and a schoolteacher, so that interested me, and he seemed to have a good time.

Sometime later—which was my style—I called him up and asked him if he was available for dating. I wanted to be clear about saying that from the get-go, and not just, "Would you like to go out for a cup of coffee," or any of that stuff. I wanted him to know my intent, so I asked if he was available for dating, and he said that he was. So we started getting together from time to time and did a lot of talking. He was divorced, as was I, though I don't have any children.

I found Paul enjoyable to be around. We had fun. It was easy to talk to him. I remember one night sitting on a couch playing some kind of board game together, and I thought it was interesting that he would do that. I was interested that he had children because I liked the idea of being involved with children and I liked kids. He also had a dog, and it was important to me that he liked kids and dogs. Paul had a responsible job as a school-teacher, so I wouldn't have to be concerned about somebody who could not be responsible in terms of career or finances.

We weren't sexual, and he wasn't very physically intimate in terms of hugging or kissing and was even a little bit standoffish. After a few weeks, I concluded that he must not be interested in or attracted to me, so I really didn't want to continue with him. One night, we were down at the local bar and I said to him that I needed to talk, because I was just going to say, "OK, this isn't going anywhere..." I like to be very clear about things and state clearly what I'm feeling, and not just not call someone back or whatever. I didn't want there to be any question about where I was coming from, and how people deal with each other is a big issue for me.

So I said, "I'd like to talk to you away from the bar. Where can we go?"

He said, "Why don't you come over to my house?"

I actually had not spent time at his house, and he had this house with a fireplace, so we lit the fire and sat down in front of the fireplace. I basically told him that it seemed to me that he wasn't interested in being physical with me and didn't show any physical intimacy, and that since he wasn't attracted to me, I didn't want to continue trying to date him.

Paul then shared at that point that his reason for not being physically intimate with me was because so often in the past when he would have sex with some guy the first night, it just never really went anywhere afterwards and was just pretty much over with. And he was not interested in doing that anymore and was more interested in a LTR and that's why he wasn't initiating anything physical that could easily lead to sexual stuff. So I found out then by asking him those specific questions that he was attracted to me, that that wasn't an issue, and that night we ended up being sexual as it turned out.

That was in the fall, and we dated quite a bit and were sexual from then on. It took a while before he introduced me to his children, and since his children were there quite often, I didn't sleep over during those times. But at some point between then and the following June, he did introduce me to his kids, and I started to get to know them. He also introduced me to his folks somewhere in there.

Interestingly enough, I could easily say to people, "I love you," so I could say those words to him fairly easily and I did, but to him that was another big issue. For him to say those words, he had to be at a certain point in a relationship. I remember it was around Valentine's Day, he made a Valentine card—I think I still have it—and the words "I Love You" were on there but they were mixed up on the Valentine, and it was something about "These words are in me but they just haven't all gotten fit together yet," or something like that. It was some indication that he was getting closer to saying "I love you," which he then did tell me on my birthday in April.

I moved into his house then on June 1st. So we used to celebrate three anniversaries, and we were each responsible for one. I was responsible for the first date in November. He was responsible for the "I love you" in April, and then we were both responsible for the anniversary of my moving in on June 1st. That's how we used to playfully do all that stuff.

We are sexually exclusive, and it's interesting how that's worked out. We'll always be talking about other men. "Oh, he's hot." "Do you think..." "Oh yeah, he's really hot. Oh God, let me have him!" And blah, blah, blah... All this chatter which we're constantly doing, and for us, it is healthy that we let the other person know who turns us on, whether they're in front of us or on TV or in a movie or walking down the street. We'll be teasing each other, like on the cell phone, and I'll say, "Oh, just a minute. There's this really hot guy going by. Oh my God, you should see him!" So there's a lot of openness about that, yet I think there's probably a certain amount of fear of stepping into that arena, too.

As a therapist, it makes sense to me that, in relationships, if you are not sexually exclusive—and there's a whole range of how people do those contracts with one another—it can also interfere with the relationship in a variety of different ways. I mean, even when you're young and hot-to-trot and infatuated with each other, there's always someone else out there who's such a perfect specimen. You can always find someone more beautiful than your partner because the world is full of so many beautiful bodies, and that doesn't change over time. And as you get older and your body ages and you can look in the mirror and see that you're not as physically attractive as you used to be—and since as a culture, we favor the youthful body—if you just base a relationship on physical attractiveness, over time the relationship will certainly diminish. It needs to have all these other factors that make it work and last.

But getting back to your question, I think there's a certain amount of fear that if we step into that arena that we would use those sexual escapades to bring us pleasure, and sometimes people do that to avoid dealing with issues in the relationship that need to be dealt with. So if we have an open relationship and I'm pissed off at my husband, and some guy comes on to me or vice versa and we have a tryst that meets my little attachment need for the day or night or whatever, then it's easy to just slide by whatever issue I didn't resolve with my husband. And if you get in the practice of doing that, pretty soon you find yourself at an emotional distance from your partner, and then the relationship is in trouble.

Sexually, I suppose, there's always going to be a certain amount of routine-ness to it if you do the same thing with the same person for twenty-three years. We do try to be spontaneous. Part of it—to be realistic—we are very busy people and we are getting older and can feel tired, so it doesn't happen as often as it used to, but even so when it does happen, it's happening because someone went up to the other person because he felt like it and started being intimate and touching, wherever we are at the time. We do that and then we can be sexual in that particular spot, which is not necessarily in bed. It could be in bed but it could be anyplace in our house or on our property or wherever, so I suppose there's a certain amount of spontaneity in that. Sometimes we have porn on, especially if we want to be sexual and it's later at night and we need to get to bed. Porn helps eroticize the whole thing much more quickly.

It's really important to have orgasms, for all kinds of reasons, emotionally and physically. If you don't use it, you'll lose it, and for men, for the health of our prostates, we need to be doing it a lot! I really believe in that, so I want to make sure that we are regularly having orgasms. Not that that's the ultimate goal of being sexual with someone, because sometimes we don't and sometimes we're just making out a lot. That's part of it, too: sometimes we make out and sometimes we don't, and by that I mean mouth -on-mouth kissing a lot, not blowjobs, because mouth-on-mouth is for us very connecting and very erotic. Blowjobs and fucking aren't the same as kissing, but of course if you put them together, it's wonderful. It can be pretty easy, maybe, for couples to not keep the kissing going over time. If we see kissing on a porn DVD, that's something we really like seeing, because it makes what we're looking at seem more real to us; we want there to be that love attachment thing going on there.

Paul and I are very affectionate and touch each other a lot regularly. Also, as guys—in contrast to our experience of being married to women—we do a lot of rough-housing, which is something I never would have done with my wife. We'll push each other around and wrestle and occasionally punch each other, though not hard; just stuff that feels natural to do with a guy. I would NEVER have had any desire to do that with a woman, and she wouldn't have liked it. It's basically goofing around.

We also tease a lot, which has been somewhat disconcerting for our friends over the years, as we're pretty animated in our bantering back and forth. Currently we have our own endearing terms for each other which are not pretty, like "Fuckwad" and "Butthole," and things like that. We've switched recently to German, so now he's an "Arschloch" or a "Dummer Esel" or a "Saukerl," and last night a friend was teaching us those words in Russian. So we can now use these words in public in the United States and get away with it, since most people don't speak German or Russian. But they're terms of endearment for us, and that's part of our relationship. That certainly would probably not feel good for other people, but it feels good for us!

We have slept together most of our lives in a full-size bed, which is ridiculous. We need to get a bigger one, but haven't done that yet. We have two bedrooms in our house, and what has happened over the last year is that Paul has had two operations, a hernia operation and a hemorrhoid operation, and with the hernia operation, it became easier for him to have a whole bed to himself where he could be held up by pillows in different ways, so he started sleeping by himself during that time.

Then when that was over, we started sleeping together again, with him getting up in the middle of the night and going into the other room so he could really stretch all out. So that may be our pattern now for the ongoing time. Sometimes, when I come home from work I'm way later than he would want to be up, so he's in bed sleeping already. But it's something we try to do every night that we're home together, so at least we can start out together and cuddle.

We also read out loud to each other. That's something we've done all the years we've been together and we really enjoy picking a book together and reading a chapter or two when we have time before we go to sleep. That's been a very connecting thing.

Interestingly enough, in our seventh year—I always think about the seven-year itch—I was involved in way too much stuff. I was working on my degree almost full-time and was working full and part-time, and we had a family, and we got estranged there. Paul really got hurt when I spent a weekend away and didn't ask him clearly enough if it would be OK to spend this weekend away with a female friend who was moving out of state. She and I had been really close for many years. So I went away that weekend, but Paul and I had to work on reconnecting again for the next month or so.

I believe at that point he had considered whether he wanted to be in the relationship or could handle it or whatever, but I remember that was a scary time for the relationship. I even recall where we were when we started working it out. We were in this forest on a weekend retreat with some friends and we were by ourselves and we started to bridge the gap again.

What we call love is that initial infatuation with connecting with someone who on several levels meets needs that you have, and it's recipro-cated. So there's that early glimmer where it feels like I'm falling in love with somebody. The pleasure chemicals are going on in my brain, and I'm feeling really good about being with this person, and there are not a lot of red flags coming out which are interrupting that pleasure thing.

After a while, when that starts to dim, I think that what increases the connection is each person becoming more vulnerable and open and honest about thoughts and feelings and fears and concerns and hopes and dreams that they have. When you share those with the other person, he is respectful and caring about listening, and then he shares his hopes and dreams and fears and you reciprocate the caring back and forth, so that you become very much known to the other person and he becomes vulnerable and lets you in on these so-called secrets that he doesn't want everyone else to know or maybe haven't shared with anyone else. So all that needs to happen, and there needs to be a lot of communication going on.

Then part of that love piece is going through the times where there are conflicts and feelings get hurt and are there is anger and whatnot, and for the love to continue you have to reconcile and get through those feelings and the expressing of them. And that's dangerous because you don't know if the other person is going to respect you or reject you or whatever it is he might do. But if you can work through some of these reconciliation cycles and you know that you've done so before and you can do it again, that—to me—fits into the love contract. That this person cares enough about me to work through some discomfort or distress or fears in the relationship to make it to the other side, and then being able to really enjoy that feeling of relief or reconnecting again. Because if that's not going on, what I would call the love contract is fake, and the relationship is not going to last.

Most likely in any long-term relationship, you do become somewhat codependent—it's probably just part of the deal—so there's always that balance/struggle where, if my partner's depressed or angry or whatever, how much do I have to participate in that? Can I just step back from it and care for him and see that he has to work through some of the stuff, or how much do I have to get in there and fix things or make things better for him? I think you have to get that worked out in a relationship so that it isn't too codependent. For example, I have to go to a conference this upcoming weekend and I really don't want to go alone. I'd rather be with Paul at our place, and I would like for him to come along, but it's not possible... So I can feel that codependent piece right there.

Other parts of me are saying, "It would be good for you to be out there on your own and have another adventure. You can do it!" And of course I can do it. I've done it before but I'm honest with the parts of me that are stuck on him, that want to be around him and to play, and if he's not around I'm lonely, at least some of the time!

Paul's more introverted, and I'm more extroverted, so I feel like I want him to tell me more—for instance, about his day—and if he's not in a space to do that, he's not going to do it. He sees me often as talking too much, sharing too much, being too open, but from my perspective, there are times when he will really kick in and share a lot of stuff. If we're having a fight, his way to do some of it would be to say, "I don't want to talk about it,"— just not wanting to go there—where parts of me want to go there, go there, go there... I want to talk this thing to death! So working out things like what we do when we're hurt has been an issue over the years between the two of us.

In one of my marriage vows, I said, "I have never been bored for one minute in all the twenty years we've been together," and that's the truth, because there's enough teasing and play and goofing around together. It's not a relationship of two people who are just so fond of each other they just sit together and cuddle and "Oh sweetie pie this," and "Oh sweetie pie that.'

There's a certain amount of tension between us. He has a part of him that's pretty critical. Like for instance when I make breakfast—I make breakfast most of the year until summer comes—he seldom praises what I make. He makes observations about my cooking: "Hmmm, you put an awful lot of onion in this..." He may like it but he's not saying that, and a lot of times what he's saying sounds critical to my ear. So that critical part keeps me on edge a bit, not just relaxing into "I know he's going to love whatever I make for him," or "It doesn't matter." No, it really matters. Every fucking meal, it matters! I don't get hurt by it very often anymore. I just hear it and start laughing and wonder, "What is he going to criticize today?"

One thing Paul said in our marriage vows was that one of the things he liked about me was that I will take all that stuff from him, because he knows that he cannot take it. As soon as I start being critical of him, he has a little-boy part that immediately gets pouty or whatever. But it's worked out for us that we can tolerate each other in that way. So it isn't a relationship where you can take the other person for granted very much, because you definitely have to be present and need to be ready not to get defensive! It's a sort of dance really. I feel like we're dancing all the time.

We're very interested in all kinds of spiritualities and all kinds of religions. The older I get, the more I am distancing myself from the theology of my youth, and do not accept it anymore. I still have a strong Christ attachment, but there are aspects of Christianity that don't make sense to me, and I have some leanings towards Buddhism, mostly in the Zen meditation arena.

Native American spirituality interests me. So does pagan stuff, though family and friends would not even like to know that I consider that to be worth exploring. My church background was very strict and rigid, and I'm just about as far as you can get in the other direction now. Paul grew up in a church, too, but did not go through any of the fundamentalist stuff I went through. I did attend church for a while early in our relationship but stopped attending after we moved to the country.

Paul and I have always read spiritual books of all kinds together. We easily share many of the same spiritual beliefs, which is a huge issue for a relationship. Because we are not seeing each other as goofy regarding spirituality, we are very comfortable that way, and those ethics and beliefs have to infiltrate everything that you do and say eventually and affect how you deal with life's many problems. So that's really nice for us. We don't have that issue in our relationship of any kind of distancing around spirituality and we can go to the same retreats and things, even though we came from very different perspectives in the beginning.

Being with Paul, I feel a lot of freedom to be who I am and I feel a lot of respect from him for who I am, and also support for all my shortcomings and frailties and insecurities. He knows them all and loves me anyway. And that's what any human being needs, that total acceptance, so that I can then just explore whatever I need to explore inside of me and not be afraid, like when I was younger… "Oh my God, what if somebody found out that I was thinking this or that or did this or that?" I don't have to worry about that. I just get to share what's going on, and he gives me feedback or joins me in it or whatever and he's always encouraging me to expand or go further. Sometimes he has ideas about my career that are fun to listen to. Just generally speaking, it's been quite amazing that I ended up in this relationship. It's as good as I could have imagined.

Because we knew we would never be able to marry, we had a blessing-type ceremony when we were together fifteen years. There were all sorts of mixed spirituality folks present for it, and that was really nice. We had a good time and a lot of people came. We used some of the marriage-type pieces out of John Boswell's book, *Same-Sex Unions in Premodern Europe*, and our kids sang and talked about our relationship and what it meant to them. So we thought, well, that would be it.

Then when the marriage thing was made possible in our state, I asked him to marry me. I thought, "This is just too cool. We have to do this!" He didn't say yes right away, which really blew me out of the water. I couldn't fucking believe it! So we talked about it. But it was quite a big deal for him to think about because it caused him to re-evaluate our relationship again.

He hadn't shared this with me, but a year or so before that, he was grappling privately with the fact that he did not like how I had aged physically. I look quite a bit older, really a lot older, than when we got together, and the wrinkling of my skin and things has been pretty dramatic. A part of him just did not like that. He did not want to be with a guy who looked that old and he didn't tell me about it because he knew it would hurt my feelings a lot. Later he did tell me what he was feeling, and of course I was hurt, because I don't like the way I have aged and look either, but of course, there's not much that I can do about it. I don't have the money and I probably would not do a lot of plastic surgery.

That was interesting, and he worked through it on his own, and during that whole time, I did not notice it at all. I was just physically glomming on to him and hugging him and all that stuff, and there was a part of him that didn't want that. So I think that entered into his hesitancy about saying "yes" right away, but it really caused him to look at our relationship, because marriage is a big step.

I was pissed, like "After all these years, you even HESITATE?!!!" He knew that it really pissed me off or that I was hurt. But then I had these parts of me that came up with this plan because I knew that he liked jewelry. Part of me didn't put a lot of stock in jewelry because I thought it a waste of money. Paul particularly liked diamonds, and I had never bought him any diamonds. So I went to our local jewelry store, and they had one ring for a man with five little diamonds in it I bought it and gave it to him. He was really blown away, and I asked, "So would you marry me?," and he said, "Yes." And away we went. That was very powerful.

Then what happened is that our families kicked in. My brother, who lives in another state, found out via the Internet that gay marriage went through in Connecticut and called and said, "When are you guys going to get married?" He really wanted us to get married, and I just thought, "Wow! What's this all about?" Our neighbors also stopped by and said, "Are you guys going to get married?" And "Can I come to the wedding?," and all that kind of stuff. It was just unbelievable.

Ultimately both sides of our immediate family came to our farm and they helped clean it up and beautify it and set up everything for our wedding. They were here for two days, and we had an incredible event. A lot of sharing of love—I can't even describe it—it was just overwhelming.

What we understood was that this was extremely important to our family. They wanted the world to understand and validate this relationship that they had been witnessing all these years, to bring it up the caliber and standing of any straight relationship. That just blew us away. It wasn't at all like we had to be concerned about "Do you want to come to our wedding?" They almost forced themselves on us! They were amazing, and talk about glimmerance and good feelings and lasting, wonderful memories... I will never forget it as long as I live. It was just way over the top. WAY over the top! It was best day of my life, and I didn't even know that it could be like that.

I think spirituality is very important in a healthy relationship, having some sort of shared understanding of the meaning of life, or a shared attempt to find meaning in life. It's helpful to have shared expressions of spirituality, to read about it, to experience it, even if it's something of a hard concept to pin down.

For a long-term relationship to succeed, there needs to be a certain level of physical attraction, although that wanes. Especially when you start out a relationship, there has to be enough physical attraction to get the thing going and keep it going. Hopefully you are emotionally compatible as well. It could be an issue if one person is really high-strung and the other is really laid-back. Financial responsibility is important as is responsibility in general; you can't have one person carrying the whole load and resenting the other person for not doing his share. There also has to be some agreement on the fidelity issue and there needs to be the ability to work out differences and conflicts, to work towards reconciliation, for the relationship to work long-term.

When you explore the potential of a relationship, you have to ask a lot of questions in your mind about the other person, about all these different issues I was just describing. It's important to take the time to really evaluate those things clearly and to reflect on them so that you don't see things through rose-colored glasses and overlook some big potential blocks to future happiness, just because his body is so hot or he has so much money or whatever. You want to be aware of enough key qualities in the person that match up with what you need in a relationship before going to the next level with a potential partner.

CHAPTER 12

STUART AND JOHN

"Being open to intimacy and being open to enjoying the wonderful differences people may have is actually what makes life interesting. I think sometimes in this world we close each other off, and it seems that people often have lists of "You must be like this," and "You must be like that..." I've never had such a list and if I did I might have ruled out some terrific people. Have an open heart and an open mind. Be open to meeting someone where they are and to exploring what makes them wonderful, which may be in ways which are unexpected to you."

In 1987, twenty-somethings Stuart Gaffney and John Lewis met at a political fundraiser in San Francisco. The devoted couple has been a major force in the marriage equality movement for years, appearing frequently as eloquent spokesmen for the cause in both press and media. Stuart works as Communications Director for Marriage Equality USA, www.marriageequality.org, where John is employed as Legal and Policy Director. Happy to be married, they make their home in San Francisco. A Milwaukee native, Stuart is also a gifted nature photographer.

Stuart Gaffney — (John Lewis)

We have now been together for twenty-six years. John and I met in 1987, and our life together has been a joy. When we met, I was twenty-four going on twenty-five, and John was then twenty-eight. I had come out publicly in college and moved to San Francisco after graduating in January of 1985. I'd had three significant relationships when I was in college, and that time when I moved to San Francisco was actually the longest period of time I had been single.

One evening, I went to a party with a friend. He had said it was a political fundraiser, and I was very interested in politics so I was happy to be invited and was really just going there to be with friends. It turned out that the host of the party was somebody I knew from activist work, and he introduced me to a very nice-looking young man named John. As I recall, we shook hands right over the fruit bowl. My recollection of that evening is that we just started talking so easily and naturally. It seemed like we spoke the same language, and it felt to me that in a sense I'd already known him for a long time.

John was very familiar, and the word "familiar" comes from family, and that's how I came to feel about him very quickly; that he felt like family to me. About a week after I met John, a friend of mine from college was visiting and asked me, "Have you met anybody new?," and I said, "I think I've met my future husband..." I just thought, "He's the one!" Sometimes people ask, "Well, was it love at first sight?," and I think the best answer to that is that it felt more like family at first sight.

Very quickly, we started spending a lot of time together and not surprisingly—since we met at a political fundraiser—we found that we both enjoyed being politically active and being part of the political process together and advocating for our own rights and for social justice more broadly. So one of the first things we did after we met was to get together and go to the candidates debate. It was wonderful to feel not just that I clicked with this person and felt so much in common personality-wise, but that we also shared a broader world-view together.

While relationships can be interesting in the ways that you differ, in so many ways, we were on the same page. My first impressions proved to be very accurate, and we spent a lot of time together. John and I met in March of 1987 and then moved in together officially nine months later, in January, though in effect we were really living together before that.

It's worth noting that we met during one of the worst points of the AIDS epidemic in San Francisco, so while we felt very serious about each other and very close to each other very quickly, the wisdom of the time was in some ways to proceed with caution. So there was a slow, steady progression of becoming more intimate in all ways. Perhaps we were more measured because of the place and time in which we met.

We are sexually exclusive, and that's a conversation we had fairly early on and an agreement that we made. We talked about it to explore each other's feelings about it, but it was not something that was controversial for us. It was a fairly easy decision that we made together and have not needed to revisit. I don't feel any intense "temptation," which almost suggests uncontrollable urges, as though I can't help myself. What maybe has come up for us are issues of how close we've become to other people. This would include situations like becoming close to another friend, a best friend, or if you feel like you're friends with someone as a couple, but in fact that person is closer to one of you than the other, or maybe in how you deal with friends you had from before you met.

Over our now-many years, I'm sure there were times when we've become close to other people but, speaking for myself, I haven't experienced that really as temptation. It's more just something to navigate, and I think it's a dance that all couples, regardless of what agreements they may or may not have, do encounter and work through. How do you balance your individual sense of who you are and individual ways in which you may become close to other people, and how you interact with people as a couple, and how you interact with each other?

One aspect of our relationship is that John and I tend to do the vast majority of things together, so we actually see most of the friends that we have together. Maybe that also reduces the sort of random ways that temptation might come up, since I may spend less time on my own than some other people may do in their relationships. Over many years there are some people I've become close to as friends that John maybe has not become close to. These have been primarily people I've worked with, and friendships can have emotional intimacy, too.

Sometimes we joke about "work husbands" or "work spouses" that people have. I've shared an office with the same man for over twelve years now, which is a pretty long relationship, and I'm very fond of him, but I don't experience any temptation with him. He is, in fact, a married gay man and he's not a close friend of John's, but I see him all day almost every day. So keeping our exclusivity agreement has not been very difficult for us.

We are still sexual today, though we haven't been sexual today, yet! Keeping an open dialogue with each other is really important. Of course, some people love talking about sex, but I think sometimes it can be challenging to talk about intimacy, and it can bring up insecurities. I won't say it's always easy, but we maintain a commitment to talking about all aspects of our relationship. Anything and everything need to be open to being on the table for discussion, and sex is certainly one of those aspects.

John and I brought two important skills to the relationship which really complement each other: John brought a very strong commitment to open and honest communication and a very strong conviction that such communication was extremely important for both of us as individuals and as a couple. I brought an innate ability to love unconditionally, and I think those two things together have really helped us to navigate a lot of situations. John's communication skills have helped us to talk through challenges or problems, and I think that the feeling that's contained within unconditional love has made it feel safe to do so. That would apply to talking through any questions we might have about how to relate to each other physically, and also more broadly, how to keep our relationship vibrant and healthy and how to grow and change together.

It's hard to express what it feels like to be with someone for twenty-six years. That's a really long time. The vast majority of my adult life has been with John, and we are each other's home. We've created a life and a home together, and that's what a relationship of this duration is really all about. We're growing old together. This is the person I'm spending the rest of my life with. This is the person who's going to care for me, or I'm going to care for him in old age. It really brings the wedding vows to life. We're all familiar with "For better or for worse," and "In sickness and in health," but over time, you live out these vows and they're no longer just words. They become "Oh yes, I remember when he nursed me through an illness," or "I remember when I was there for him in a time of crisis." Those inherently deepen your sense of intimacy and bonding and all contribute to a feeling that you're on a shared life journey together.

Having been extremely involved in the marriage equality movement for over a decade now, it feels like the most natural thing in the world for us to be holding hands or being arm in arm, whether we're in wedding gear, activist gear, or just being ourselves. At least in San Francisco, people often recognize us on the street as husbands. I'm sure that over time, we vary in terms of literally how cuddly we feel day to day. I try to tell him I love him multiple times every single day. I'm not sure if I say it every single time we talk on the phone—I probably don't—but I almost feel like I do, because it's really important to be expressing what's in your heart. John is extremely open-hearted, which helps create the atmosphere that makes me want to kiss him when I come home. I want to hug him. I want to tell him I love him and that I missed him during the day. That just feels good to me too.

My experience of love includes the experience of meeting John and feeling that he'd already been written in the book of my life from the beginning. It may sound silly to answer someone who is earnestly asking you, "How do you know that you've met somebody special or you've met the right one?," with "Well, you'll just know." But in some ways that's very true. It's just a feeling deep down inside. At first there's the excitement of, "I just met him!," and it's new, it's thrilling, even overwhelming.

Over time, those tingly, excited, initial feelings of love evolve, and it's not that it becomes less exciting, but it takes on a different, more profound sense that this is the person you're sharing all facets of your life with. To me, even as I say this to you now, it's almost too much to take in. Even though we see people do it all the time, there is something intangible about it... How do two people at the same time decide to make a relationship happen, and they both want to do it with each other? It's easy to say that it's magical, but it is. There *is* something magical about it.

John and I definitely have different communication styles. Speaking for myself, when I get upset or a certain kind of upset, I tend to get very quiet. So that may communicate that I'm upset but it doesn't help with why I'm upset and it doesn't help resolve it. John's style is more the reverse, where if he's upset, he tends more to tell me so, which does help us communicate about it. It doesn't necessarily mean though that just because he tells me about it that we can resolve it. When I'm upset, my instinct is to shut down. I'm aware of it happening but it's hard for me at that moment to say, "Wow, I'm shutting down now, but that means I'm not talking to John about it..."

Over time, it's gotten easier in the sense that we're more aware of it— he's aware that that's something I do, and I'm aware that I'm doing it—but speaking for myself again, there's something that feels instinctive about it to me. I don't want to say that in a fatalistic way, like it couldn't be changed, but though I can observe it happening, it doesn't mean that I can just snap myself out of it. We can talk about it afterwards but we don't have a perfect solution to it while it's happening.

We went to couples therapy for a "tune up," which health insurance at the time covered. We'd been together close to twenty years at that point, and over two decades, there are things that can build up, things you haven't talked about or found a way to talk about, or maybe one of you feels has been settled but the other does not. It was helpful to have somebody else be there to facilitate a conversation about "course corrections." Sometimes it's helpful just to have a third person there saying, "Wow, that was a really long time ago, and you're still thinking about it?" "You're still upset about something he said sixteen years ago?" And that doesn't mean that that solves it instantly, but it is a good reality check, and it's something that a couples counselor can be uniquely helpful with.

I was brought up in the Unitarian church, which is a bit more abstract in the spiritual direction than most churches. John has had a very long-standing interest in Buddhist practice, and while I would not say that is my practice, I think in some ways I'm very receptive to it, and parts of it really resonate with me. I've certainly learned a lot about it through John. So it's not my spiritual path, but to the extent that I might want to at certain moments in life draw on some spiritual wisdom, that would probably be a source that would resonate for me.

Our senses of humor are a little bit different but are probably comple-mentary. It's never a source of friction, but there are some times where we don't always get each other's humor. John is a bit more laugh-out-loud and he enjoys telling silly jokes. My sense of humor tends to be more subtle or ironic or involves wordplay and the like. Like any couple, we could laugh more, but we do have our fun. We are certainly spontaneous with each other. "Hey, I feel like going for a drive, or a hike," or "I feel like going to this movie..." We both try to keep our lives happy and interesting.

We have shared finances for a very long time now. John and I bought a house together three years ago, which may not be as big a commitment as marriage, but it's a very big commitment nonetheless. It felt extremely natural to us to buy a house together at that point. I'm not saying it wasn't scary for us, since the value of real estate in San Francisco is pretty scary in and of itself. But we've been sharing expenses for a very long time, since about our second year together, when we basically said in effect "What's yours is mine."

John and I spent a year traveling all over the world. It was amazing and wonderful, and it brought us closer together actually before it even happened. This was a shared vision, and we needed to share it as a vision in order to make it happen. We needed to both want to save money for it, we needed to both be willing to give up our jobs to be able to do it, and we needed to be able to agree on places we wanted to go and on the style in which we wanted to travel. We also needed to feel like it was fun and not work! It was a process of a couple of years just to plan for that moment, to be able to do it, so it already felt like a dream come true. I quit my job. John was able to negotiate a year off from his job, which in itself was a huge accomplishment. Obviously money can always be a stressful issue, but it was, "OK, this is how much money we have. This is the style in which we say we want to travel. Can we make this work?" Most things fell into place pretty naturally, so that was wonderful, and it really made it possible to do the trip. The whole experience felt like a dream come true.

I had always wanted to take the Trans-Siberian railroad, and John had really wanted to go to Vietnam, which was just beginning to open to tourism, and we did that. He had worked with Southeast Asian refugees before we met, and being able to visit the countries the refugees were from was particularly amazing for him, and I got to learn a lot about it by seeing it through his eyes. So the trip was a lot of lovely give and take. During the year, each of us got sick at some point, and being travelers, it meant that we were sick in inconvenient circumstances, to say the least. So being there and supporting each other, caring for each other through that, brought us closer together as well.

I mentioned that I've learned a lot about spirituality through John, and one of the things he wanted to do in some of the places we went in Asia was to visit spiritual sites. This is something that I would not have naturally thought of or really even known to do, but some of the things he brought us in contact with were really mind-blowing. Every three or four years, there is a mass pilgrimage in India where over ten million people descend on a particular spot in the Ganges, because it is the most auspicious time to bathe in the Ganges. This is something I'd never even heard of before, much less witnessed, but to be there was just beyond words. That was certainly one of the highlights of our trip, but it was also a gift that John gave to us, because he knew to make it happen. Going on a safari in Africa was also extraordinary and incredibly beautiful, in a way that is hard to describe.

Our wedding day, exchanging vows, and then the journey of working for marriage equality, are our greatest life adventures together so far. But on the other hand, this year of traveling around the world is right up there. Certainly before we got married, I would say it's our biggest adventure together. We could put them hand in hand and say we got to have the honeymoon before we got the wedding! When we married, we had been together about seventeen years, but we had never had a ceremony or exchanged vows, though we were utterly committed to each other.

Sometimes you don't really understand rituals until you experience them, and though we'd been to countless other people's weddings, we had never had that kind of a moment for ourselves. And because the opportunity to marry in San Francisco City Hall in 2004 did arise spontaneously, there was almost a magical beauty to it. Before we knew what happened, there we were exchanging vows and being pronounced spouses for life, and because of the way these weddings unfolded and because John and I were able to be there at the very first moment—there was no time to invite anybody or to plan a wedding—it made it very intimate. We were in City Hall, which is a big, beautiful, and busy building, so we were not truly alone, but in some ways it felt like it was just the two of us there at that moment. It was very personal and very profound.

Recently we went back to Washington, DC, for the Supreme Court hearings and marriage equality cases. During that time, one of our nieces, who's now a freshman in college, wrote us a spontaneous note. She said how grateful she was to have us in her life and how much she admired us for standing up for who we are, and how that was really such an important model for her in her life, to be who she is and also just to stand up for social justice in ways that are meaningful for her. It's amazing just to be able to touch another person's life in that way, and it was very obviously sweet of her to take the time to share her thoughts with us. There's a political aspect to her message too, and the reality is that she's known us her entire life as Uncle John and Uncle Stuart—we've been together longer than she's been around—but she's now of voting age, and the first time she ever voted, she voted for marriage equality in Washington state, where she's attending school, and she voted to re-elect the first President to come out for marriage equality. That's also a nice illustration about how social change is made.

I learn so much from John, and he helps me be a better person in so many ways. It's certainly a challenge for any couple to grow and change both as individuals and as a couple in a relationship, and no relationship is going to be perfect in being able to maintain the ideal balance between individual freedom and your identity as a couple. But over time, we've been able to share a lot of amazing adventures which have brought us closer together and allowed us to grow and change. It may not be surprising, since we met at a political fundraiser, that we've been very politically active in the marriage equality movement.

Just as there was some spontaneity to our marriage, we didn't know that we would spend the last decade now working for marriage equality together, and through this experience, we have grown and changed together in ways we just could never have anticipated. We've now led rallies together and written press releases together and been interviewed on live national TV together. We have been through really difficult, heartbreaking losses and have also been at the table when there has been lots of conflict. These are unexpected ways that we've changed and grown.

We've learned more about each other and discovered new and different skills we didn't even know we had. How could you know when you meet somebody, "Oh, this person might be good to advocate for social change with..." "This person might make a good MC at a rally with thousands of people..." You just don't know until that happens, but in our case, it did. In ways big and small, being able to grow and change together would seem to me to be a key to a successful long-term relationship, and this has been a wonderful way in which we've been able to do that.

We obviously believe very strongly that relationships can be a wonderful thing, and it certainly continues to be a wonderful thing in our lives. I couldn't imagine life without John. He's Mr. Wonderful to me. But I think for people who are looking for a partner, concepts like Mr. Right can be challenging. It conjures up, "Have I met the person I'm destined to meet?," instead of "Have I met someone wonderful with whom I can maybe make a beautiful thing happen?" John and I have talked about this. We also hesitate to say "Relationships take work," because it just sounds laborious. We know they take effort, but hopefully, it's in a good way. It isn't always fun to be in the trenches, but hopefully it feels good to be working to make your lives better together.

Being open to intimacy and being open to enjoying the wonderful differences people may have is actually what makes life interesting. I think sometimes in this world we close each other off, and it seems that people often have lists of "You must be like this," and "You must be like that..." I've never had such a list and if I did, I might have ruled out some terrific people. Have an open heart and an open mind. Be open to meeting someone where they are and to exploring what makes them wonderful, which may be in ways which are unexpected to you.

SECTION III:

COUPLES TOGETHER
THIRTY TO FORTY YEARS

CHAPTER 13

LARRY AND GREG

"He comes from the grand old W.A.S.P. male tradition of keeping it in. I come from the grand old ethnic tradition of lettin' it out. I come from a family where you yell and you scream and you throw the crockery and then you say "I'm sorry, I love you," and you move on. He comes from a family where you keep it in and you develop a wine problem."

Lambda Award winning novelist Larry Duplechan met his husband Greg Harvey nearly four decades ago when they were both students at U.C.L..A. One of his most popular novels, *Blackbird*, a semi-autobiographical tale about a black teenager coming of age in the 1970's, was recently made into a film. Larry is also a talented cartoonist and musician, and works by day in the legal field. He and Greg, a banker by profession, live in the L.A. burbs with their cat, Mr. Blue.

Larry Duplechan — (Greg Harvey)

Greg and I have been together for thirty-eight years, which is amazing. Here's how we met... I was a singer and a soloist with the U.C.L.A. Men's Glee Club, and Greg saw our Spring concert and saw me on stage and heard me sing and thought, "I've got to meet that guy..."

The next school year, he auditioned and got into the Glee Club, largely in order to meet me. I thought he was cute in kind of a square/straight sort of way. He thinks he was very obvious in his wooing of me, but I didn't get it for about six months. Greg was my straight bud, and we got to be friends. Until the night he pounced, which was a mutual pouncing, I guess. So I liked him, but it took a while before I understood what was actually going on, and I was actually pursuing someone else, which also complicated things.

I'm not one for going after straight guys—there's no percentage in it—so I didn't really pay a lot of attention to this "straight" friend of mine. I was going after someone I knew was gay, only to find out that this guy wasn't interested in me at all, and Greg was actually the friend I turned to for the shoulder to cry on about that! So that's how that happened.

Things developed. We kissed and made out and we didn't really turn back from there, though we didn't have sex the first time we made out. We were on Glee Club tour and were sharing hotel rooms with other guys, and it was a rather furtive type of grappling in this hotel bed, in the hopes that our straight roommates did not return to the room. But that was kind of it for both of us; we just fell into dating each other right there.

At that time, Greg was about to finish college, and I was about to finish my sophomore year, so it was understood from the beginning of our dating that when he graduated he was not going to stay in Los Angeles. He was from San Jose and he assumed that he was going to go back there, where his family lives. And at the beginning, it was like, "Yeah, OK, this is really nice and I like you and we have good times and things in common, and then when you graduate you'll go and we'll kiss and we'll—you know—always have Paris."

And the closer it got, the more difficult that idea became. It became a you-know-what-or-get-off-the-pot situation, where we either had to decide that we were going to have some sort of commitment to each other or we were going to have to say goodbye. We'd been together about three months by then, so Greg wasn't yet out of college, but that's the point where he decided he was not going to move away, and we did move in together at that time.

We've never been sexually exclusive. I prefer that term to monogamous, because we've never been married to anyone else. We've always been each other's number one for thirty-eight years, which to me is monogamy; but we've never been sexually exclusive. We cheated at first and then we've been various forms of openly, brazenly open, over the years. But again, it's a lifetime, so it kind of depended at what point in the relationship you took the snapshot, but we've been everything from cheating behind each other's back and lying, to being completely open, to having Wednesday nights off, to having separate boyfriends, to having a shared boyfriend to... We've really run the gamut on that one. We don't fuck around much now, mostly because we're older and we don't have that kind of energy any more. But we did, and I'm neither proud nor ashamed of it; it was what it was. We don't date outside the relationship anymore, but we did for a while. So currently, we're just middle-aged and settled. It isn't so much that we're actively monogamous; it's "Who has the time and energy for *that*?"

We certainly are sexual together, hallelujah. It's certainly what makes being de facto monogamous okay, that we still have really good sex with just each other. And we're really attracted to each other for whatever reason, and that's just not something you can quantify. I don't know why that is, but we're both attracted to each other physically, so we both want to. And we're pretty darn compatible in terms of who goes where. Now, the pretty side of monotony is familiarity, which means you know what you're doing, and there's really something to be said for that. More and more in our dealings with other men, I found that the excitement of the newness was often negated by the clumsiness of the newness, like "Oh, you don't like that... You like that over there... Oh no, not here, there..." And the great thing, at least for us, is that you know where it is and what each other likes, so the routine-ness of it is not for us a downside.

We are affectionate every day. We kiss each other every day and we express our affection for each other every day, so sex can really be, "I'm itching. Will you scratch this for me?" It's like, "Great, we've got fifteen good minutes, Let's go!" And we can do it and it's great and we sweat and we cum and yell and make noise and then we get on with our day. It certainly doesn't have the excitement of immediacy and newness that doing the twenty-three-year-old construction worker has, and every now and then you do like to have that, because new is new and there's no substitute for "Oh, isn't this different..." But overall, same 'ol, same 'ol is not a drawback for us.

Today, at this point in our collective career, I think we value each other very, very much. We appreciate what each of us brings to the marital table. I very seldom feel taken for granted, and I like to think Greg doesn't either.

We're very "please and thank you" kind of people—that's just how we were raised—so I think we have a very healthy appreciation for one another. It's not even something I have to put an effort towards, because I think he's pretty awesome in most ways. But our appreciation for each other hasn't always been that smooth, and there were times when I could not have said that.

We were really young when we started dating—I was nineteen and he was twenty-two—and we were one another's first gay relationship and we made a lot of mistakes on each other. One of them was along the lines of taking the other for granted: "I'm going to do what I want to do because I know he'll still be there..." But that was all part of the process in that we more or less grew up together. In certain ways, I think, "Gee, wouldn't it have been nice if we could have both gone out and sown our wild oats and acted silly and gone through two or three guys and made our mistakes on them, and then come back when we were more mature..." But it didn't happen that way.

At least twice we were close to ending the relationship. One time, we actually sat down and talked about selling the house, and how we got through it is that we didn't break up, which I know sounds terribly flip and I don't mean it to be. But I think every day you agree not to break up, because you always can. So if you've hit whatever bumpy patch you've hit and you've hit it to the point where you're actually discussing splitting the assets, at some point you either sign the papers or you don't, and at that point, we just went, "Do we really want to do this? No, Let's not. Let's do another day. Let's do tomorrow, then let's do another tomorrow..." That was fifteen years in. So we've done another twenty-plus more years of tomorrows after that, but yeah, we talked about it.

And because we started so young, we were kind of making it up as we went along. We didn't really have any role models, so we didn't know how this was supposed to go. We didn't realize, for instance, that you're not going to feel passionately in love with your partner every single day. You might go a while, and then you don't. But if you don't hang around through that point when you think, "I'm not really in love with him...," you don't then discover that—guess what?—it comes back. Who knew? Passion comes back? But when you're thirty you think passion has moved out; "I gotta move on and follow it..." And instead, we hung around, and passion returned. But it was a horrible time to go through. We had a couple of years where we were miserable every day, but we waited it out, and it got better. And that life lesson was that when people tell you that things can never be the same, they're right. Things can never be the same again, but things can be good again. And that's something you don't know until you get through it.

I think that if love doesn't deepen over time, then you should leave. Our relationship and love has certainly deepened. Every now and then, I'll be at the office, and Greg will call me from his office and say, "I just had a wave of I-love-Larry and I just wanted to let you know..." I don't think you can have that—truly—when you're dating. I will be going along and doing my little work and suddenly think, "Wow, we've really been through a lot, and he's really been by me..." He really is my best friend—and people just cringe—but he really is. And he's not perfect, but when it comes to "If I really need someone, is he there?" Yeah. Pretty much all the time.

I think the depth is something that comes of just staying. You come to appreciate your partner more all the time just because you have so much history, so many stories, so many things that you've been through together, that if your life flashed before your eyes you'd go, "Damn! He's really been there for me. Almost all of the time." So that cannot help but deepen one's regard for one's partner.

Currently, at this stage of our relationship, at this age—and a year or two ago I might have said something different—love is accepting your partner completely, good and bad, just accepting him for who he is and staying. That's a lot of it. There's the day to day you take care of one another. We have a very high regard for each other and respect for each other and we like each other's company a great deal, probably more than anyone else. I can't think of anyone else I'd rather just hang around with all day, every day. But the big life lesson for me, I think, in being with the same person for so long is just realizing that you take a person as he is, for everything he is. You take the whole thing. You get the whole package—good, bad, and indifferent; this is it—and you either stay or you don't. And on a daily, weekly, monthly, yearly basis we've both decided to stay, thus far.

We don't have a set of written agreements or rules in our relationship, other than things like: you don't just not come home at night. If I'm going to be a half an hour late because I'm stuck on the freeway, I'll call, because Greg's home making dinner. To me, that's not a rule, this is how you treat family. Things like: if you meet the twenty-three-year-old construction worker, you'd best have a rubber on. Things like: you look after your health and mine. If that's a rule, then it's a rule. Rules are things you have when you're dating and just getting started because you're just getting to know one another. We might have put our respective "lists" together thirty years ago, but darned if I remember!

One of the cool things about the house we live in today is that it's really large, so on those occasions one wants space apart, you can just go to another wing of the house. But because we both have full-time jobs, we don't see each other all day. It's not like we're padding around the house tripping over each other all day Monday through Friday. We're not around each other during the workday, so basically we have a couple hours after work and we have weekends and vacations. So if anything, we try to find time to spend together.

I very seldom feel closed in by the relationship. Sometimes I'm concerned when I do have to spend time away, that he might be upset with me. For instance, a few years back, our church was putting together a rather elaborate stage show for a charity that the church supports, and I had a featured role in it. So instead of Thursday evenings at choir rehearsal, I'd be gone two or three evenings a week for the month of June, rather than one evening a week. That was difficult, because we're very routine-oriented people and at 6 p.m. everybody's home and you sit down and have dinner. Again, it's a consideration thing; before I volunteered to do this show, I was like, "Are you sure this is going to be OK?," and Greg said, "Yes."

A big communication hurdle for us was the fact that Greg wasn't particularly good at communicating for several years. He comes from the grand old W.A.S.P. male tradition of keeping it in. I come from the grand old ethnic tradition of lettin' it out. I come from a family where you yell and you scream and you throw the crockery and then you say "I'm sorry, I love you," and you move on. He comes from a family where you keep it in and you develop a wine problem. So it was a big cultural difference for us and it took like ten years before I felt like we could actually have a conversation about something that wasn't pleasant, and everybody knew that everybody loved each other at the end of it and we were going to move on. I had to learn not to yell, which was tough for me, and he had to learn to be more verbal, which was tough for him.

We went to couples counseling exactly one time. It was at a time when we were about to break up and it was a desperation sort of move, and it worked. By that point, we were a one-issue couple, and that issue was monogamy. We sat down with this straight, female, Jewish, middle-aged therapist, and fortunately—probably because we were culturally so different from her—she was able to cut through a lot of our crap and she did it in an hour. And we really just kind of picked up from there.

We have taken very different spiritual paths. Greg was brought up in the Methodist Church, though they weren't really big churchgoers. I was raised in the Black Baptist Church and I'm a questioner so I was never comfortable with people telling me to take it on faith and shut up. It was just never something I could do really well and I left the church shortly after high school over the blatant homophobia of the church. I studied every religion and did Tarot and Ouija board and trance channelers and all that shit people did in the '80's.

Then, by the time I turned forty, I found that I was starting to want to go back to a church, for various reasons. I had read Joseph Campbell and had a very different sense of what I believed and didn't believe, what religion was, what myth was, and what its role was going to be in my life. I found that I could go back to church, as long as I was confident that there wasn't a huge umbrella of homophobia hanging over it, and be pretty comfortable in it.

So a couple of years ago, Greg and I as a couple joined a Presbyterian church—not a gay church, just a very open, loving church—mostly because we really loved the music department and we both still sing, and we like the senior pastor, this really cool straight woman who is just one of those people who just seems to exude love wherever she goes. So for us, oddly enough, it's one of the centers of our life together because we have mutual friends there and we are accepted completely as a married couple there. But that's where we're at, a couple of good churchgoing homos!

We have very few conflicts and disagreements anymore. I mean at this point, what have we got left to argue about? What usually happens is that one or the other of us has gotten up on the wrong side of the bed or had a bad day and is just feeling snarky, and one of us will say something, and the other one will get his feelings hurt. And we'll just retreat to our separate corners—literally—and probably not sleep in the same bed for that night, which means that nobody sleeps very well at all, and then by the next morning somebody will say "I'm sorry, I didn't really mean that...," and that will be it. But golly, there's just not a whole lot we haven't dealt with at this point, other than deathly illness. People fall out about money and sex, and we've pretty much got both of those things dealt with, so usually our conflicts are really small because we've done the big ones already.

Among our friends, Greg and I are kind of the longest running show in town, and mostly people sort of look up to us. We don't know anybody who's been together as long as we have. I don't like to give the impression that I think being married is the best way to live. It's just the best way for me to live. It can be unhealthy for people to think they need to have another person in their life to be happy, rather than realizing they're happy already. Marriage is simply not right for everybody.

I know for a fact that if Greg and I hadn't found each other, I'd be with someone else, because I'm a "coupler." I knew when I was ten that I wanted to marry a man; I wanted to be in a relationship with someone. It was never a question. But because I'm so happy being married, people have sometimes taken that to mean that I think less of someone if they're not married, which is totally not the case. Our best couple-friends have been together eight years, and it's like a second marriage for both of them. One of them comes out of a marriage of twenty years, but it was miserable for fifteen. We're hanging more with long-term straight married couples, though not by design. They're just people we know from church or from college or whatever.

Now and then, we still surprise each other. We'll be talking to other people, and they'll ask a question or something, and Greg will say, "Blah,

blah, blah...," and I'll turn around and go, "You're kidding! I had no idea you felt that way!" It is surprising that you can still be surprised by a person after all this time, but every now and then it happens. Also, we're both the type of person where if we see something, we'll think, "Oh, he'd love that," and we'll pick it up. I tend not to say, "Oh, let's wait for the birthday," because tomorrow's not promised. So either one of us at whatever time will come home and find flowers or a gift of some kind.

Humor-wise, Greg and I crack one another up. We always have. As you know, if you know somebody for a long time, you collect inside jokes, so we can convulse one another with an eyebrow raise. We have so much history now that somebody will say something, and Greg will just look at me, and we'll just laugh 'til we cry. We both have an odd sense of humor in that we tend to find odd things funny and we find some of the same odd things funny. One of the things I really treasure most about the two of us is that we do laugh a lot.

We've spent our entire adult lives together. One or the other of us will point things out like, "I've lived with you longer than I lived with my parents," or whatever. To say that I've spent most of my life with him is an understatement, so there's an awful lot of finishing each other's sentences, and I tell people that we can both communicate in eyebrow raises and grunts. There's just so little that needs to be said anymore.

We are married. As of August 30, 2008, we are legally married. We've always both been so adamant that we didn't want kids. I think we had that conversation once. Which is great, because we've known couples for whom it was an issue, that one person wanted them and the other person really didn't, and kids are something you both have to want. So we uncle.

To have a long-term relationship, you both have to want it. I've seen so many couples where it's obvious that one person is doing all the work, and the other person is just kind of inert. To really work, you both have to want to be in the relationship and you both have to want it enough to work for it. And that's something you deal with daily. When it looks like things are going south, you have to deal with it more aggressively and you decide any number of times in a relationship whether or not you want to do another tomorrow with that person. But you both have to be there. You both have to want it. You need to talk about sex. Like I said before, that was a big hurdle for us, because you have to talk about your feelings, you have to talk about what you want, what's good, what's not good.

And for us, we have enough in common and we have enough difference, too. That's not something you can work at; that comes under the heading of who you both are. I think we have a good balance of similarity and difference. We're not good at the same things, which is great, so we fill in a lot each other's gaps in terms of our skill sets, physical and emotional and otherwise. That, I think, has contributed to our being able to deal with each other over several decades; we're each good at different things.

We're so much a unit now at this point that it's difficult to even consider what my life would be if he wasn't in it. We each have a life but we also have our life together. We plan everything around who we are as a couple. You work and spend and save and plan for the thing that is your marriage. I often tell people that we have merged into one large black-and-white homosexual!

CHAPTER 14

CHRIS AND ANDY

"I never thought I'd fall in love. When I came out I just assumed I was going to be alone, and then I met Andy and we've been together longer than anybody else in either one of our families, including our parents."

In the late 1970s, Chris and Andy first crossed paths in a St. Louis dance bar. A subsequent meeting in Kansas City launched their now three and a half decades-long relationship. Residents of the Portland, Oregon area, Chris is retired from the management field, while Andy is still active as a physician in the Veteran's Administration system.

Chris — (Andy)

Andy and I will be together thirty-four years in May, 2013. At the time we met, I was twenty-four and had been out of college a few years. Andy was then twenty-five. I had come out in college, between my junior and senior years at Kansas State U., and had confided in three of my fraternity brothers, one of whom felt the need to tell the rest of the fraternity. This was in Kansas in the mid '70s, and I was told not to come back.

I moved to Kansas City, where I attended grad school at U. of Kansas City and was also working part-time. A friend of mine and I had gone to St. Louis one weekend to see a Monet exhibit at the St. Louis Museum. While there, we went to a gay dance bar and had a number of drinks—this was at like one or two in the morning—and some people came up to talk to us. Andy was part of that group and he came over to introduce himself to me. When he put out his hand to shake my hand, apparently I didn't shake his hand or even talk to him, and actually turned away. So he thought I was quite the asshole, but I was his type because I'd grown up in Hawaii and was a blond surfer boy.

The next day, my friend and I went to the art exhibit, and Andy was there with his sisters. I didn't really remember him from the night before, but he and his sisters were literally standing in front of us in line, and he said to them, "Oh, there's that guy I told you about from last night!"

His sisters were like, "Yeah, he is an asshole... He doesn't even act like he knows who you are!"

So we saw each other—I think it was fate—and then my friend and I went back to Kansas City.

About six months later, we were at a bar in Kansas City for something. Andy was then in medical school at the U. of Missouri, and he came to Kansas City and happened to be in the bar with his friends. He told his friends, "There's that surfer boy I think is so cute. I'm going to go over and ask him if he wants to dance..." So he approached me and asked me to dance, and since he was not my type, I said, "No, thanks," and turned away.

Then again, just by luck, the next night we were all in the same bar, and his friends thought it was hilarious that he was chasing me around and that I didn't even know who he was, so they bet him free drinks that he would not come up and ask me to dance again. He did come over and ask me to dance, and again I said, "No, thanks."

Then I remembered that he was the guy from the night before and I said, "But if you want to buy me a drink, you can buy me a drink." I was really a prima donna. So he went and bought a drink and as he approached he tripped and threw the drink all over me. I just thought, "God, this guy is such a BOZO! I just can't believe this..." But then we ended up talking all night in the bar.

He asked me to go home with him, and since I was a sort of the Mary Tyler Moore of the Midwest, I said, "I don't go home with people when I first meet them."

He said, "Well I have to go back to medical school tomorrow," and I said, "The next time you're in town give me a call."

The very next night he called me and said, "I'm going to be late for school, but I'm staying in town to take you on a proper date." We went out on a date that night and moved in together two weeks later—just like a couple of lesbians—and have been together ever since. We did, of course, have sex the night of the date. I wasn't *that* prudish.

Andy was really smart, and we had good conversations and just got along well. He wasn't my type, though, because I liked tall, dark and handsome guys, and he was an All-American, boy-next-door type. I liked bad boys, and he wasn't that, but we clicked and moved in together. Andy was in his last year of medical school, and I moved to Columbia to be with him and worked in the hospital where he was in school. I'd told him that I was going to be moving to L.A. to become a famous screenwriter, so he agreed that if I would stay with him the last year of his medical school, he would move to L.A. with me.

We moved to L.A., and Andy did his residency at U.S.C.L.A. County Hospital, while I tried to become a famous screenwriter. With my art, theater, and journalism and marketing background, I ended up starting a chain of stores for Universal Studios and eventually became vice president of the Oregon Museum of Science and Industry. I retired about two years ago when Andy developed prostate cancer, to take care of him and our two Golden Retrievers, one of which was blind and the other had cancer. Andy had his prostate out and has been cancer free ever since, fortunately. But I took care of everybody, and that was really my job.

Andy and I have always been sexually exclusive and early on made that commitment to each other and have stuck with it. We've had friends who've had open relationships, but I don't know of many of those that lasted forever. One of the guys usually ends up liking somebody they have sex with, and the relationship breaks up over it. For us, after thirty-five years together, sex today is not as exciting as it was when we were young. With Andy's having had prostate cancer, it's not as easy as it used to be either, but one good thing is that when you've been together this long, you know what the other one likes, so you work with that.

We're both pretty affectionate. Andy is a lot more comfortable with public displays of affection, though I've never been as keen about that and have always thought that was something you should do when you're alone together. I'm sure he wishes I would hold his hand in public and stuff, but I just don't do that. At home, we're affectionate and we'll rub each others feet when we're watching TV. We like to cuddle in bed and we've always slept together, too.

I can't define love. It's this weird thing. It just is. I never thought I'd fall in love. When I came out, I just assumed I was going to be alone, and then I met Andy and we've been together longer than anybody else in either one of our families, including our parents. And we've worked at it. It's not like we've never fought, but we just somehow complete each other. We've had friends who've fallen out of love with each other. They find themselves getting bored, or the relationship loses some of its excitement or whatever, but for us, our love has deepened over the years. It's different today. It's not like when you're first in love and you want to have sex three times a day. It's different. It's deeper. I don't know what either of us would do without the other. It would be very odd.

I've had kidney stones and broken bones. Andy hasn't had much the matter with him over the years, and his prostate cancer was the first sort of life-threatening health crisis we've dealt with. Going through experiences like that makes you feel like you're about one hundred eighty-two years old. You come to terms with your mortality, which is somewhat strange.

It was odd that Andy had cancer at the same time that our dogs—who were like our kids—did. Andy's sister's husband also had cancer at that time, so we just went through a really hard period of about four years where we lost everybody except for Andy. Those experiences help you to put everything in perspective and to become clear about what your priorities are.

We both work at not taking each other for granted. I'm a little more temperamental and outgoing and I do my best to keep Andy on his toes, so that he doesn't take me for granted! We're very opposite types of people. Andy is very intellectual and soft-spoken and doesn't have big mood swings, where I do. Being so different from one another is probably why our relationship works for us. We're different types interested in different things, and for Andy and me, it just works.

We both enjoy humor and laughter. My humor is more pronounced than his. I read *The New Yorker* and cry at the cartoons. Andy doesn't understand any of the cartoons, and I have to explain them to him, which kind of defeats the whole purpose. He likes Ted Baxter from *The Mary Tyler Moore Show* or Kramer from *Seinfeld*; the more goofy, off-the-wall, obvious humor. I love British humor, New York Jewish humor, witty humor, and really mean humor like Joan Rivers; that kind of stuff makes me laugh like crazy. Andy doesn't laugh as much as I do. One of my big goals in all the jobs I've had is to tell all the people who work for me, "If we don't laugh every day, we're not doing our jobs right!" I really love to laugh.

Communication-wise, sometimes I need to talk more than he does, though I am also the worst when it comes to fighting. I'm not a fair fighter. When I get really mad, I won't talk to him at all. So I want to talk things over, but if I'm really mad, then I just cease to speak altogether, which is hard for Andy to understand. Usually it takes me a day or two to unwind again. Now as I've gotten older, I don't have as many mood swings, so it doesn't happen very much any more. Andy doesn't like it but he's accustomed to it. He wants to keep talking, but when I've gone over the edge, I don't talk.

We had our first dog for thirteen years, and when she died, I was completely devastated and really went off the deep end and wouldn't speak for a couple weeks. I was really angry with him, though I don't know why exactly. Finally, I went and saw a psychologist, and she helped me through it. But I really did shut down for a while there.

We're domestic partners here in Oregon, and if they had legal marriage here, we would get married. Andy thinks it's really important. I think it's important that we have the right to do it, that we have the same rights as straight people. Having the piece of paper is not important to me, but being able to marry or not marry is important to me.

Andy and I have been together so long now, I can't imagine us not being together. I'm sure we'll be together until one of us dies. Back when we lived in California, we did talk about having kids for a while. But once we got our first dog, Samantha, after a while, we liked the fact that she didn't get pregnant, have drug problems, or need to go to private schools. So we never did have children. My sister is our best friend, and we helped her raise her children, who are now twenty-one and twenty-three, and we're very close to them.

When you get together with someone, there's this whole thing you go through where you become less selfish. You let go of putting your needs first all the time, which I think makes you a better person. Andy's very altruistic and moral and would never do the wrong thing ever, under any circumstances. And not that I was out there robbing banks or anything before we got together, but I want to live up to his standards.

Relationships are harder than you think, particularly at the beginning. Andy didn't have much when we got together, but within the first month, we put everything in both of our names, the bank account, the car, whatever we had. The house—everything—is in both our names. We made that commitment to one another and I think that helped to keep us together, even through the rough periods. Going back to the thing about selfishness, you have to let go of that for the relationship to really last.

Having sex the first time you meet somebody may not be the best way to start off a relationship. I think it's better to get to know somebody, even a little bit, so the sex becomes an outgrowth of the feelings you're having for the other person, rather than just screwing someone after exchanging only two words. Starting with sex can make it difficult to build a relationship afterwards. Sometimes you can meet someone you don't really like, but the sex is fabulous. You would no more want to be in a relationship with him than the man on the moon. Sometimes with the person you're destined to be with, it may not be sexual fireworks the first time, but it gets better because of how much you care about the person.

I think it must have been fate that Andy and I got together, with him chasing me around for a year, and I didn't even think twice about him early on. Andy might say it was more persistence. Probably it was a combination of the two, but I'm very glad that he didn't give up on me.

CHAPTER 15

BRIAN AND RAY

"To me, love means transcending self and one's own needs and finding union with someone who is doing the same for you. It can take many years to get to that place. Love is multi-layered like an onion, and there are several inner layers you'll never get to if you don't stick with it."

Nearly four decades ago, Brian McNaught and Ray Struble met as roommates in Boston. Their friendship slowly became physical, and their feelings for each other grew into the deep, loving bond they share. Now retired, Ray worked for many years as an investment banker. Brian is a well-known author and educator on lesbian, gay, bisexual, and transgender issues who has contributed immensely to raising consciousness and to advancing the cause of LGBT rights over the years. Brian's newest book, *Are You Guys Brothers?* charts his and Ray's relationship across the years, and can be found, along with an array of his other resources, on Brian's website, www.brian-mcnaught.com. Married in Canada in 2003, the two enjoy life together in Ft. Lauderdale, FL and in Tupper Lake, NY.

Brian McNaught — (Ray Struble)

We'll be together thirty-nine years in May. I was twenty-eight, and Ray was twenty-five when we met as roommates in Boston in 1976. Ray, and another member of Dignity, the gay Catholic organization, had found a wonderful, three-bedroom apartment, and they needed a third person. I was in Detroit when we first talked about whether I was interested in joining them. They had heard that I was thinking about coming to Dignity's Boston -based national office to work. At the time, I was sort of a "star" in the gay

Catholic world because of my civil rights battle with the Archdiocese of Detroit, which had fired me from my newspaper job with them when I came out. In the small pond of the gay Catholic world, there weren't any other lay Catholics who were as well-known publicly.

When the chair and vice-chair of Dignity/National found out that Ray and I were going to be rooming together, they said, "You stay away from him. He's fragile!" I thought, "What the hell are they talking about?" I guess they wanted to make sure he didn't get swept up into my gay activist world.

Ray and Patrick, the third roommate, drove out to meet me as I drove in from Detroit. They wanted to make sure that I didn't miss the exit on the Mass turnpike and get lost coming to the apartment. They flashed me down, and Ray walked over to get into the car with me. I told him this morning that I remember exactly how he looked. He wasn't my type, but he was handsome, seemed like a really nice guy, and I felt immediately comfortable with him. I'd always been mostly attracted to Mediterranean-type guys with dark hair, and Ray's hair was more strawberry blond, so there wasn't an immediate physical spark. There was an emotional connection though, especially since my barking Irish Setter settled right down. Ray was not intimidated by nor uncomfortable with him; he jumped right into my car and into my life without hesitation.

When I walked into the apartment that they had moved into a month before, I saw that Patrick, the other roommate, had already started decorating in colors and styles that I thought were horrible. Ray and I connected when I asked him whether he liked the look of Patrick's things, and he said, "NO!!!" So, we had something of a joint crusade of slowly moving Patrick's things into his bedroom, and changing the look and feel of our living room.

My grandmother had a home nearby, and since I had a car, I took the guys out to meet her. Ray was always more polite, attentive, and interested than Patrick was. I really admired and appreciated how quickly my family took to Ray, and he took to them. I was also very impressed by how hard he worked and how honest he was. We shared the same values and passion for civil rights and didn't seem to disagree on anything. Our taste in things was very similar in terms of furnishings, and he was always very complimentary and appreciative of my cooking and my decorating around the place. So we became a team pretty quickly and we also started having sex, within the first couple of weeks, I believe. But it was not sex with the intention of establishing a long-term relationship, because we had each recently come out of relationships. And it was the '70s, a time of free love and open relationships. This was pre-AIDS of course, and one-night stands and going to the baths were a part of the culture.

Although I didn't have much in the way of sex with others while he and I were together, nor did he, we didn't make any agreements that this was a romantic relationship, nor that we were a couple, until Christmastime. Ray was in Wichita with his family, and I was in Detroit with mine. I called him and suggested that he stop in Detroit on the way back to Boston. I picked him up at the airport and realized immediately how much I cared about him.

To me, love means transcending self and one's own needs and finding union with someone who is doing the same for you. It can take many years to get to that place. Love is multi-layered like an onion, and there are several inner layers you'll never get to if you don't stick with it. It just doesn't happen immediately.

Everything we experience is in the context of the relationship. When you kiss somebody you've spent thirty-nine years with, the kiss is in that context. If you had Alzheimer's and kissed your spouse, you might enjoy the kiss and find the other person attractive, but the kiss wouldn't represent anything deeper than the moment. It wouldn't contain any molecule of history. When you're together in an ongoing relationship, your mind, body, and soul have changed because of your association with this other person, and that can only happen with time. Now, that doesn't mean that time will guarantee it. Time can also create contempt, and hatred, and resentment. If you don't choose to love the person you are with, then you are not going to be happy. You have to choose love, and to act lovingly, to be in relationship. You don't just wander into it and ride it. You can do that, but you'll never experience love at the depth you might otherwise.

In the early years, Ray and I said it was going to be an open relationship. We said that sex was not what our relationship was about. We insisted that our relationship was completely about growth. So, there's never been a time in our lives in which we said that the relationship needed to be monogamous.

Sexuality is continually evolving. I find myself in lust with people. Ray and I both playfully comment about people in television programs, movies, and in magazines who we find attractive. The older we get, the more comfortable we feel talking with each other about our attractions without feeling threatened by doing so. There was a piece this morning in the *New York Times* about an affair that ended a major career and a marriage. Is one sexual encounter enough to end a relationship?

People often surprise themselves with what they think their response is going to be, and how they actually react. I was thinking about it, and I have a double-standard. I could have sex with tons of people, thoroughly enjoy it, feel like I was connecting with them, but not feel that it in any way threatened my relationship with Ray. But if he had sex with someone else, I would have a much harder time with it, since I struggle with jealousy and control. It's not that he hasn't had sex with people, but we usually don't talk about it the day after. If it happens, it happens. It has happened infrequently in our relationship.

I don't know whether it's having turned sixty-six, or the experience of selling our summer home in Provincetown, but I've been becoming more aware of letting go. Simultaneously, I'm more focused on Ray and our years together, and how incredible the experience has been. Looking back, I would describe myself as not fully aware for much of our time together. I was very focused on gay liberation and helping people, writing columns and answering letters, and doing whatever I could to advance the cause. I really felt the weight of that on my shoulders. That was my passion, and I think that at one point in my life if I had been asked to choose between working on LGBT equality and Ray, I would have chosen my work, because I felt it was a ministry in many ways.

Even though I've moved away from a theist spirituality, I really always felt "called" to do what I was doing. Today, I now have the time and the focus to really understand what incredible companions we've been over these many years. It doesn't mean we haven't had fights—those are pretty normal, especially when you're tired or hungry—and we've been through a lot together, but he's very truly my best friend, and when we're apart I feel it.

One of the things we're trying to get our arms around now is saying goodbye to each other. We're only in our mid-sixties, but Ray's back is so bad that he sometimes wishes he could just die, and not have to deal with chronic pain anymore. So we're both focused on what an amazing journey this has been, and of how grateful we are to have done it together. If we've found ourselves attracted to other people, we have played it out in our mind, and realized that after the initial satisfaction of lust, we wouldn't want to go to the movies with that person; we'd want to go with our partner. We wouldn't want to travel to Europe with them; we'd want to go with our partner.

This morning in the hot tub we started kissing, which is not something we would typically do there. I mean, we kiss several times every day, but not passionately. I wanted to communicate in that time with the embrace and the kisses how much I love him. I wanted Ray to feel totally, unconditionally, completely loved, so that when he died, he would never need to wish that he had that experience. The time we had this morning was quite extraordinary and satisfying. If anyone ever asks me, should Ray die before me, "Did he ever really feel the love that you have for him?" I would comfortably say "Yes."

One can surmise after years of being together, after all of the things you've done for each other, all the gifts, and all of the compromises, that you have been loved. But, to actually hold the person's face in your hands, and look into his eyes, and completely shut out all other things, and focus on him as a unique person who has given you the gift of his life, is quite an amazing experience in both directions. Ray adores me, and I feel it. I feel completely loved by him. I can't imagine that anyone else would love me as totally as he does.

The experience in the hot tub this morning was quite wonderful. It wasn't orgasmic. I've had prostate surgery, which makes ejaculation more difficult. Both of us are on so many damn meds—Ray, especially, for pain—that it makes even getting an erection more difficult. Neither of us bothers taking Cialis or Viagra because we don't feel any need to perform, but it was wonderful getting a good erection this morning from kissing and caring. It wasn't about getting off.

I find that I'm much less interested in the work that goes into sex or masturbation today. It's too much trouble, and I really don't miss it. If I started in again, I'm sure I'd remember how fun it can be. But things can change with age, operations, and medications, and I think that's one of the things men need to be mentored on, because otherwise those changes can come as quite a shock. Men so associate sex with their masculinity. I've personally had the benefit for years of participating in human sexuality trainings where I presented the gay component. There would also be people talking about the impact of aging, so I was quite prepared for the changes. But for most guys, there's so much tied up in getting a hard-on.

Ray and I are very affectionate with each other. Almost everyone— sisters, nieces, nephews, neighbors—who come into our house talks about how much affection and love they see. Ray and I kiss when we get up, we kiss goodbye if we go out to the store, we hug, we dance together if there's music we like that comes on while we're watching television, we kiss before we go to sleep, and we hold hands in bed and in the car. There's lots and lots of intimacy in our relationship.

There's not only touch, but also care. There's a lot of sensitivity and thoughtfulness, of watching out for what the other needs. Does he have his soft drink? Is it time for his nap? You change your schedule to accommo- date the other person's in order to be with him. It's a very intimate relation- ship.

It's very easy to take someone for granted unless you stop yourself consciously, and choose to focus. I think that for people who are forced to get up early and go to work, who can't even call home, and then get home late, it's probably hard to focus on what they have at home. But the more time you have to yourself, the more opportunities you have to be conscious. We have found in our own relationship that when we start to take the other person for granted, and start to think about our own needs over our partner's, that's when we have trouble. So being conscious of the other is really important to building and maintaining a loving relationship.

Since the beginning of time, people have tried to name it and give it a shape, but when people talk about there being a "higher power," I really think it is something that is available to them through the love they have for another person. You don't even have to be in a relationship to experience it. You could be serving the people in a slum in Mumbai, really go outside of yourself, and experience a higher power. It seems to me that the only way to experience the sublime is to get outside yourself and love something or someone else selflessly.

Being out has been essential to the success of our relationship. If one of us were in the closet, it would simply not have worked. Choosing each other over our families was essential. You can't have two masters, so our loyalty is to our spouse and not to our family. When both of us stopped drinking and using grass, and chose to live sober lives, it was really important for our relationship. Leaving the Catholic church, and actually rejecting any dogma, was essential for our growth. We're both independent thinkers. It's not helpful to us to have others tell us what we have to believe in order to experience spiritual growth. We need the freedom to experience it ourselves.

You always have to have the option of leaving a relationship. You have to have the belief that you are not stuck, because if you feel stuck, as many people do due to their children, their finances, or because they're in high-profile romances, it's going to have a significant impact on the joy that you experience daily.

We laugh about the fact that throughout our relationship whenever things got tense, really tense, we'd each be decorating our apartments in our minds, contemplating which china to take, and which art, because you always have to feel you have an escape. We have had days and experiences of, "Fuck you!" "Well, fuck you!," and then we would laugh after a while.

Both of us can go to the back of the cave when our feelings are hurt, when we just withdraw, shut down and don't talk, and we've had periods where that was really painful. I think you get wiser with time, and we both have been helped with therapy. We've had to become aware of how our behavior impacts the other, and we've had to learn to sit and listen without being defensive. If somebody had told me these things when I was young, I would have said, "Yeah, yeah, yeah..."

Regrettably, so many of these lessons you have to learn yourself. But an important lesson for us in our relationship was learning to just listen to the other. You don't have to solve the problem or the feeling the other person is describing. If you sit and just ask him to talk to you about how he's feeling, he can feel heard and understood, where an hour before, he was feeling that you had no clue how he felt, and how your behavior was impacting him. Learning to say, "I'd really like you to tell me how you're feeling, and I promise not to interrupt you" is extremely important.

I wouldn't be who I am without the relationship that I've been in. I have no idea who I would be, but I know it would not be a person I would like as much as I like myself now. I like who I've become, and I know that it would not have happened without my being in relationship with Ray. I don't know that I ever would have stopped drinking. I think it would have been very easy for my ego to guide my life. I probably would not have dealt with issues of sexual abuse, and would have been stuck as a co-dependent romantic who unhappily tried to manipulate the world to meet my needs. I know very clearly that I would not have become the person I am now, and would not have achieved what I've achieved without Ray.

Ray and I are both really nice people, and I think that our kindness in the world is actually what facilitated our coming together. If I hadn't chosen to come to Boston, we wouldn't have met. When Ray and Patrick found out that I might be thinking about moving there, they called and we talked on the phone. I know that I felt instantly comfortable with Ray on the phone, and I do believe that you get back in life what you put out, that goodness begets goodness.

We laugh together all of the time. Ray loves my sense of humor, and he thinks I'm very funny. He's my best audience, so I'm constantly acting up and making comments with him and in groups of people. I love making people laugh. I can be funny and irreverent and shocking. But humor is definitely an important component of our relationship.

I constantly have projects going on. He came up this morning, and I had all the pants from the closet on the bed, insisting that we had to try them on, and if they didn't fit, they were going to the thrift shop.

He said, "I see you started a project again..." But he always goes along with it and doesn't fight me. He doesn't say, "I'm not in the mood for this," or "I can't do this." It's really helpful to "sit loose in the saddle" in a relationship.

For the first year with Patrick, we kept an accounting of who put what money in for rent, etc. After the first year, Ray and I had joint accounts. He made more money than I did, but neither of us made much money. We just said, "If we break up, we just split everything fifty-fifty." Later on, he made a lot of money, and I didn't. Then, when he retired, I made money, and he didn't. Our attitude is that, "There's nothing in the house I think of as mine."

I love beauty, and creating beauty, and Ray loves my taste. He loves my eye, and I've got a good eye. I'm not talking about creating a well-tailored room. I'm talking about having an eye for balance and beauty and whimsy. We have nice homes. But if I lose it all, I'm fine, too. Not long ago, we had to sell a home, and put things in auction. Initially, I didn't like it, but once the decision was made to sell, I found it very freeing. Going through the pants to see what fit earlier today, and going through bookshelves, and grabbing books and things we don't use, has been a great experience. I love getting rid of stuff! I also have things that I look at and love, and would be sad if they were burned in a fire, but they're not me; I still have an identity and a personhood without them.

When Canada passed gay marriage in 2003, we decided to go there immediately. We'd had a civil union in Vermont on our twenty-fifth anniversary, but that wasn't marriage. When we flew to Ottawa to get married, we did it not for legitimization but because it was an historic opportunity. As two people who were an important part of gay history, it would be insane not to participate in something we helped to make happen. We told our two best friends at the time that we were doing it, and they decided that they wanted to come and get married, too, so the four of us went up.

Ray and I found the experience to be very moving and affirming. We knew that our relationship did not need the blessing of church or state in order to be legitimate, but it was nice to be on the inside for once in many,

many years as opposed to looking through the glass from the outside. It was nice having the immigration person at the airport say, "Good for you," when we answered his question about why we had gone to Canada. Having been fired for being gay before moving to Boston, I had walked through life on a certain level with my hands clenched, preparing for a fight, and so it's nice to relax and open your hands up, feeling that you're safe and valued.

You have a choose to be in relationship. You can't wander through life hoping it happens to you. You have to put yourself out there so that you see people, and they see you. Invite people to dinner and encourage them to invite you if they have single friends. Do some reading about love. I had read Erich Fromm's *The Art of Loving* long before I was in my first serious relationship. Do some homework, just as one would do some homework on parenting.

Relationships don't just happen. People think that all you have to do is give birth and suddenly you're a good parent. You have to do some work and think about it, and also be aware too that sex is the wrong motivation for a relationship. If you want hot sex, then make sure that you find someone who's into an open relationship because your sex with them is not going to stay hot. After a while, it's like having sex with your brother, and you have to re-frame it. Or if you don't, then some other aspect of the friendship is going to suffer because if we keep people as our lovers as opposed to our partners, then something gets sacrificed.

You're not going to have it all. People say, "I'd like to be in a relation-ship." What are you doing to make it happen? If you're home watching TV six hours a night, seven nights a week, you're not going to find a relation-ship that way. You have to be available, and as you get older, you have to shorten your criteria. "Well, they have to be cute and twenty-five and smart, and they can't smoke or drink, and they can't do this, and they can't do that...." If there's one person like that, there's already a line waiting!

You have to be very clear on what it is you're looking for. Why not look for someone who shares your values, and who you want to spend time with, someone you see as a really good friend who eventually becomes your soul-mate? That's far more important than whether you're getting sexually satisfied. Because the person you see at twenty-five who is really hot is going to change; his body is going to change. His family may be prone to baldness. You may be marrying someone who is prone to weight gain. You just don't know! So as you go into it, think through what it is you're hoping for. Make the decision that you're interested in a relationship, and then put some effort into it.

You need a good sense of humor, patience, compromise, self-sacrifice, and most of all, open communication to be in a successful relationship. Learn to say things in a loving way. We're not all great communicators, and sometimes the way we communicate something can be really upsetting. We don't intend to be, but we're gruff.

You can change. You can learn to say things differently, in a way the person can better hear you. And if you can't do it on your own, then get help. Go to couples counseling. Ray and I did lots of couples counseling and individual counseling, and both were exceedingly helpful. When we were having some trouble a few years ago, we went to a therapist who said, "You guys expect too much. You have a wonderful relationship." We realized that he was right. So we've got a great running automobile. It doesn't mean that there aren't parts rusting or that it backfires occasionally, but it works, and it's carrying us to where we want to be.

SECTION IV:

COUPLES TOGETHER FORTY TO FIFTY YEARS

Chapter 16
Byron and Dennis

"Back one time when we were in college, I was cooking a pot of Campbell's chicken soup but I didn't slowly warm it up and slowly pour the water in and whisk it so that it was real smooth. It came out with lumps in it, and he said, "You fucked up the soup!" I said, "I did not!" That's when I threw one of my fits and I said, "God damn it, if you don't like my soup, HERE!," and I threw the whole pot against the wall."

Byron Roberts and Dennis Merrill met forty-five years ago in Louisiana. After relocating to California, they worked for the San Joaquin County Human Service Agency, Byron as a social worker and Dennis as a program manager. Now retired, Dennis continues to perfect his craft as an outdoor photographer, while Byron continues to volunteer and advocate for change on a variety of social justice issues. They are now married.

Byron Roberts — (Dennis Merrill)

We've been together forty-five years now. Since I'm a few months older than Dennis, at the time we met he was twenty-three and I was twenty-four. I had pretty much come out not long after high school and in 1965, when I was twenty-one, I moved to New Orleans for a year. What a great way to sow one's oats that was! As I tell folks, I just had one gentleman caller after another and I loved it. I met lots and lots of hunky, handsome guys and happened to be the recipient of their largesse and I happily took it.

My best friend at the time, Diane, a lipstick-dyke lesbian, and I moved in together with the understanding that we were both just going to have fun and screw whatever we wanted to. We wanted to have a good time and enjoy our life together and we weren't going to let anybody come between us. I had moved there first and gotten the apartment off-campus at L.S.U., and she moved in afterwards. One night, we got dressed to the nines and went out to a local gay bar, and darned if Dennis didn't walk in with his fag-hag girlfriend. So Diane and I are sitting at a table and I'm fawning over him, and she says, "Well, go ask him to dance!" That was back in the day when people slow danced together, body to body.

Being the prima donna I was, I said, "Hell, no! If he wants me to dance he can come over here..." So after panting for like an hour, Dennis sidled over to our table and asked me to dance. I said, "Sure." Wouldn't you know he asked me to dance to *Hey Jude*, the longest god-damned song in the world. It was very slow, and he was a smooth slow dancer and oh my God, I was loving it!

All of a sudden, in the middle of the song, I got nervous and my knees began to knock, and Dennis asked, "What's wrong with your knees?" I said in this very deep baritone voice, "Well, I went to the gym this afternoon and I did a lot of squats and then didn't drink any orange juice, so I have a lot of lactic acid..." I was so excited and so devastated and I thought, "He is so cute and so sexy, and God, what a dancer he is!" He asked me for a couple more dances, and all I can say is that things just started changing very quickly. We went home and tricked that night. Those were the days when you had one-night stands, and that's what I thought it was going to be. The chemistry was amazing and in fact, after about three times, he said, "Do you really want to do it again?" I said, "Why not!?"

Dennis didn't want to have a relationship, and I didn't want one either, but I think fate had something else in mind for us. After a few weeks of going out to the bar dancing and socializing, Diane and I got to know Dennis and his friend Carolyn really well and we became good friends and Dennis and I became bedmates. Diane said, "You're falling in love with Dennis," and I said, "I think I am..." She said, "You *ARE*. There's no question!"

She had a girlfriend in Mobile and she said, "I'm going back to Mobile," which she did. That left me without a roommate, and since Dennis was living on campus, I said, "Why don't you just move in with me? You won't have to live in the dorm." So he did, and that was that. It was a rather whirlwind romance. He fought it like hell. I fought it, too, but I think I fell in love or passion first, before he did. Dennis kept resisting it and saying, "Can't we just be tricking friends?" I responded with, "Excuse me... I'm not some two-bit whore!"

When we first decided we wanted to have a relationship, a lot of guys wanted to have three-ways with us. Dennis was willing, and I said, "No way. I'm not going to have sex with a third party."

He said, "Why not?"

I said, "I'm just not!" I came from a very puritanical family and my sexual morays were pretty much aligned with the standard heterosexual format of "Once coupled, you stay together and remain faithful." But we did make a verbal contract, that "Whatever I don't know is none of my business, and what you don't know is none of your business. I don't ever want to hear about it if you have sex outside our relationship and you'd better make sure our friends don't tell me you did."

I've abided by that, and I have no idea if Dennis breached it or not. Maybe in anonymous ways. Certainly not in affairs; neither of us has ever had an affair. We live in Stockton, California, which is in the Central Valley, eighty miles from San Francisco. We used to have "mental health weekends" just to give each other space, and we had friends in the city, so Dennis would go over to the city once a month. Another weekend I would go. To this day, whatever he did in the San Francisco, I have no idea, never asked him, don't care. What I did I never shared with him, but I never had an affair, and never had a hard time resisting the temptation to have one.

Certainly these days, sex isn't of the degree and intensity that it was in our early years. There's much more love and affection and touching and hugging and cuddling. After forty-five years with the same person, it's not exciting sexually any more to me. At the same time I think we're actually more intensely in love and more intensely affectionate than we were in the early throes of our relationship, where it was more sex and passion but less in-depth, seasoned love. Our relating is very deep and affectionate and we hug and kiss each other often. We're around each other a lot so we're always embracing each other and saying affectionate things to each other. It's a very intense, deep, romantic relationship.

We've never slept apart except when we had fights. I have a very strong temperament, and if he makes me really mad, I can go off the wall easily and throw him out of the bed and say, "Go fucking sleep in the guest bedroom!" I can stay really mad for a long time, where he does not. But he's stubborn and won't be the one to give in. I just hold out until he yields, which is something I learned from my mother.

Our experience of love has grown over time and Dennis and I have definitely become more patient with each other. It seems that the first several years of a relationship are really the most difficult, because you're both doing lots of testing. No matter how long they last, in most relationships, there's that testing phase, which happens in the first three or four years. *Who's going to do this? Who's going to do that? Who's going to be the boss? Who's going to be subservient, or is anybody going to be either?*

The early years are filled with conflict and passion, and you're having to work out lots of issues and develop what your role is in the relationship and who's going to do what... Our relationship has continued to deepen over time and we have a great deal more respect for each other and more patience than we once had. There's no question that the romance, the affection, and the degree of love, compassion and empathy for each other has grown over the years.

From very early on, Dennis and I have carved out space so we could have time apart. We have always worked together. I worked for the Human Service Agency in San Joaquin County as a social worker in Child Protective Services. Dennis worked at the same agency and had the same hours— we had the same holidays, everything—so we would go to work together and we'd come home together. But throughout that thirty-one-year career and before that, we always made and had time for ourselves. We respected each other having space. It was very important to me that neither of us smother each other.

Dennis and I have a lot of things in common that we love to do together and a lot of things that we jointly agree on. But he is very intellectual and musically inclined and has his artistic interests that require a lot of quiet time, alone time, focus time, and he'll sit and listen to an opera in the family room by himself and read the libretto, which would bore me to death. I have a masters in social work and am much more social, ethereal, and very politically active and engaged, where the only thing he cares about is writing a check and pulling a lever. So we allow each other the space to indulge our separate interests.

I learned long ago not to disturb Dennis when he's on the computer doing his photographic/artistic work. You're not going to get his attention, and he's going to be very annoyed! And don't mess with me if I'm deeply engaged in my Facebook communications! But in general, I think we have great communication skills, whether that communication is silent, passive, or direct.

Many years ago, we made an agreement that if either of us felt taken for granted, we would say, "Stop. Let's take a break here. We need to talk..." We try to keep the channels of communication open, though obviously no person is going to be successful in that every day, every week, every month. There are times I say, "Don't take me for granted, God damn it!," or he might say the same thing to me. Or, "Don't try to tell me what to do!"

Dennis is the gourmet cook. Back one time when we were in college, I was cooking a pot of Campbell's chicken soup, but I didn't slowly warm it up and slowly pour the water in and whisk it so that it was real smooth. It came out with lumps in it, and he said, "You fucked up the soup!"

I said, "I did not!"

That's when I threw one of my fits and I said, "God damn it, if you don't like my soup, *HERE!*," and I threw the whole pot against the wall.

For a short time afterward, he stopped telling me how to cook. Later, after we moved to California, we agreed to an even-steven cooking schedule: one night he cooks, and the next night I cook, and whoever isn't cooking for the night cleans up. Well, I quickly caught on to the fact that every time he cooked he used every pot and pan in the damned kitchen and I thought, "I'm getting the short end of the stick here. He uses every bowl and pan and utensil we own, and I have to wash them all!" When I cook I often will use one pot, because I love to do stews and soups.

Relationships require constant work, and stubbornness can be our greatest stumbling block. Dennis and I have never been to counseling together but, fortunately for us, more often than not, he's very willing to discuss conflicts. Since I have a degree in social work and did counseling, it's helped me to bring some useful meet/negotiate/compromise skills to the table. That doesn't mean that I have all the answers to our conflicts. It just means that I'm usually more willing to discuss such things, though I can also be very stubborn in a conflict and just go into the silent treatment when I get really angry.

We are both Christian-based in our value system, but we don't believe in all the orthodox bullshit. Organized religion is not for us and I'm sure that our homosexuality has a lot to do with the fact that we left the church. We were not accepted or wanted, and why would you want to belong to an organization which is constantly telling you you're going to hell? I'm an agnostic and an intellectual about religion and I believe that you can have a very strong set of principled beliefs and live a good life and be a good person regardless.

Dennis's sense of humor is much more witty than mine. His humor is more sharp and he has a very clever and quick wit. We both have a great sense of humor and we don't take ourselves that seriously. We like to surprise each other with things. Dennis brings me beautiful flowers, and I will see beautiful flowers at the store and I'll pick them up and bring them home for him. I call those "just because" flowers.

We're very close to our families and we're very lucky. The first time I took Dennis home to meet my family, they accepted him and fell in love with him. The first time I met his family, not long after we had fallen in love, his dad and mom and siblings totally accepted me. So we've been very fortunate that way. We go back every six months to Mobile and Baton Rouge and New Orleans to see family and friends and we have done so throughout our relationship. We keep our friends close. It's really important to have those supportive relationships in your life.

We moved in together within three months of meeting each other. Dennis had no money, and I had no money. I had a stipend that I got from the federal government to go with my scholarship. He had a small student loan and a little spending money, so we pooled our funds right from the beginning. We never had separate monies at all and we had a cardinal rule: *Your money is mine, and my money is yours, and if it's under twenty-five dollars you can spend it on whatever you want.* It was like, "At least consult me if you're going to spend our money." We've moved up the amount over the years so that he doesn't have to come home and ask me if he wants to spend one hundred dollars on something. We've never restricted each other on buying essentials like clothes; that is outside the agreement. But if it's a "tchotchke" or something fun, at least let's agree that we should spend it or can spend it. For many, many years I was the bookkeeper of the family and kept all the books.

I've been a longtime civil rights activist and can remember at age five feeling that something was wrong when I heard my nanny called a "nigger." I've stood up and fought for virtually every major racial, ethnic, and political issue and have worked in the area of gay rights since I came out. Dennis is much less political and was much more subdued about his sexuality than I was. When we had an opportunity to get married in California six or eight years ago, I asked him to marry me, and he said no. I asked him why. He said, "Because as long as they have the DOMA, we're registered as domestic partners in California and we have the same rights as straight people and we're not going to get any extra rights getting married." So I let that go, even though I really wanted to get married. He didn't see the need.

He said, "Do you really think that after thirty-nine years, getting married is going to make any difference?"

I said, "No. It's the principle of the thing. I want my civil rights and I want to exercise them."

Well, he didn't see the need, so I just let it go. Now when the Supreme Court knocked out DOMA recently, many more federal rights accrued to us, so I said again, "Will you marry me?" He said, "No," and when I asked why he said, "I just don't see the need. What's a piece of paper going to matter?"

I said, "Dennis, it's the principle of the thing. I want to enjoy the process and the rights. I fought hard for this civil right for us and for others."

He replied, "No," and I said, "Fuck you!"

So I pouted and didn't speak for two weeks, and he came into the living room one day and said, "So when are you going to talk again?"

I held up my big, ostentatious anniversary ring that I've had for forty years to him and said, "When you turn this damn ring into a wedding ring!"

He said, "Oh for God's sake, if it's that important, alright!"

He said, "There's one condition. It's gotta be small."

I said, "How small? We can't marry each other..."

He said, "You can pick who marries us. I don't care."

So our state assemblywoman and her partner married us here at our home. Our two closest gay male friends were here along with a straight couple whose wedding we'd stood up for forty-one years earlier. Just the eight of us. We had our ceremony and then went out to dinner. I loved it. I was excited for three weeks getting ready for it.

After Dennis said yes, it was amazing. I felt like a teenage girl having captured the big man on campus! I don't know what the psychological and emotional factors all were, but it was just exciting. I got really giddy about it and got excited about selecting flowers and everything, and Dennis and I did everything together. We selected the guests, the cake, and the restaurant together, and he really got into it or at least impressed me that he did!

Getting married was a real big deal for me and I got a great big emotional high from doing it. Because I'm a social activist, I'm on a great big high for the entire nation and community of lesbians and gays who choose to marry or plan on marrying and I'm certainly happy that I have the federal benefits that I wouldn't have had. Dennis was aglow the whole time.

Once he broke down and agreed to do it he became—reluctantly at first—very engaged in the process. Dennis is a very private person, but I have intuitively sensed that he's very comfortable with it and he's happy that we finally got married. We've both been pleased and impressed with all the accolades we've received and also by how supportive and caring people have been.

A very good friend is a columnist for the local paper and he was going to do an article on us and he said, "I want to do it six months after the wedding and see how things are..."

I said, "Michael, do you think that after forty-five years, six months is going to make a difference?!"

Dennis and I happened to go to a street party in Stockton yesterday, in midtown, right in the center of old downtown. We were sitting outside at a table at this restaurant, and it seemed like every lesbian and gay and straight person we know had come to that event, and they all rushed up to us to say, "Congratulations!" It was so exciting and fun and warm and positive to have all that reinforcement. We've not had one rude or negative comment or reaction to our marriage and wedding.

Neither of us have ever wanted to be parents. Working in child protective services for thirty-one years with foster children, I got my fill of children every day. Dennis is a very paternalistic person and he helped raise his little sister, who is sixteen years younger than he. He and I are Uncle Bryon and Uncle Dennis to a ton of kids and now their kids, so we have had the vicarious satisfaction of raising kids through our friends who have children.

Being with Dennis has made me so much more mature and patient and much more respectful of other people's needs. I've become a better listener and a kinder person, too. I was pretty much self-centered and very spoiled. I was an extremely spoiled child by my parents, by my nanny, and by my only sister, among others. Dennis has spoiled me our entire relationship, so I'm a very spoiled person, but I like it and accept it and don't apologize for it, yet I don't take it for granted.

When I was younger, I was less appreciative of the special attention I used to get as a child and as a young adult. But being loved by Dennis has given me the opportunity to extend love farther and broader than I could have on my own. Had I not been loved in this way, I don't think I would have become the loving person I feel I am today. I can honestly say that I unconditionally love most of my family and friends and colleagues, etc, and I don't put conditions on it.

Loving yourself is vital, too. I hated myself when I was young and wanted to kill myself several times. You can't grow up in this culture as a homosexual, especially in the Deep South in the years that I grew up, and not have it affect you in a profound way. I was born in 1944 and already at five years old, I was aware that I was gay and I knew that I couldn't even tell somebody that. I didn't know what it was but I knew it wasn't something to bring up at the breakfast table. I felt that I was the only one on the entire planet with those feelings and I was lonely and miserable and wanted love and affection and was attracted to every male character on television at the time. I knew I was attracted to men and that it was about sex. It caused me to live in a very lonely cocoon and I felt depressed and isolated. Coming to grips with my sexuality was the greatest gift I ever gave myself.

It's still tough out there. My partner and I help out with the LGBT Center here in Stockton and I'm just amazed at how many young kids write in to these websites that give free advice, and they still feel like they're the only person in the world like them. Even with all the publicity we have, all the stars and athletes and politicians we have, there are still a lot of kids who live very singular, isolated lives, who don't know that there are other people like themselves.

Back when I was growing up it was even harder, but it's still hard. So when I'm on Facebook or the Internet and Dennis is saying to me, "Can you please do a load of wash? Could you please unload the dishwasher?," I'll say, "I'm busy." He doesn't know that I'm typing maybe a five-paragraph response to a sixteen-year-old teen who just posted, "I think I'm gay and here's why I think I am. Do you think I am?" I'm responding because I love that and because I worked my whole life with kids and I still care very much about doing whatever I can, even if it's an anonymous Internet response to a post.

If a relationship is going to become long-term, it certainly helps to start out really being in love. Then you have to really fight, fight yourself, and fight with and for that relationship. Fight your own detrimental instincts. Never take anything for granted, and you really have to do a self-checkup on a regular basis. I can go back all the way to when we first met and can remember thinking, "I don't want to lose this relationship. I want Dennis to want to keep this going, so what can I do?" It's a constant struggle in a way and it never ends if it's going to last. Dennis and I have worked very hard on our relationship. We've had some knock-down, drag-out blowouts and really had to work through some troubled times. It is not a bed of roses.

In a relationship, you have to offer more than just taking. What can you give to it and are you willing to make the sacrifices and/or the modifications to yourself to make it work? It can't be all me, my, mine. For Dennis and me, it's been constant growth, constant struggle, a constant check and evaluation. We've had the good fortune of having an extremely supportive and supported relationship, with lots of loving, caring family, co-workers, bosses, extremely close friends, both straight and gay. All of them have contributed very much to making our relationship work too. As Hillary Clinton said, "It takes a village."

Dennis spoils me. He brings me coffee every morning in bed. He draws the drapes every morning so I can have fresh sunshine. He opens the door so I can hear the birds. He brings me my iPad and then he departs to the living room and has his quiet time and reads the *Chronicle* while I read the local paper online and start doing my Facebook postings.

He does the yard work. Dennis does all the shopping and ninety percent of the cooking, so you see I'm a true prima donna. I'm lazy. I could go the whole day and do nothing. I'm lucky, and he does it all without making me feel guilty. He's a gourmet cook and fixes dinner most nights and serves it like it came out of a fancy kitchen. We sit and have dinner together and watch the news and then after dinner, I clear the table. We are truly retired and we have matching recliners so after dinner we sit in our recliners and hold hands and watch a movie.

Many years ago, we could only meet guys in gay bars. Today we have so many outlets and resources. If you'd like to meet someone, go to a place where you might find someone who has mutual interests. If you're religious, go to a religious setting, for God's sake. Try Barnes & Noble. You don't want to be introduced to some drunk who only goes to the bar and drinks and smokes if you're not interested in a smoking, drinking partner. Give yourself an opportunity to go to a variety of places and venues. Expose yourself. You're not going to meet anyone sitting in your own backyard. Internet dating is really big now, and I have a number of friends who met their partners via the Internet.

It helps to know what you want, what type of relationship, what type of partner. When you meet someone are you physically and sexually attracted? The first test of most relationships is sexual attraction, and I believe sex comes before love. It's the most natural, animal, basic process there is. So sex is essential, and you hope it becomes compatible. From there you start the gardening, the hoeing and the planting and the feeding of that garden together. You help each other tend it and make it work.

Our relationship has its own momentum now. Obviously, if you're in a relationship for forty-five years—even five, ten, twenty, thirty—you have so many people ask you, "What's the secret?" Man, if I knew the secret, there'd be a hell of a lot more people bonded together and mated for a much longer time than most people are! I don't know what the secret is. Dennis and I have a magical bond and I can't really explain it. I can only say that I love him, he loves me, and we enjoy life together very much.

CHAPTER 17

JOHN AND CHARLIE

"My advice is to pray hard for a lifetime companion. When you meet the right person, all those fears and misgivings about feeling crowded and so forth just fall away. With the right person, you can't get enough time together."

It isn't often that I get to interview one of my personal heroes, so it was a special honor to be able to interview John McNeill, one of the true giants of the gay and lesbian community. A renowned psychotherapist, ordained priest, teacher, theologian, author, and scholar, John was a prisoner of war in Nazi Germany in 1944 and 1945, during the harrowing latter days of World War Two. His contributions to the modern gay liberation movement are profound, and it would be nearly impossible to overestimate the dramatic impact he and his works have had on the church and society since the early 1970s.

John's groundbreaking 1976 book, *The Church and the Homosexual,* and his subsequent works on gay liberation theology have been translated into numerous languages and continue to be widely read around the world. John co-founded the New York City chapter of Dignity, a support group for gay Catholics, and was dismissed from the priesthood when he refused to be silenced by the Vatican on LGBT issues. A humble, brilliant, and deeply spiritual man, John McNeill and his works continue to shed a great deal of beneficial light around the globe. Filmmaker/friend Brendan Fay (*The Saint of 9-11*) recently produced a superb new documentary on his life and works, titled *Taking a Chance on God.* www.takingachanceongod.com. Together now for almost fifty years, John and his longtime partner, Charlie, a retired electronics engineer, live in Florida.

John McNeill — (Charlie Chiarelli)

I had frequently prayed to God to meet someone with whom I could enter into a loving relationship. Charlie and I met in Toronto, on New Year's Eve. At the time, I was teaching at Lemoyne College in Syracuse. The Vietnam War was on, and I took an anti-war stand. I was giving lectures in the area that the war was immoral, and therefore someone with a strong conscience should refuse to serve. Well, a lot of my students took me seriously and refused to enter the draft and the Army and sought to be conscientious objectors, to have that status recognized.

But the Army refused to recognize that category, so to avoid going to prison, they fled to Canada. So I had a whole group of young men in Canada and I used to go up and visit them on occasion. This was New Year's weekend of 1965, and I went up as usual, and while visiting there with my former students, I went to a gay bar in downtown Toronto called the Saint Charles Bar. It no longer exists, but at that time, it was perhaps the most important gay bar in Toronto. While I was there, I was introduced to a young man named Charles, so I met Charles at the Saint Charles Bar! At the time I was forty, and he was thirty. That was New Year's Eve, and we immediately took to each other.

He brought me home with him and the next day we went and visited his parents in Hamilton, Ontario, which was his home originally. From then on, I would visit him in Toronto, where he was working, and he would visit me in Syracuse, where I was teaching. Finally he got a job in Syracuse and moved to Syracuse. So that was the beginning of our relationship. We knew we wanted to be together pretty quickly; a matter of two or three visits back and forth. I felt very definitely that this was an answer to my prayer, and I remember saying a lot of prayers of gratitude to God, too.

We were sexual right away, the same night we met. For a long time, we were sexually exclusive, and then at some stage—maybe ten or twenty years into our relationship—we realized that it would be even better if we gave each other permission to have sex with other people, if he wanted to or if I wanted to. So for the last number of years, we've had an open relationship. If Charlie wants to make a date with somebody, he does, and if I want to, I do, and it works for us. It makes being with Charlie less like being trapped into a narrowing of our lives!

Having an open relationship in no way crimps our freedom. We've never really found ourselves emotionally drawn to anyone else, and since our primary commitment is to each other, the love gets stronger over the years. So other people can't really challenge that. I don't know why, but I know it's a fact. We are still sexual together. We still meet each other's sexual needs, and it's still a great pleasure. In fact, it doesn't become routine because there is a type of intimacy that grows over the years.

I have always said that the primary pleasure involved in sexuality is not the physical pleasure, but the experience of intimacy, of closeness, of oneness with another human. And that encompasses all areas, emotional, spiritual, and so on. I have also always held that there are many experiences that have no definition because definition means that the mind creates one meaning. But to experience love... Like play, it can only be experienced. There's no definition, there's only the experience. But I definitely know what the experience is, and the experience is a very heightened intimacy, almost like becoming one with the other person. Charlie and I are also very affectionate and we hug and kiss and cuddle. That's always been important to us.

Charlie has an extraordinary sense of humor. I've written about a couple of things. At our first breakfast, he poured wheat germ over me, and when I asked why he did that, he said, "It says right here on the bottle, "Pour this over your favorite fruit!" That's a typical humorous action, and Charlie has done thousands of them. For example, when I told him I was going to make God my primary love object, he said, "That's fine with me, as long as he'll help with the laundry..."

Occasionally, we've had breakdowns in communication, and that's primarily because as a child, my stepmother Katie was always critical of me; everything I did was wrong. So I felt my self-confidence constantly undermined, and whenever Charlie gets critical of me, I re-experience Katie and get pretty angry about it! But that's not often. It's strange how deeply conditioned we are by our childhood experiences. But we've never had any big crisis or been close to ending the relationship. Ever. My stepmother used to say to me almost daily that I was a ne'er do well and would never be able to make a living, and that's because I was always lost in books. She thought I should be out fixing cars!

The number one key in a relationship is to never go to bed angry. Reconcile. Apologize if you did something that made the other person angry and ask forgiveness. Have a lot of give and take because frequently you may do things that make the other person angry, even if the relationship at a deeper level is even stronger than the anger. Charlie is excellent at that. He can get very angry, and then an hour later, it's gone.

Spiritually, I take very seriously the statement in scripture that God is love. And if anyone loves, they know God. I have always believed that this includes a gay love relationship, which is a genuine human love and therefore contains the Divine. It's another way of knowing God. That certainly has been the fundamental belief system for me in my relationship with Charlie for the last forty-seven years.

Charlie is on the same page about that, too. He is—how can I put it?—religious, but it is more unspoken and undefined in his case. I've been doing a lot of reflecting on that and writing about it and as a result I have articulated a spirituality. His is unarticulated, but nonetheless real.

Both of us go to church. We feel like exiles from the Roman Catholic church because of its homophobia and we can't go to a Catholic service and hear our love denounced as evil. So we go to Metropolitan Community Church, and here in Fort Lauderdale, that is Sunshine Cathedral, which has over one thousand people every Sunday, and a large number of them—maybe over half—are exiled Roman Catholics.

I often say that we're brought up to believe that God is love, but if we didn't experience human love, we couldn't know what that means. Our first experience of the love of our mother and father made it easy for us to understand what was meant when we say God is love. God was a father or mother loving us like our parents do. But I think that as an adult, I would never have really believed that God is love had I not experienced forty-seven years of human love from Charlie. That made the concept of God's love very concrete and very real to me.

We went to Canada, to Toronto where we met and were married there by a judge on September 8, 2008. It was a powerful experience, and the primary reason was because many of Charlie's family were there, as well as my family from Buffalo, New York; my nieces and their husbands. So we both had sizeable numbers of our family there, and to have them share our marriage and to be there approving and applauding was a very deep experience for us, since most of our life we felt like we had to keep it hidden. My parents and older brothers were homophobes, but that was never the case in Charlie's family. His parents were from Sicily and they were very accepting. My family was right out of Ireland, Irish Catholics, and even heterosexuality seemed sinful to them!

Our sex life is certainly a big factor in keeping our relationship growing. We continually meet one anotherr's sexual needs, and that keeps it very vital. The other factor is our awareness on both sides that we're mortal and we only have this certain amount of time together and we have to make the most if it. Every day is a gift! Especially since I'm eighty-seven, and Charlie is seventy-seven, so we know we don't have too much more time together. I do assume that there is an afterlife and I definitely anticipate that we will be reunited there. If God is love, and anyone who loves knows God... God's love is eternal, so if our human love is a sharing in Divine love, then it has to continue beyond death.

If you want a loving relationship in your life, pray for it. Scripture says "Ask and ye shall receive, knock and it will be opened." So ask God. Secondly, ask yourself what, if anything, you're doing to prevent one. As a psychotherapist, I saw that many of my clients would get very fearful if somebody started getting close, feeling that if they allowed themselves to depend on that person, they could always be hurt badly. So to avoid that, they would immediately break off a relationship that started getting too intimate. The best way through such an impasse is to put underneath your human love a deep spiritual relationship with God so that if the human love gives way—and in Charlie's and my case, it's going to give way when one or the other of us dies—then you still have the spiritual love to depend on and to keep you going.

I've also always been aware that a gay person needs community. That's why forty years ago now, I founded Dignity in New York City for gay Catholics. It's always been a support group for gay and lesbian Catholics, and our motto was "Dignity is not something you can give yourself, but it is something we can give each other." I always knew you needed a community of people who accepted and felt blessed by their gayness and who were willing to share that very positive stance with each other and support each other and so forth. The organization is still going strongly. In fact, I went up to New York for the fortieth anniversary just about a year ago, and we had a huge celebration. The City of New York even issued a proclamation honoring me for the gift I gave the gay and lesbian community by founding Dignity. So that was nice.

We do have a small group of friends, though most of them are single. There are very few male couples with whom we have formed a deep relationship. I don't know why. It's just the way things worked. We do love kids and appreciate them, but it never occurred to us to become parents. We have many friends who have children, but it just never occurred to us to do that. We have two cats, and have always had cats.

I'm inclined to think that every gay man goes through an adolescence, where he wants to experiment and meet different people and doesn't want to be tied down. And then it's part of maturity to desire a deeper intimacy and stability. The first typically precedes the second. In other words, I think there's a maturing process that goes on. Some people never mature. But the average person does mature and needs greater stability and assurance of the other person's continued presence.

I think that as humans, we get horny and we need sexual release, and if you can find someone who will share that with you, that's a good. It's nothing bad. And if it's the right person, then you'll move in together and continue doing it and become partners! So if that hasn't happened yet, it's possible that you just haven't met the right person yet. My advice is to pray hard for a lifetime companion. When you meet the right person, all those fears and misgivings about feeling crowded and so forth just fall away. With the right person, you can't get enough time together.

SECTION V:

COUPLES TOGETHER FIFTY TO SIXTY YEARS

CHAPTER 18

WARD AND GEORGE

"How lucky I am to have found George, and now to be able to stick with him to the end is just magnificent. Each day is a surprise. Every morning is a revelation. That somebody this wonderful could love me is, for me, just astonishing. It's a miracle. We find ourselves staring at each other across the table and we choke up. Both of us are the same way."

* * * * *

At age twenty-five, Ward Stewart was operating a Greenwich Village art gallery when a slim, twenty-year-old student with the Martha Graham Dance Company walked in. The two clicked, and Ward and George Vye have now been together almost sixty years. As a registered nurse, Ward worked in the very epicenter of the AIDS epidemic in New York City. George continues to work as an artist and book illustrator. The pair married in Canada and again more recently in Seattle, where they now live.

Ward Stewart — (George Vye)

George and I have been together fifty-six years. He was just twenty, and I was twenty-six when we met. After finishing the Army and being discharged, I got a job in a little art gallery/frame shop on Eighth Street in Greenwich Village. George was studying dance with Martha Graham and came in shopping, looking at some drawings I had by an artist named Iris Brody, now long dead. We struck up an acquaintance and struck up a spark and struck up a fire together. It was not a long courtship.

He struck me initially as somewhat shy but he was handsome and adorable. Oh, my, he was gorgeous! I fell like a ton of bricks. We each fell for each other and were in love that night while we were fooling around. He was the first person I had met who I thought I might like to make my life with. George moved in. The next day, we went by subway to get his stuff out of his rooming house, and he moved into this little tiny loft I had. It was very primitive, and the rent was fifty dollars a month. There he was, and there I was, in that "snug two by four where we kept house," to use Bertold Brecht's line.

I believe our meeting was luck. I'm a deep-dish atheist, except I have a soft spot for Fortuna, Lady Luck. Fortuna is the Roman goddess of luck and she's very much alive. I don't dare say ill of her. It was just pure, crap-shoot chance that we met, but I met the perfect guy for me, and vice versa. All those millions of people in New York bumping along together, and there George was. I had always wanted to live my life with somebody and I never thought I would do better.

Fifty-six years is a long time, and we have not been exclusive. We always wished we were and we failed at that. There were other people on and off, mostly off, through the years. George had a long interlude with someone else, but he never really left. He stuck with me. We were still always committed to getting to the finish line together and staying on these horses together until we got to the end. That was always our wish.

We're not really sexual anymore. I'm eighty-three and I had my prostate revamped, which took away my erectile capacity. We hug and kiss and cuddle a lot, but there just isn't much genital action between us. I get up in the morning and the first thing we do is hug and kiss and cuddle and we celebrate another day. We've got another day together, a gift from Fortuna, and we get all mushy about that. We may be fools, but we're having a hell of a good time!

It's not easy to define love. Various clichés come to mind like, "He completes me." I never ever wanted to hurt or harm him, and I just hope we'll be together until one of us pegs off. But I don't know what love is. I have no definition but I do feel it. We say it to each other constantly. Love for us has become better over time. We're smarter, more aware of each other. It has moved from hotsie, hotsie, to cozy, cozy, and the two of us have just stuck with it over the long haul. It's important to try to be as nice as you can to your partner. Be kind and loving. I don't think there's a lot else. If you have angry feelings and hostilities and so forth, keep them to yourself. Neither George or I had internal *Sturm und Drang*. We just haven't. We're simple, sunny souls and we're happy that we found each other.

We have never exchanged "high words" so that anybody more than six feet away would know we were fighting. It's happened that we've become frustrated with one another and turned on our heels and gotten cold for an hour. We've never really had a fight. We don't argue or find purposes that push us apart. We just don't disagree on much of anything really. George and I laugh constantly. I suppose our sense of humor is similar as we seem to laugh at the same things. We have similar interests and similar tastes in movies and television and art and music. We both find Madonna and Lady Gaga to be abominations. We're very fond of opera and *bel canto* and we love beautiful singing.

Both of our families were absolutely magnificent. All of my old New England family approve, though it wasn't until we'd been together for some time that it was spoken of. Remember, this was back in 1956, and we were sailing on uncharted waters. It was something new. My mother, a psychiatrist, had been born in the late 1800s and she knew perfectly well what was going on. She loved George dearly, and he loved her. The three of us traveled together, but we never discussed our marriage. Once she scolded me for not being nice enough to George. But she was a nineteenth-century person, and we simply didn't discuss it.

We're both passionately American and we wanted to stand equal in our society, and this whole same-gender marriage was really hatched in our then-immediate vicinity, in Hawaii, thirty-five years ago. The Hawaiian Constitution was rewritten so as to take out the gender divisions and separations and inequalities, and that included the marriage law. It was amended to recognize no reason why two citizens shouldn't marry, and I was part of the crowd that jumped on that.

George and I were domestic partners as soon as that was available, and then as soon as marriage became available in Canada, we went there and married. We went there with a couple of friends and took a suite with bedrooms for all of us. A terribly amiable man came with gorgeous, white,

Christian hair. He was a dreamboat! He had a satchel with him with equipment for any type of marriage you could want, and we told him we wanted an absolute minimum of pious thought. He did a ceremony for us, and we got married.

It was very pleasant in Canada, and same-sex marriage was still new there, but everybody seemed to get the point. A cute little girl in a bank where we had to get a license for two or five dollars was just delighted to see these two semi-elderly gents come in and get married. She thought that was wonderful, and the Justice of the Peace, the marriage officiant, thought so, too. It was an entirely pleasant, although not very grandiose, affair.

Then we married again in Washington, and that was done in a beautiful park by a dear, dear friend. It was very nice but it was not a big deal. It did not vary our commitment to each other at all. It varied our relationship to our government, which was the only real change, and we have federal and local protections, which is very nice.

Under George's attention, I have grown enormously, and so has he. We've grown old together. We're elderly. He's bald, and I'm entirely grey-haired. We're old farts and we've gotten here together. If I'd never met him, I think I would be in a very different place. I have known other long-term friends with whom I might have formed as pleasant and joyous a relation-ship, but the odds are against it. The odds are against successful marriage anyways, especially without being able to marry and form a contract. The poor straights only get it right half the time, and I think we probably do less well.

We've always merged our funds. We really never even discuss money. For years and years, we never had any but we never felt poor. We just *were* poor! Most of the time, I made more money than George did, but it was never a question as to who was contributing more. That never occurred to us. Now after having hop-scotched through real estate, we're in a much better place today. Social Security isn't very generous, and since neither of us have any great taste for spending, we're fine.

Being parents would have been nice. We both came from family backgrounds where children and grandchildren were cherished. I suspect we both would have been good parents, but when we were at the right age, we just weren't prosperous enough and couldn't have afforded it. There's no great disappointment in that for us. It was just, "Oh dear, wouldn't it have been nice to have somebody bringing home grandchildren..." It simply didn't happen.

After that first tiny loft, we moved to a little cold-water flat in the very belly-button of Greenwich Village. Later, it was a large, luxurious, rent-controlled apartment in a rundown building on the Upper West Side and then we finally bought a 1900 house in Staten Island with a nice view.

By then, I was a nurse and I enjoyed the bejeesus out of nursing. I worked on the Bowery with the homeless. In the early 1980s I began volunteering an evening a week at a community health center, which started out as a service to junkies and young drifters who'd ended up on the street in the East Village, and it gradually changed over as HIV became a nightmare. Our patients began dying of this horrible disease. They'd come in with the flu on Monday and they'd be dead on Friday. We knew nothing about what it was, and the medical establishment in general was terrified and didn't know how to handle these people. We didn't know the vector of the thing, and people were dying like flies.

So I did that for years and I would have paid them to let me do that work. It was both heartbreaking, as well as immensely good to be able to reach into that cesspit and do something and help. I met people I'm still in touch with, beloved friends, people I cherish, who survived that.

Martin, one of my dearest and closest friends survived that, and he said to me once, "You people in this clinic, you touch me like you love me." I said, "Well, we do! Of course we do." He'd been through a few other clinic situations where they just recoiled in horror... "Oh God, you've got leprosy. Get out of my sight!" We couldn't do anything about it except love him and support him.

I worked with people who were just amazing. We had a love feast, a wonderful time. It was a time of heroic efforts and enormous good deeds by ordinary people. It was just God's work; it was wonderful. I was in that and of it, and the work was gratifying to the absolute max. It was gorgeous! I was lucky. Fortuna again! I was just lucky to have picked up those useful skills and have them tapped at that terrible time, to have them used and appreciated. I was truly blessed.

The transformation I've seen in society in my lifetime has been just absolutely astonishing. I went into the Army because I was too timid to tell them I was gay. Three years later, George got called in and just said, "I'm gay. Don't bother me." That was the end of that. And now I wear funny clothes and gay striped handkerchiefs that I stick in my breast pocket, and if anyone doesn't like it, fuck 'em! I've walked in the Fifth Avenue parade with the New York City police crowd, along with the boyfriends, the spouses, of policemen. There have been profound changes and there's still more to change.

For people under the age of forty or so, it's a different world, and they completely perceive it as it is, and the old farts are full of shit! Their marriage is being attacked. Please! I wouldn't touch their marriage with a twenty-foot pole.

I'm eighty-three, so my ticket is about to be punched. I'm way past my sell-by date. I'm medically a little shaky and have some cardiac arrhythmia, controlled diabetes, and murderous arthritis, which has me in a wheelchair. I'm pegging out, though not for a year or two or three, probably. I doubt that I'll make ninety. That's just the way it is. We don't talk much about it except that we're both very much aware that our clocks are ticking. We're having a wonderful time, but it's not forever. That awareness has—to a fantastic degree—made us appreciate each new day all the more. Just intensely so.

How lucky I am to have found George, and now to be able to stick with him to the end is just magnificent. Each day is a surprise. Every morning is a revelation. That somebody this wonderful could love me is, for me, just astonishing. It's a miracle. We find ourselves staring at each other across the table and we choke up. Both of us are the same way. And I'm not a very pretty article, but he still looks on me with a wondrous gaze. That's a surprise. He seems to me a miracle. When he comes walking towards me in the street, my heart goes pitty-pat. There he is! Wow, I haven't seen him for two hours! My soul rises, and it's a miracle every time.

CHAPTER 19

GEORGE AND JACK

"We're affectionate, and I've often said over the years that the high point of my day is sliding in bed with him at the end of the day, and it still is."

* * * * *

George Harris and Jack Evans met in Dallas in 1961. Founders of the Stonewall Professional Business Association, they are both retired from residential real estate. Jack and George also founded The Dallas Way, a GLBT History Project, which can be found online atwww.thedallasway.org. Now in their fifty-third year together, the two gay community pioneers had a recent church wedding, to which they invited EVERYONE, and—not surprisingly—a huge overflow crowd showed up to celebrate along with them.

George Harris — (Jack Evans)

We've been together fifty-one years. At the time that we met, I was twenty-six and Jack was thirty-one. I had gotten caught up in that purge at the Pentagon in Washington in 1956, at the time of Eisenhower and J. Edgar Hoover, and had gotten thrown out of the C.I.A. There was actually a book written about all of that called *The Gay Metropolis*.

A good friend of mine who was in the State Department got thrown out, too. He was from Secoville, a suburb of Dallas, and he said, "We need to get out of this town or they're going to kill us," so I said, "I'm ready to go!" Well, we left about 5:30 in the morning and drove all the way through to his hometown, Secoville. I didn't want to live in a suburb so I came to Dallas and checked in at the YMCA. They had a residency here at the time downtown, which was like twelve dollars and that included maid service! They also had a wonderful cafeteria and homemade food. As you can imagine, the YMCA was quite active and it got the nickname of "The French Embassy" among our little group, because all the married men would come in on the weekends for entertainment. Occasionally a cowboy would wander in from West Texas, so it was a lot of fun and it was a reprieve from running from the vice squad, which was in all the bars arresting people for just looking at one another.

Everything was underground when I came to Dallas in 1956. They only had a couple of bars, gay bars, but people were afraid to go in them because they might be arrested. So most of the kids would gather 'round the display windows at Nieman Marcus. They kept their lights on until midnight, so here you'd see a bunch of queens staring in the windows, one eye on the fashions and one eye on the street. I was there one night and I looked down the street and saw this sailor and said, "Oh my... I'll go down there and check out our naval forces..."

So I started down there and out of the corner of my eye, I saw this white Ford going down the street. Well, back in those days Dallas didn't have any one-way streets, so he saw the sailor and did a U-turn in the middle of the street, the door flung open, the sailor gets in, and they drive off. Well, I got a good look and saw who was driving that car.

Sometime shortly after that, when Jack and I were formally introduced, I said, "I've seen you before. Don't you drive a two-door white Ford?"

He said, "Yes, how do you know that?" I said, "That's another story, but I've seen you."

Jack and I had a mutual friend, a British fella, a wonderful man who was an antique buyer for Nieman Marcus, and he was going around the world on a trip for two clients. One was a Mrs. W. A. Criswell, who was the wife of the senior minister at the First Baptist Church here. She had a renowned collection of antiques. The other lady was Mrs. Ima Hogg, who was the governor's daughter and a very wealthy woman. So our friend was giving himself a bon voyage party, and we went and there we were—and that's where Jack and I met.

We didn't get together right away. After that we had gone to a parade in town, some type of parade, and we met and he gave me his card. It said "Emmons Jewelry, Newark, New Jersey," and I thought, "Oh Lord, I've met a diamond merchant!"

Little did I know that he was selling costume jewelry door to door and was about to starve to death. I was working at night trying to finish off my college education, so we were a pair! We didn't have any money but we fell in love and we've had an incredible journey.

Sex is usually what brings gay people together. It brought Jack and me together, but it's not what keeps us together. You are forced to determine how you want to live after the passion wears off. We often laugh that we went to bed and didn't get out of bed for three days. We called in sick at work and had a great time.

The atmosphere for gay life in those days was just tough. Twenty-four hours a day, you lived in fear of losing your job, because invariably, when they had a raid and gay people were caught, the newspaper would print their names. Consequently, people were just devastated and they'd literally have to leave town. One doctor from a very prominent family here in town was caught in a raid and had to go to Canada to practice medicine, so we lost a lot of good people. But Jack and I had decided that we wanted to live together and we got a little house and set up housekeeping. I was working in the motor freight industry, and he was in savings and loans, and we had a good life and developed a lot of good friends. We had mostly weekend dinner parties, and we hardly ever went out. That was just the sign of the times.

We started off monogamous, which is important because you have to build up trust. You have to have a sense of direction as to where you want your relationship to go. I remember one time Jack and I went to San Francisco. Before we got together, he'd had a relationship with a flight attendant with Pan American who lived in San Francisco, and he wanted to see him, so we went out there. He was a very charming man, and I enjoyed meeting him, and didn't feel that he was a threat or anything.

While we were there, Jack wanted to go to the tubs, the baths. I was a little shocked but intrigued. The place was called the Embarcadero, and we went there. I was extremely nervous but I decided that it wasn't that big of a deal, and that if he enjoyed it, it was fine with me. We did determine afterwards that that wasn't the way that we wanted to live. I think so many kids today make the mistake of being too stringent and laying down some pretty heavy rules, and after all, we're human and we're subject to error. But after that experience, we just didn't want our relationship to be like that.

Oover the years, you change. Your values change. Your bodies change, and sex is not as important as it once was. Somewhere along the line, it becomes secondary and then even farther down the line. In talking to young kids, we try to caution them to be careful not to set too many rules, because there's always someone out there who is cuter and prettier and you're going to be disappointed and hurt and so on.

We have been fortunate that we've always been able to count our blessings. We're not sexually active anymore due to medical problems and medication and age. We're affectionate, and I've often said over the years that the high point of my day is sliding in bed with him at the end of the day, and it still is. That's a great emphasis in our lives at this point. We've never slept separately.

We travel a lot with a younger couple, and they always laugh because they hardly ever sit together on an airplane, and we demand to sit together. When we go out to dinner, I want to sit next to Jack. This couple will have a dinner party and they'll say, "We're going to split up all the partners tonight at the table, except for Jack and George, because they don't like to be split up." And we don't. We enjoy sitting next to each other and being close.

I see love as caring. You have to make sacrifices sometimes and Lord knows, you have to be patient. Fortunately, in our relationship we never had any real battles. I was brought up in a very volatile family and I promised myself that if I ever grew up I would not have that kind of relationship, so I don't argue. If he gets upset about something, I'll just listen to him and not say anything. I determined a long time ago that whoever wins in an argument is going to lose anyway. There are no winners in a lover's argument, and it's best resolved when you have cooler heads and can talk about it at a later time. But the older we get, the closer we get to each other.

We try to comfort each other and be there in the good times, as well as in the bad.

You have to work at a relationship. It has its challenges every day, even at our age, but they're not insurmountable. There are all kinds of demons out there. We don't have an alcohol problem and, thank the Lord, we don't have financial problems. We've come to an agreement on a lot of things. Politically we're on the same page. We have the same church faith. I was extremely fond of his parents, who were very good to me. They're both deceased, but we had a great relationship. Jack knew my parents. But I think if you're living and breathing, you're going to have challenges. You can't avoid them, but how you approach them and how you handle them is really who you are.

We've really had a good life and I don't have any complaints at all. Jack and I started out in a small house we paid fourteen-five for and we loved fixing it up. We moved from there to a big house that took us forever to restore, but that was also quite enjoyable. We sold that and went to a high-rise and loved that experience. Now we're in a townhouse that we've enjoyed putting together, but with our age, it's getting tougher working three levels. So in spite of our getting it to where we really love it, I see that down the road, we will have to make some adjustments.

Jack has emphysema and I have COPD, so we both have lung disease, which is a not very good for navigating three levels! But we've seemed to handle it pretty well so far.

Later in life, I took over our finances, and it has been bothersome to Jack in some respects, because I'm not very transparent with our investments as to what's going on. It's not that I'm trying to hide anything, and he gets irritated about that. But I have developed a system where I will record monthly everything in the accounts, the account numbers, where every bit is and how much, so he can refer to it and not feel insecure. I'm not as open a person as he is and I don't like to discuss my business with our friends.

Back when Jack and I got together, in the early days, we had separate accounts. After a while, we determined that we weren't going to get anywhere that way, and we liked re-doing houses. At that time, two same-sex people could not get a mortgage in the state of Texas. Two same-sex people could not get insurance on a car, so it was always in Jack's name because his brother-in-law was a well-to-do man in West Texas who owned savings and loans and he made our loans for us. Later, when they changed that act in the legislature, we both went on, but to enable us to acquire these little houses and do what we wanted to do, we had to pool our resources. It's much better from our perspective to do that.

After fifty years together, it's easy to take each other for granted, and I do every day, and I'm sure he does me! But I don't know that it creates a problem. Recently we were down in Destin, Florida, and this straight woman was down there with us, and she laughed about the way Jack and I communicate and said, "That is so indicative of people who've been together so long. Y'all can read each other's minds!" She said, "You can anticipate what he's going to say."

Jack and I certainly have a sense of humor, and I like to say that we're both retarded. I'm the jokester. I think it's essential to have a good sense of humor if you're going to make it. This is a tough world, if you think about it.

I'm not too crazy about surprises, but I like to surprise him. We were in Palm Springs not too long ago and we went into this art gallery, and Jack saw this piece of art and said, "Wow, I just love that..." I thought he was going to buy it, but he said, "Oh, we really can't afford that," so we went on. Soon after he wound up in the hospital with a very serious lung situation. I didn't think he was going to come out of it. Well, after he got out of the hospital, I decided that I wanted to have a party for our close friends, and I told this friend that I wanted him to call this place and buy that piece of art and have it shipped. He did, and when we were all together, he brought out the painting. It was a great surprise to Jack, and he thoroughly enjoyed it. Those kind of things just give life a little spark!

We've never come close to separating. In our day and time, it was so hard to just stay together, because nobody was for us. Everybody was against us, and we hardly knew anyone who had any kind of a lasting relationship. They were roommates. It was very hard, and the first ten years were awful. We had financial problems and were trying to get a direction in our lives and in our careers. Whenever we would get to a point where we had a problem, one of us would come home and fix a pitcher of martinis. So if we ever walked in and saw that martini pitcher on the cocktail table, we knew we were in for a discussion! Sometimes Jack would get mad and he'd say, "I'm going to move," or "I'm going to get an apartment," but that would blow over. We never did have any serious moments.

We're very close to our church. It's a United Methodist Reconciling Church, which means that the congregation has voted to accept gays and lesbians and anyone else, so there are no limitations. We have a lot of straight friends we enjoy and we like the aspect of worshiping with straight people and gay people. Our church has a straight minister, a young man, and his wife is a Hispanic family court judge, and they're very, very liberal and they make big waves in the city, which is easy to do because Dallas is so damned conservative!

Being a red state, it's hard to get anything done here, but we thoroughly enjoy our church. Jack grew up in West Texas as a Presbyterian. I grew up in a church, too, and we always lament the fact that none of our friends go to church. We don't bother people about our religion. I hate it when people try to coerce somebody to go to church—you either want to go or you don't—but our friends know that we go and that we love it. We enjoy the people we meet there quite a bit and we see them a lot socially. So we have the best of both worlds; we have the gay world and we have the straight world, and it's fun to bring them together.

We'd get married if it meant anything. A lot of these kids are running off to New York to get married, but why? If only we could get our rights from the government... They claim that there are nineteen rights that we are entitled to, so absolutely we'd get married in a minute if it meant something. The way it stands, if one of us died, we could not get the other one's Social Security. In the straight world, the wife gets the husband's, or the husband gets the wife's automatically. So there's still a lot of injustice out there. Jack and I have never had any commitment ceremony or any blessing or anything. We've just always felt blessed that we found each other.

The most important thing in a relationship is you've got to care. You've got to have compassion and you've got to be patient. You have to have the faith that it's all going to work out. You've got to love. You've got to love unconditionally and have a lot of hope that it will work out. There ain't no guarantees, for sure!

When we were in Washington last week at the White House, this ambassador friend of ours whom we went to see had this darling little boy there as an assistant. He was young and just cute as hell and he was a former speechwriter of Obama's. He was from Florida and he was openly gay. He told me he had a partner who works for the C.I.A. in Oregon and I said, "Have mercy, how do y'all ever get together?"

He said, "We both enjoy our space and we get together once a month."

I said, "That's the strangest relationship I've ever heard of!" If I'm around five years from now, I'd sure like to know if that relationship is still going on. But anyway, I'm going to write him and in this note I'm going to tell him that I hope he realizes how far we've come, because I got thrown out of the C.I.A. for being gay, and he's going around Washington telling everyone about his lover. We've come a hell of a long way. I couldn't believe it!

As a kid, I was so introverted. I had a very difficult background growing up in the backwoods of Mississippi and I grew up with horrible segregation, unbelievable treatment of blacks. I have four brothers and a sister, and the only thing that held us together was our mother. We lived out in the country and it was very, very tough going because we were just coming out of the Depression and it was tough, tough, tough. I had always been a small person and had to be a fighter, had to scramble to get anywhere, and was very untrustworthy and didn't trust anybody.

I was just an angry person. Then I met Jack. He has always been a very peaceful man, very open and happy, and I thought, "Well I'd like to be like that." So I've changed tremendously since I was a young man, through meeting him, and I hope that I've helped him on the other hand in some regard. I think that's what makes a partnership, that you help each other. We've had an extraordinary journey, I'll tell you that. And I hope it keeps going for a while. I'm not ready to see the light at the end of the tunnel yet!

SECTION VI:

COUPLES TOGETHER
SIXTY TO SEVENTY YEARS

CHAPTER 20

JOHNNY AND LYMAN

"If you meet someone and you want a relationship together, work on it. Just don't run into anything. Go slow and take your time and do it right. Have no secrets; that's the secret."

* * * * *

Johnny Dapper and Lyman Hollowell began their sixty-five year love affair when they met the day World War Two ended. Johnny worked as a Hollywood set designer for such classic films as *All About Eve*, *The Day the Earth Stood Still*, *Oklahoma*, and *Guys & Dolls*, while Lyman was a film editor for such films as *The Robe*, *All About Eve*, *Miracle on 34th Street*, and *The King & I*. The recently married couple were the subjects of Paul Detwiler's sweet, uplifting 2010 documentary, *Johnny and Lyman: A Life Together*, which won numerous awards and is available on DVD. I'd hoped to be able to interview both men for this book, but Lyman had died several months before I first spoke with Johnny. It was an honor for me to be able to interview Johnny Dapper, now in his ninetieth year.

Johnny Dapper — (Lyman Hollowell)

We met the day World War Two ended in 1945 and were together for sixty-five years. I was born in 1923. Lyman was born in 1915 and was ninety-six when I lost him in July of 2011. At the time we met, I was working at 20th Century Fox, and the announcement came that with the surrender of Japan they were going to close the studio to celebrate the occasion. In the process of all that, some people there said, "Let's go out and have lunch!"

So about six or seven of us piled into cars, and someone said, "Where's Lyman?" Somebody else said, "He went home."

"Oh, let's stop by where he's staying and pick him up."

"OK..." So we did that.

Lyman was renting a room from a secretary who was working at Fox, and she at the time was away on location with her boss, so he had the place to himself. When we went to the house, it was an absolute wreck. Someone said, "Lyman, we're going down to the beach. Why don't you come along?"

He had another fellow there he was entertaining who he was hot for when we picked him up, a fellow worker from the studio. So all of us piled back into cars and went down to Hans Drive-In in Santa Monica. While we were there having lunch, I suddenly remembered that I was having a dinner party that night at my house. I made this realization while I was taking a leak in the bathroom at Hans Drive-In, and I thought, "Oh, my God, I've got to get out of here and I can't take these people with me. I have to ditch them..."

I told the group I had to get home because I was expecting some guests. I asked Lyman if he'd like to come to a party but I told him, "I can't ask anybody else and I think you'd understand..." He said yes, he understood.

I had a house in Hollywood at the time, and Lyman said, "I have to go up to Hollywood. Can I go with you?" So Lyman and I took the bus, and when I got to my house, they were partying it up already.

It was a two-bedroom house, and several of the guys stayed overnight, while most of the guys went home. Of course, sex will have its way, and the guys who stayed over ended up sharing beds for the evening. Lyman got in bed with a good friend of mine. My friend left early in the morning, about the time the street cars started to run, which was around 4 a.m. So when he left, I got up, and like a good host, I got into bed with Lyman. The rest of the story you know!

In the morning I got up and was fixing breakfast for everybody, when who should drive up the driveway but my mother and dad and my siblings! I told them we had been partying the night before and some of the guys took the girls home and some of them stayed over, and that worked just fine. After breakfast, I suggested we all go down to the beach, and we did.

From that first night on, Lyman and I were monogamous. We never got around or fucked anybody else. We did have a few friends we liked but we had slept with them before so there was no need to do a reprise. For Lyman and me, sex never became routine. I loved him very much and that was reciprocal. There wasn't anyone else I wanted, and he felt the same. It just happened that way. I can't explain it, and if you think you can, good luck!

We weren't affectionate in public but we had our circle of friends and we lived among them. Lyman and I always slept together and shared a bed every night. We were very compatible, extremely compatible. I loved him with all my heart, and he received that and loved me back. We never broke up or threatened to take our record collection and move out—any of that stuff—and I can't remember any great differences that got in our way at all.

We never had any troubles or fights. It was quite remarkable. We just lived life as it came along. Our falling in love happened pretty quickly. I liked the idea of living with someone, and it just worked out. We invested in real estate and we both worked at the studios, and when things were slow and maybe one of us would be laid off for a while, the other one picked up the slack. Lyman and I did our expenses fifty-fifty and we each kept our own accounts. It was fifty-fifty all the way and that worked out fine.

We had wanted to get married for a long time and we said, "It will come around, so we'll just wait..." In the meantime, we lived together as partners until that came to pass and then we were home free. Our neighbor was a minister, so he and my sister and a couple other friends got together at our house, and we got married that way. A simple ceremony; we didn't do any big thing. We had our honeymoon first, in Laguna.

Lyman and I traveled a lot, so we never had pets. To sustain a pet, you should have constancy, instead of pawning them off on someone to take care of them while you're running around overseas. That isn't fair to the animal. The two of us went around the world three times. The first time we went around on a planned trip offered by TWA. Then as time went along we would go back and visit people we knew in Europe or in Asia, and we just ended up going around the world three times.

Losing your partner is really hard. Lyman and I talked about what it what it would be like to lose each other. We knew it was inevitable one day, but we didn't dwell on it. When the time came, we'd deal with it then.

Lyman had been ill early in the summer, and it settled in his appendix, which became very inflamed and ruptured, and he died quickly. I've had some friends who have been very helpful and supportive. There was no great breakdown or any emotional scenes. Lyman wouldn't have wanted that, and I didn't want that either.

I think of him often and I miss him dreadfully. I'm terribly lonely and I miss the sharing and I hope that I'll be able to share again someday, but I just have to keep going. I don't have any great answers; you just have to do what you do. My health is very good and I'm grateful for that. Your true friends will help you through.

If you meet someone and you want a relationship together, work on it. Just don't run into anything. Go slow and take your time and do it right. Have no secrets; that's the secret.

We were both just about as sensible as can be and our lives were pretty well thought out. I did most of the cooking. Lyman handled most of the finances. He didn't want to cook and didn't know how to cook. I like to cook, so that worked out. He didn't do the dishes because we have a dishwasher. I remember one time many years ago, we were out looking for a new apartment.

We had looked at several and had narrowed it down to a couple of them, so I said, "Which of the two or three apartments do you prefer?"

He said, "Oh, I prefer the second one we looked at."

I said, "OK. Can you tell me why?"

He said, "Yes. It's got a dishwasher."

Why fight City Hall? We took the apartment.

CHAPTER 21
ERIC AND EUGENE

"We're quite different, and he really does irritate me a lot, but I've never loved anybody the way I love him."

* * * * *

In 1953, Eric Marcoux met his life partner Eugene Woodworth through a mutual friend in Chicago. The two moved west and settled in Portland, Oregon, where they recently celebrated their sixtieth anniversary together. A former monk, Eric worked as an art teacher and a psychotherapist, and co-led with Eugene a popular series of personal development workshops for gay men back in the 1970s. Formerly a dancer, Eugene was employed as an engineer in the electronics field. The couple are practicing Buddhists and live with their thirty-three-year-old blue and gold macaw.

Eric Marcoux — (Eugene Woodworth)

Eugene and I were twenty-three and twenty-five when we met sixty years ago. He's eighty-four and I'm eighty-two, so I now sleep with an old man! Next June will be our sixtieth anniversary. My background is that I went into a cloistered monastery, the Trappist monks in Kentucky, when I was almost fourteen. My family wasn't Catholic, so it was entirely my choice. I just knew in my heart that I absolutely needed to do that, and I felt very at home there.

What got me to the monastery? After joining the Catholic church, I began to read books about the saints. Reading books about the saints revealed to me that the recently discovered joys of masturbation would send me to hell for eternity. I remember clearly the night I sat reading *The Lives of the Saints* and realized I would go to hell and burn eternally if I masturbated again. So that began a long spell of trying to do the holy things I read about to keep myself from whacking off. I could go for two weeks at a time, which I think is a heroic thing for a young teenager. I fasted and prayed and slept on the wooden floor of my closet instead of in my bed. I followed the examples of the holy people I read about: I fasted from food and water for days at a time, slept on the bare wooden floor, and beat and cut and burned my body; my body which "failed" me over and over. It became my enemy.

One day, in confession, having yet again confessed "the sin of self-pollution," I was told by the priest to do more penance, to pray more, and to "Go to the Trappists..." I had never heard that word before. I looked it up. Three months later, I was in the monastery. Even though my mother deeply disapproved of this move, she was also dedicated to allowing me to make my own choices.

At twenty-three, I was sent to another house to study and stopped in Chicago to visit my mother. While I was there, I met a man. I was barely conscious of what I was about to do. I was carried away emotionally. We spent three glorious days in bed together. It was an absolute revelation to me. At the end of the three days, I prepared to go to the other monastery where I was headed, to continue studies, and all the guilt came upon me and I called my abbot and told him what had happened. He said to me, "You know, Brother, your simple vows, your temporary vows, are going to expire soon. Just stay there and let them expire and don't come back." So in the course of that brief conversation I was moved out of the twelfth century and into the twentieth.

A few months later, I walked into a restaurant, and there was my friend, Nathan, sitting at a table with a companion whom I'd never seen before. Nathan asked me to come to a party that evening, and I said, "Thanks, but I'm going to a movie with friends," and I went and sat at a distant table.

What happened next was a paranormal experience: I could feel something lift me under my armpits and walk me back to the table, and I said, "Nathan, I've changed my mind. I want to come to your party. Why don't you introduce me to your friend?" That's how I met Eugene, sixty years ago this upcoming June of 2013.

Nathan, who introduced us, was a man I had met a few weeks earlier. He was something of a sexual mentor to me. When he suggested coming to the party, I thought it would be a party where people would sit and chat. I didn't realize that after a certain amount of chatting, they'd all remove their clothes and go off with one, two, or more people.

Eugene pulled me into a bedroom and we made love. I had been living in the twelfth century and was a bit shocked by the whole thing. I was wonderfully innocent, but also intensely in lust. Our togetherness was an enormous experience, and Eugene and I continued to see one another. Several months into it, we decided that we were indeed in love with each other and went off and had a honeymoon. Two years later, we decided to move to Oregon.

Nowadays, when Eugene and I make presentations at universities about the needs of elderly gay people and we share an autobiographical piece, Eugene describes our early days this way: "We met. We made love. And then we courted." That's a not-uncommon sequence for human beings to experience in a new relationship.

We were sexually exclusive out of innocence and naiveté for many years, and that was OK. Remember that those were days when people like us could live without even knowing other gay people or knowing very few, so we didn't have other people to exchange ideas with or think about different models of how to relate, so ours was a monogamous one. In the late 1960s and early 1970s, we were more sophisticated, so when Eugene would go to Seattle, it was taken for granted that he'd go to the steams or the bars and have fun with other guys, and I would do the same thing. Then later we'd talk about our experiences with great joy and delight. But there was a kind of territorial definition which forbade us from calling and saying, "I'm next door and Ted and I want to go to bed together. I'll be home late, dear."

The geographical distancing was an important factor. There were also a few occasions during those years where the two of us would be involved with a couple of other people in sex play and pleasure and affection. But what has characterized our relationship is that neither of us has ever wanted to be in love with another person. The polar opposite of that, perhaps, is just using people, but we were most definitely not thinking of sexual play with others as just using people. That sounds awfully noble, but that's exactly what we quite consciously committed ourselves to.

Eugene had had a very extensive sexual life before he met me, and I really hadn't had any at all. I'm very grateful that I had the opportunity in the 1960s and '70s to play around with other guys, to discover what it was like to be in bed with various men. And now it's been a long time since we've particularly even wanted to have sex with anybody else. After a certain amount of that experience, it was like, "Oh, I know what that will be. I don't need to do that. It's too much of a hassle."

We frequently say to our straight friends that one of the things we love about being in a same-gender relationship is that we can look at other people and talk about other people sexually. We enjoy looking at pornography together and having a good wank at the same time, and it isn't that I want to be with those people; it's another form of very powerful intimacy with this man whom I love very much. A "nooner" used to refresh us; now it knocks us out for two days. We don't have sex as much as we used to, but our sexuality is very important to us.

I'm very grateful for the Internet. I discovered it in 2001, with great interest, as a male and as a psychotherapist and as a Buddhist practitioner. I found myself learning so much about human beings and their needs and their desires, and some of them I'd just as soon know very little about! But I am incredibly grateful for the sense of how it is to be human and to be sexual in all sorts of ways, without having any need to go out and do them.

Eugene and I touch each other a great deal. We sleep in separate beds now, which started out with snoring. I have sleep apnea and I sleep with equipment, but every night, he tucks me in and we say "I love you" many times for the next five minutes as he gets himself into his own bed, and that's meant as a goodbye because one day it will be a goodbye. In the morning I get up and crawl into bed with him and we cuddle for a while.

During the day we touch one another frequently, hand on hand, hand on face, we lean into each other... We really like touching one another, and verbally we're also very warm and affectionate. Our pet bird is really jealous.

I have trouble walking. Our legs have gotten bad as we've gotten older, and mine are quite bad the last year or so. So I ask Eugene to do things for me frequently, but I constantly assess, "Is that going to be an interruption or too much for him?" It's just part of my mental equipment to be thoughtful about asking him to do things for me and not taking him for granted. In 1994, when I started going back to visit my old monastery—I'd go for two or three weeks at a time, two or three times a year—I would find myself frequently thinking about him and how much I like him.

He's a good man, though he drives me crazy because our behavior patterns are singularly different. We're quite different, and he really does irritate me a lot, but I've never loved anybody the way I love him. When I'd travel, I would think a lot about him, not so much in the sense of "Oh my God, I'm missing him," but just, "This is a good person, and I'm glad that his life and mine are connected."

We're both very egotistical, because we're human beings, but as our obsession with our narcissistic needs has softened and matured with the years, we see more of one another as someone we're cherishing in and of and for themselves and not just an extension of our own needs. That's a conscious stance that we both have learned and have held for many years now, from our spiritual path as Catholics and then Buddhists and also from things we experienced in the human potential movement in the '70s. Those things contributed immensely to our consciously working to develop a sense of the other person as valuable and lovable in themselves, and not just an extension or function of our own needs.

I have the inclination and vocabulary to talk about feelings whence they arise—what they're doing and where they might go or shouldn't go—and Eugene doesn't have that particular passion. There have been times when his disinclination to talk about emotions has been problematic. He's learned to at least sit there and let me go on and on and on, and not in a wounded, victim-y way. He's patient with my need to articulate stuff and to get feedback. He's very direct and honest.

We've never been secretive about our feelings with one another. We've had some tough times, but I don't think either of us has ever, ever seriously said, "I need to get out of here." I'm very committed to telling people that if their relationship is really toxic, they should get the hell out of it. But difficult is not the same as toxic. Difficult is something that can be worked with.

We're more patient now and we've weathered challenging times, but we've never been on the verge of separating. It isn't as though our relationship is always in the process of being worked on but—and this comes from my monastic training as a novice—it was made clear that the spiritual path could be very sweet for a while and then it would inevitably get very dry, and there would be times when it would be very bitter. And there would be times of doubt about its validity, and then times when it would be sweet again … In other words, a committed relationship requires love and patience.

Eugene and I are both practicing Buddhists in the Tibetan tradition, with a minimum of cultural "drag." We were practicing Catholics for many years. We actually tried to be celibate for a while, though that was not successful. Thank goodness. One of my monastic friends, a young abbot, said to us one day, "Forget worrying about it. Love one another and be grateful to God that you have this relationship," and we took him at his word and continued practicing as Catholics. On our twenty-fourth anniversary, we decided to make a commitment to one another. One of our friends is a rogue Franciscan, who married us. We had a wedding ceremony here in the house with a couple hundred people.

I had first become interested in Buddhism back when I was a monk. In 1970, a great Tibetan Buddhist teacher came to Portland, and I made a decision: "This is the path I want to follow. I'll set the other one aside. I really need to step into another thing." So I began practicing and studying, and eventually one of the important lamas in the tradition appointed me as a resident lama of a small group of people who were students. I've been doing that for about twenty-five years now.

Buddhism is a wonderful model for working with one's mind and emotions. It is extraordinarily subtle, easily available, and very, very powerful. It has helped me immensely in cultivating greater patience and in being there for people in a way that my own narcissistic needs don't cause trouble. It's just a damn good working model. I am committed to not perceiving it or teaching Buddhism in terms of "Now this is the real truth, compared to other truths." It is simply one of many ways of working, and for the people for whom it works, it works very effectively.

I'm very grateful to be in a position where I can help pass on to others what I've received from the tradition. Eugene considers himself a student of mine. He doesn't have the same passion for intellectual modeling that I do but he practices with the same degree of commitment and interest in making himself a kinder person.

The only way we can learn to be gentle and kind and of value to people in the world, as well as of value to ourselves, is in relationship. That doesn't necessarily mean in a primary, intimate relationship. We humans are wired to be in a group; we need to be a piece of a group. Loving Eugene teaches me how to be kind to other people and kind to myself as well. I don't think one can wake up out of one's cultural ignorance except in a relationship with another person who can push the buttons—the buttons of love as well as the buttons of irritation and impatience. There are other types of intimate relationships, such as teacher and student, which can serve this purpose, too.

Eugene and I like to do impulsive things for one another. He'll bring home a pot full of those lovely orchids that show up in the shops these days, that wouldn't have been available when either of us were young men. He's more inclined to do that than I am, but he tells me that I surprise him sometimes with the food I make for him. I'm the chef, but as we've gotten older, the meals have gotten simpler and simpler and simpler. In fifty-nine years, I've made three or four meals a day, almost all of those days, with rare exceptions, and I'm kind of tired of being inventive! But I must have been a short-order cook in another life. Rarely do I plan a meal; I simply go to the refrigerator and look in and go, "What do I do now?" I even surprise myself sometimes with what I come up with.

Eugene has maintained the more regular jobs over the years, so it was natural for me to assume the responsibility for things that I would have time to do, like cooking. We were vegetarians for almost twenty years, though not for great philosophical reasons. These days I don't cook meat, though I don't consider bacon meat anymore—I've decided it isn't meat—and I will put some in the oven periodically so we can have crispy bacon. I really don't like handling meat anymore. Much of our protein comes from dairy products, and I sometimes cook with tofu.

When Eugene and I moved out here, I met a nun who was the head of the art department in the local college, and she was very intuitive and insightful about me and she insisted I go to art school. So I got a degree in art and I taught painting and figure drawing for fifteen years. Then I got interested in psychotherapy and I took the necessary training and did private counseling for many years.

In the 1970s, Eugene and I experienced human potential trainings, and there wasn't really a place that was safe for gay men and women to do trainings of that sort, so I was actually asked by someone to do one of these intense emotional workshops for a small group of gay men and I ended up doing those for fifteen years. Then the Buddhist thing started, and my energy went into that direction. That's what I've been doing all these years. But all of those activities have related to one another very nicely from my perspective.

From the beginning, Eugene and I have pooled our monies. We each have an account in common and a small account on the side. It's just more convenient sometimes to be able to do it that way. But for all practical purposes, all the cookies are in the same cookie jar, and we both feel that that's really important.

It looks like marriage will be legal in Oregon within a couple years, and I remember that we brought this question up with an attorney we were consulting a few years ago as we began to realize we need an executor for what little bit we would have to leave behind. He said, "People your age are usually advised to get divorced. It's financially far more beneficial for you. It has to do with catastrophic illness: if you're married, all your funds are considered a lump, whereas for two separate people, only one of them would have to spend down whatever little he or she had saved." So we probably won't marry.

Eugene tells me that many decades ago, we had a conversation about "Wouldn't it be nice to be parents," but I don't remember it. I am really good with adults and interacting with adults and have been ever since I was a small child, but I'm not comfortable with children so I don't want children. When people say, "How can you not have had children?," I remind them that I have many children, only they're adults! I've been a teacher all these years, hopefully a teacher of importance to a few people.

For our fortieth anniversary, Eugene and I were talking about having a Buddhist ceremony. The husband and wife abbots of the Zen Buddhist temple here—dear friends of ours—said, "We haven't done anything yet for the gay community particularly," so they gave us the space and hosted the whole thing, and we made our vows to one another and integrated them into a piece of the Buddhist text. That was our fortieth.

When it came time for our fiftieth, we wanted to renew our vows, and they said, "Good. Do it here. Use the temple, and we will host the whole thing and prepare all the food." So we had a formal repeating of our vows, and we found more mature ways of expressing them on our fiftieth than we had on our fortieth. I'm sure we'll do something similar for our sixtieth.

I'm very grateful for having the Buddhist path as a heritage. I'm not a true believer in the sense of "This is the only way to go." Thank you, no. That's not so. But it really nourishes me—same with Eugene—so this was really a very important path for us. We renew our vows together once a month. I wrote the vows for us, and they're inserted in a very simple way into a kind of Buddhist verbal envelope, and we do that every month.

On occasion we forget. We forgot this month. But remembering to renew our vows has really been an important piece in our training of loving one another, because we might be having an argument about something and I'll say, "Well it's time to go to the shrine room and do our wedding vows..." There we sit across from one another, reciting words that bind us together and remind us of our commitment. I have tried to persuade many people—I don't know how many successfully—who, after they write their vows, to at least repeat them to each other, if not every month, at least every six months.

This goes back to my monastic training: it's helpful to have a belief that it's good to be in a relationship in a particular way. In the monastic environment, it was the belief that it's good to be a relationship with a community of other people on a spiritual path, and that one's growth is dependent upon how we interact with one another, whether it's with the community or whether it's with this one other person in a marriage.

So believing that it is good for people to be married in general, with some very definite exceptions, is one of the sustaining elements in our relationship. It's in the background when things are difficult or when we're bored or just tired.

One of the things we find is that our bodies are old, and sometimes one is incredibly more vulnerable to emotional discomfort than when we were younger, so it's important to have that commitment to being with this person even when it's difficult. It's being attentive to knowing what it is to love somebody and be willing to work on things. Be willing to be bored with somebody and know that you love them even when you're bored with them and when they're bored with you. Again, it's the ups and downs, the passage through the flower garden into the vegetable garden into the fields and into the dry fields and back and forth again...

It's important to cultivate a real interest in how people are and be willing to see their positive qualities but also to recognize that the things we don't like about them come from their own wounds. And not to just see someone as a function of making me happy, and above all not to think that one person is going to make one absolutely happy. It's not the task of anyone to make anyone else totally happy. I am so grateful for my companion. I am so grateful for my lover. The thought that someday he or I will die and leave the other alone is very difficult, but nonetheless we both know that in a very real way we're on our own now as well. So instead of "You've got to fill this hole that's in me," it's "Maybe we can both hold hands next to the hole."

Obviously a relationship is a lot more than sexuality, but I also think that a relationship without sexuality is lacking something really important. It's been our experience that because our bodies are tired it gets easier to go longer without having sex. I know there have been times when I've said, "We really need to make love even if we don't feel in the mood for it." And I think this is one of the gifts especially that gay men can give to one another—the willingness to talk about sex and to be honest about our needs.

I think that this type of discourse is part of the healthy discourse for our contemporary society, and we gay men especially have a lot to contribute just through our honesty about the whole thing, and we enjoy sharing our own perspective. Eugene and I are doing this interview now, and then the newspaper wants to do one, and we've been in the newspapers more than a few times over the years, which is all well and good. But I keep thinking, "God, there are other couples out there!" I'm tired of just seeing my picture or seeing Eugene and I as sort of being the archetypal old gay men who haven't killed one another and are therefore somehow admirable...

About six months ago, a woman was here from an important New York marriage equality organization, and she said, "You know, it's interesting that of the many men working for me, those who are in their fifties and sixties say, "Why would anyone want to get married? I am having one hell of a sex life and am not ashamed or feeling guilty about it." Whereas the younger men say, "Well, it's great to play around but I really want to meet the right person and settle down and maybe have a couple of children..." She found the contrast between the two quite interesting.

Times have changed a great deal, and these days, there's far less for these younger people to process. They haven't been marginalized to the same extent that older gay people have. I hope I can live another five or ten years to see how things shift and change, even in that short a period of time. I'm actually grateful to George Bush for having said the words "same-sex marriage" and put those words on the lips of millions of Americans, who just said, "WHAT???" And they've been talking about it ever since, and just the talking about it—whether with approval or disapproval—is so important.

CHAPTER 23

EUGENE AND ERIC

---

*"All the time we're touching each other back and forth through-
out the day and saying, "I love you, I love you, I love you." That
might be monotonous to some people, but it's very meaningful to
us. If I'm passing him in the room I will touch his back or kiss his
head or something like that, and he does the same thing with me."*

* * * * *

In 1953, Eugene Woodworth met his life partner, Eric
Marcoux through a mutual friend in Chicago. The two moved
west and settled in Portland, Oregon, where they recently
celebrated their sixtieth anniversary together. A former monk,
Eric worked as an art teacher and a psychotherapist, and co-led
with Eugene a popular series of personal development workshops for gay men back in the 1970s. Formerly a dancer, Eugene
was employed as an engineer in the electronics field. The couple
are practicing Buddhists and live with their thirty-three year old
blue and gold macaw.

**Author's Note: Although I'd been out of the closet for all
practical purposes for years, I had only come out to a select few
people at my current, mostly conservative workplace. After
interviewing Eugene, I decided to take his advice and come out
to my entire department, which proved to be a good experience.
I am grateful to both Eugene and Eric for the integrity of their
example.*

Eugene Woodworth — (Eric Marcoux)

We've been together fifty-nine and a half years. Our sixtieth anniversary
will be in June of 2013, on the 11th. Eric was twenty-three and I was
twenty-five when we met, so I'm now eighty-four and he's eighty-two.

Before we met, I was studying to become a ballet dancer. I was working for three different companies in Chicago and had a company of my own. I had tried teaching children and gave up after three classes because I couldn't stand the mothers! One Sunday afternoon, I was just sitting at a lunch table with a friend of mine—we had just come back from the beach—and we were having a conversation. All of a sudden, a figure appeared at my right shoulder. I couldn't see who it was, but there was this electric shock, and my body froze and I couldn't breathe... There was this conversation going on between my friend and this new figure, which went something like, "Eric, I'm going to have a party tonight. Would you like to come?"

And the figure said, "No, Nathan, I'm going to be going to the movies with some friends over there. Thank you for offering and see you later."

He went back behind me, and I still couldn't see him. I was able to start breathing again after he left, so we continued our conversation across the table. All of a sudden, the same thing happened; I couldn't breathe again, and there was another electric shock, and I froze in place.

So I waited, and this new figure said, "Nathan, I've decided to come to your party. Won't you introduce me to your friend?" Well, by that time, I was already deeply in love because I had turned and looked at him, and WHAMMO! What a face. What a body. I almost couldn't take it! I shook hands with him and kind of stuttered around. So we made arrangements to meet at Nathan's party, and I went home and got cleaned up. I don't know what he did.

When I finally got to Nathan's party, there was Eric, trapped in the kitchen by a very handsome, very large, husky man, who we found out later was a lawyer from New York. He wanted Eric to become his boy in New York. Well, when I walked in and saw what was going on, I thought, "Uh, oh, there goes my date..." With that, Eric ducked out from under his arm and said, "Excuse me, this is my date!"

He came over to me, and we enjoyed the evening together and then went out and had a late lunch or early dinner. As we walked in, both the waitress and the cashier said, "Oh, you're twins aren't you?," and that has stuck with us for the rest of our lives. Hardly a day goes by that somebody doesn't say, "Oh, you're brothers," or "Oh, you're twins." When we look back at our early pictures, we do look a little bit alike, and people still see it. Even our mothers were constantly getting us mixed up.

Now when we met and Eric said he was going to the movie with friends, he had stepped back to sit down with his friends at a table about thirty feet away, and something lifted him up under his arms and propelled him back over to Nathan's table. That's the second part of the story. So I think it was actually a deep magnetism of some sort, like two souls finding each other. A lot of people say that we share the same aura. That might be. I feel that we do, though I'm not sure exactly what an aura is.

It's funny, but when I shook hands with Eric and looked at his face for the first time, I knew right then and there I was going to have to give up my career as a ballet dancer and get a real job, because I was going to be a family man. I just knew that. And I did, even though I was getting really good reviews in the papers, and some of the people from New York were coming out and seeing me. I hadn't gotten around to signing any papers or anything yet, but when I met Eric, that was the end of that. Right then on the spot. I think our commitment was made even before we were introduced, so we both knew we loved each other before being introduced.

We were first sexual together at the party, very briefly. Then we scheduled a date for Wednesday night to go to the movies and also made arrangements to meet the following Saturday to take a room at the YMCA. I knew a little YMCA that was outside the main part of town—I had been there before—and we went out and got a room with a double bed and stayed in it most of the weekend.

We've been sexually exclusive throughout the years with the exception of a few years during the Age of Aquarius, when everybody was doing everybody else. At that point, Eric was going to Seattle every couple months for the weekend to visit an older friend who lived out on the island. We'd go up there and spend the night in the baths and have a good time. That's pretty much the only outside sex we ever had. We're still sexual today in a rather vanilla way. We still love each other very much and we love having sex with each other, but it's nothing spectacular. It's a commitment, a positiveness.

All the time, we're touching each other back and forth throughout the day and saying, "I love you, I love you, I love you." That might be monotonous to some people, but it's very meaningful to us. If I'm passing him in the room, I will touch his back or kiss his head or something like that, and he does the same thing with me. I never take Eric for granted because I never know what he's going to do.

As far as fooling around with other guys, I have no feelings about that at all, and if he does he does. We have an agreement that if it happens occasionally, that's alright, as long as we're careful and don't get caught or don't get AIDS or whatever. But that's only very occasionally; every couple of years that might happen. Once in a while, it happens in the steam room at the gym that we go to. We don't do it covertly or intentionally. A spur of the moment sort of thing is what I'm talking about.

We slept together clear up until, oh, about fifteen years together. He decided I snore too much, so we started keeping separate bedrooms. We still get together every morning and snuggle and say "I love you," and thank each other for coming back. We're at the stage now where it's really exciting to see our loved one in the morning, after having been apart for eight hours and not knowing whether or not he will be there. To have him walk in the room is just very, very exciting.

Our love for each other has deepened over time. Just being with somebody for a long time, it deepens. A lot of people don't allow themselves to feel that, and that's why their relationships crumble. So many people base the relationship on sex only, and then when the sex starts to get old and boring they split. That's when the relationship really begins! Our love was based on being together; we knew we were supposed to be together. That has never left. Later on, as sex became less and less possible because of our age, we still loved each other and we still do. Love will grow with the relationship if you let it, unless the relationship is based strictly on lust.

We've always lived together and have never been out of each other's sight except for the occasional vacation. Sometimes we take our vacations together and other times we take them apart. The ones apart are usually for very specific reasons. I took my vacation to visit my mother and dad, who are both now dead, and Eric took his vacation to go back to the monastery that he was in for nine years. Sometimes I went with him, and other times he went alone.

We just enjoy being together. We really do. We've been to Italy together seven times. The first time we were there, we drove a car all around Italy for three weeks and had a great time. We didn't want to take a public tour so we learned a few words of Italian and just went and explored the country on our own.

My abruptness is probably our biggest communication hurdle. He asks a question, and I will try and answer it almost immediately and sometimes am too loud and too brusque about it. Every few days, we'll go through a corrective period, where I have something to say about something he's doing, and he has something to say about my actions. But it's a very loving exchange. He's trying to make me a better person, and I'm trying to make him a better person, by our own standards.

I don't think either of us have ever felt crowded together except when I was snoring, and that was on a California king-size bed. He would roll over and push me and say, "You're snoring again!" Once he rolled over and his elbow hit my nose and broke it! It was unintentional, I know.

Eric came from a middle-class family in Detroit, and I was born into a very low-class family in Chicago, during the Depression. I was brought up a Methodist, and my family said I could go out and try other religions and see what I wanted to do. I shocked them all by becoming a Catholic when I met Eric, since some sort of Protestant denomination would have been more what they were expecting.

Later, when Eric started studying Buddhism and became a teacher, I became his student, which shocked them even more! They couldn't get over the fact that I was a Buddhist. "You don't believe in *GOD*?," and all that stuff ... But they handled it. From the beginning they accepted Eric as their second son, even though they could not understand or appreciate our relationship. They were very warm with him, as they would be with any other relative. The only difference was that whenever the two of us went to visit them on our vacation, Eric would be assigned the front bedroom and I would be assigned the back bedroom. We weren't allowed to sleep together, and I confronted my mother about that after my dad died. I said, "You know, when Marilyn comes with her husband, you put both of them in the front bedroom, but when Eric and I come, you separate us. Why is that?"

"Well uh, uh..."

I said, "Look, we *love* each other. Just like you and dad love each other, we love each other." She still had a hard time with that.

We would love to get married. There is something about marriage that is special. We've had two religious ceremonies. The first one was performed by a Catholic monk, and the other was at the Buddhist Church here. The first one was on our twenty-fourth anniversary, with the Catholic monk. At the time of the wedding itself, we had two hundred fifty people in our own home. The house was packed! People were standing in the bedroom and sitting on the bed, and there were probably another one hundred fifty people before and another one hundred fifty there after the ceremony. It was a pretty big crowd. They were coming and going constantly, and we had an open house all day long, with the ceremony right in the middle.

We didn't have a lot of notoriety at the time of the first one, other than that there was a surge of articles in *The Oregonian*, our local paper. One of them was about gay teachers. Another one was about us, and I don't recall what the third article was, maybe about religion. That was pretty close to the time of our twenty-fourth anniversary.

Then, when our fortieth came around, our friends at a Zen Buddhist church said, "Why don't you come on over here? We'll marry you." It was great. So we went over and they had a full wedding ceremony for us, and somehow the local paper again found out about it and sent the religion editor, who's a wonderful woman, and who wrote a fantastically beautiful half-page story about us. There was a half-page photograph, too.

Something wonderful which happened as a result of that article was that we were going to the senior exercise class at the gym, and had been there about ten years at that point. We were open with everybody from the very beginning, so everybody knew us, and a lot of them were invited to the wedding. So when this article came out, several people found it and thought it was great, so they hung it on the bulletin board in the exercise room.

Well, within a week everybody in the entire place had read it. They already knew us, but now they knew we were married, and it made a big difference.

Afterwards they made a point of being friendly, and it was a marvelous example of what can happen when people are fully open. That's happened more than once in other situations too, where we open up to who we are and what we are, and barriers just break down. I try and encourage everyone to come out of their closet, no matter what kind of a closet it might be; most people have one. Come out of the closet and show your real self, your whole self, and watch the difference. I sometimes say, "You might lose your family and you might lose your job, but it's worth it." It really is. It's that important.

I tend to be very loud in my laughter, especially at a television show or movie. Eric will sit back and sort of half-smile, and I'll say, "Are you enjoying it?"

"Oh, yeah. Yeah!"

"Well, how come you don't laugh?"

"I am laughing!"

He's just a quiet laugher, where sometimes, I just erupt in loud laughter. I can't help it.

Every once in a while, he'll make a special dinner for me without my expecting it, or I will occasionally bring him flowers. Eric makes our dinners, and I do the laundry. We both share everything. Sometimes I do the cooking and he does the dish-washing. I make extremely good pimento olive bread, which everybody raves about and can't get enough of. About the only thing that I prepare besides that is a vegetable stew, which we both enjoy. I do most of the shopping because he has a hard time getting around. So we drive to the store together, and he sits and listens to the radio while I go and do the shopping.

Occasionally, I'll buy him a bouquet of flowers or something special. The other day, I saw two cute little hats. They were children's hats, and one was a monkey face and the other one was an elephant. So I bought the two of them and gave Eric the elephant, so he can prove that he always remembers, and I took the monkey face because of what they call "monkey mind" in Buddhism, which is a mind that jumps around all the time.

In the late 1960s and early '70s, we went through a great series of personal growth workshops. We had heard about the first one, and Eric said, "Oh, that sounds just like something you could really benefit from." So I went through it and came out and said, "Buddy, you're going to go through it, too!" It was that good. So he went through it, too. We did the later ones, the more intense workshops, together. We went to quite a few other personal awareness organizations and different schools and teachers and learned a lot and worked for several of them as assistants too.

Finally, Eric said, "I think we should start our own gay personal growth workshops just for gay men. So many gay men just won't go to these workshops because they aren't geared really for them, and they feel like the outsiders. Even if they wouldn't be excluded in any way, they might feel as if they were." So Eric started that up, and I was his assistant, and we conducted workshops for eleven years in our own home and occasionally up in Seattle. The training would run four or five days, starting on Thursday night. That was the basic one, and then the second one was more intense and would start on Friday night. The third training lasted over three months, and was like five or six hours once a month for three months. We saw fantastic results happening to people, and they happened to us as well. Those were very bonding experiences for us.

Pretty much from the very beginning, we've had one bank account, which was available to both of us. It was mainly my job and still is my job to pay the bills out of that fund. We each have a small separate account, sort of a mad money account, that we can buy little things with and work on the Internet with. When we met, we did have a couple of separate accounts at different banks and finally decided it was a waste of time and money to do that, so we consolidated everything into the credit union. Having one primary account has worked out well for us, and everything we own is in both names or "survivor." It's a good feeling to know that family can't come in and get it after one person dies.

We never had children but we've had many pets. We started out with birds, and during the time we had birds, we also had cavies and hamsters. We gave up the cavies and hamsters very early on but continued with the birds. When we moved to Portland, we brought the birds we had along with us. After the birds died, we switched to cats. A friend of ours was raising Siamese Seal-point cats, so we got one of the daughters and loved her so much. Later we got another one, and after that, a yellow-headed parrot, and we trained him. He was a good friend and was very comfortable with both of us. More recently we went out and got a blue and gold cockatoo, and that's been Eric's bird. I keep saying that I want to have another cat, but not with a bird though. So the bird is now thirty-two and has still got another thirty-five years to go.

Consistency and continuity keep our relationship growing. By consistency, I mean we are constantly telling each other "I love you" and constantly touching each other. For a relationship to last, make sure that it's based on love rather than lust. There's nothing wrong with lust, but it may not last all that long. You need love, affection, and the give-and-take to discuss things, to allow each other to make mistakes and then to be corrective, and also to accept correction.

When we met, Eric had had very few experiences. He'd been in a monastery up until about six months before we met and was living with a friend whom he knew from the monastery, who wound up being straight after they broke up. My own history goes back a long ways, having sex with lots and lots and lots of guys and occasionally having a very short-term relationship of a week or so. But I would suggest to anybody, "Don't look for a relationship. When you meet the right person, it will come to you." I'm not saying to close your eyes. Look around and make eye contact with people and start friendships.

A lot of long-term relationships we know of started off with people who knew each other already. In several cases, the partners died on both sides, and because they were friends, they decided, "Well, let's try living together and see what happens," and they ended up being long-term lovers. That happened to at least two couples we know of personally.

But my point is not to look too hard, and if you don't get a permanent lover, so what? You can still be a healthy, attractive human being and enjoy sex with other people. We belong to a group called Gay & Gray, which is for both men and women over age sixty-five. Some are in relationships and some aren't, and we get together once a month for a lunch at one of the little local restaurants. It's just us in the great big room and we have a real good time and introduce friends to each other and so forth. Sometimes a nice relationship gets started. A lot of people drop out and a lot of people come in fresh. But it's very nice to be in a room with other people sixty-five years of age on up, and to know that you're all family.

We've talked about how we will deal with dying and we use the term *when*, not *if*. We talk about plans, such as it would be nice to have a going-away party if there's time to do it and invite all our friends. And if there's not that kind of time, then a party can be held afterwards, a wake, and just invite everybody over and have a big dinner and drinks and have a good time.

As far as the feelings of missing each other, we can't tell until that actually happens. We will certainly miss each other. The thought of missing him in the morning when he comes in, or him coming in and finding an empty bed; that's what we've talked about. There's really nothing we can do except be open in communication with each other. We both intend to be cremated, and what happens to the ashes is whatever will happen, whether they get distributed over the sea or dug into a landfill. We don't know yet.

We'd definitely like to make it to our sixtieth anniversary in June of 2013, and probably have another re-commitment ceremony at the Buddhist church. The last one was catered by the church, and I'd like to have the ceremony there at least, and then whatever else we decide to do.

There's a community center in Portland called Friendly House, about four blocks from here. We went in one day and they said, "Hey! Would you guys like to volunteer to talk to a group of nurse students?" I said, "Sure, we can try it," and we've been doing it ever since. It's an organized platform or routine that we use, and there's a moderator who gives a background of the group and why we're doing what we're doing, and then there are usually three people who tell their life story, who put a face to old age. We wind up passing out photographs of ourselves as we were in the past and as we are now, so they can relate to the changes. Everybody always talks about how hot we look in the early photo. When it comes to question time, I usually start out by saying, "Ask any question you want. We have no secrets at all. And if you'd feel better asking us when we get out to the hall after the talk is over, you can do it privately." We just make ourselves wide open.

We have a table in the living room, a beautiful old library table, and it's covered with all sizes of photographs taken from the very beginning up until the present day, about forty photographs. It's quite something to see us over all those different years and how we've changed and haven't changed. I went from being a dancer to being with Eric.

A few years back, the Buddhist church was having a talent show and they said, "Are you going to do something for us?" I said, "Well I haven't danced in a long time but I think I've got one I can put on," so I did. It was one that was very slow and quiet. There was not a lot of jumping and moving around, and it went over fine. Everybody loved it.

CHAPTER 23

ERIC MARCOUX –
ON LOSING A PARTNER OF SIXTY YEARS

Author's Note: When I learned that Eric and Eugene had gone to Washington state in early December 2013 to marry, I called to congratulate them right after Christmas. We had long since established a warm and friendly phone rapport and I enjoyed calling them semi-regularly. I knew Eugene had been struggling with congestive heart failure, and Eric quietly informed me that Eugene had died four days before Christmas. We talked at length, and I asked him how he was coping with the loss.

Several days later, I asked Eric if he would be open to interview with me, this time on what it's like to lose a partner of sixty years, and without hesitation he said yes. We did the interview approximately ten days after Eugene's death. Additional questions occurred to me later which I had not thought to bring up then, and when I asked Eric if we could do a follow-up interview, he again immediately agreed. This second interview took place two weeks later.

Six months later, we did a part three interview. Each time I was impressed—as I always am—with Eric's clarity, his total candor, and the depth of his wisdom. The loss of a longtime partner to death is a universal human experience, and Eric's sharing on what it has been like to lose Eugene is both deeply moving and profoundly beautiful. I am honored to include it here.

PART ONE - JANUARY 1, 2014: ELEVEN DAYS AFTER EUGENE'S DEATH

I've lost twenty-three pounds in the last two weeks since Eugene died, but I'm being careful to see to it that I get some protein and some fruit juice so that I'm not starving. But I might as well take advantage of what's going on in my body and my heart with Eugene's death and get rid of some of my extra weight.

I'm being really good about accepting assistance and asking for it when I need to. I have always known that was important and I've helped a lot of clients over the years to do that, but there's still been this sense of, "Well, if I were a good person I'd be able to handle this all alone..." That's simply not true, not just emotionally, but I'm now eighty-three years old and feeling eighty-three years old at times. I don't have the strength I used to have, so there are some things that I just really have to ask people and I'm able to do that now without embarrassment or shame.

Eugene and I always felt married, really from the moment we met. We did make vows to one another and a formal commitment on our twenty-fourth anniversary. Later, Eugene and I became practicing Buddhists, and I've now been a teacher in the Tibetan Buddhist tradition for about twenty-four years with a responsibility for a small group of people. On our fortieth anniversary, we had a marriage ceremony at our Zen temple, and we renewed our vows there on our fiftieth anniversary. So the irony of our recent wedding in Washington is that we've already been married twice in terms of our emotional and spiritual commitment.

So what brought us to the point that we wanted to go to Vancouver? There are some practical matters which have to do with the passing of funds from one to the other. My income is absolutely minimal, and Eugene's is very modest, consequently my Social Security is very low and his is about five times more; enough to make a difference in my life as I get older and find my own way out. So we decided that we would do that and that it would be useful, and also because for various reasons, we've become well known through the newspapers and through interviews with us; we're kind of the old poster children of the marriage equal rights movement. So we went to Vancouver, Washington and got a marriage license and three days later, we returned to do the wedding ceremony. Eugene was in a wheelchair, and our two friends—as witnesses—-wheeled him around.

There we were, waiting for the marriage ceremonies to begin, in a room with about five other couples, all waiting for a wedding. It was all very jolly, people friendly and warm talking back and forth, and then we were called one couple at a time in to the judge. The judge was a very attractive blond woman who was absolutely present. Professionally and humanly, I was just so impressed by her, her gentleness and firmness and professionalism and caring. She stood right up close in front of us and ran us through the vows, and it made us cry. Why? Because whoever had put the vows together had done a wonderful job. There's not a mention of religion at all. None. It's absolutely peak, valuable humanism, and offered ample instruction about what we should do and how we should be in the marriage without being too teach-y or preachy. And then it was over, and we came home. That was on a Thursday.

Friday, we had a meeting with the cardiologist. As the wheelchair Eugene went to be married in indicated, he was getting weaker. His congestive heart failure was making it ever more difficult to breathe and he was often overcome with exhaustion. We saw his cardiologist on Friday, and she said, "Well, I'm sorry, my dear, but it's happening faster than we had anticipated. You only have a few weeks." Now this came as a surprise and not as a surprise. We really thought there was going to be more time.

The next two weeks were spent signing up with hospice and we met a wonderful nurse, doctor, and social worker who came and visited and interviewed. A bed was delivered to the house for Eugene to use when he needed to be down on the first floor, and day by day, he had more trouble breathing and more devastating exhaustion. One medication he had to help him breathe easier gave him a mild seizure several times the first day, so it was very frightening.

Fortunately for us, we've been working for a long time with the idea of death. Our Buddhist teachings remind us in all sorts of contexts about impermanence and our mortality and how important it is to be aware of that, not as something grim and awful but just a reality, so that we're not totally surprised. And I'm grateful for that because I found that neither of us were saying, "How could this happen? This shouldn't happen..." Rather we were saying, "God, this is so painful separating from one another." So our pain of impending separation was in some ways more acute but it wasn't polluted by all the other business of, "Well, this shouldn't happen," and so forth.

I didn't know what to do during the first three days where Eugene was acutely weak and needed a little bit of morphine to help him breathe. Prior to that, I'd always known, "OK, it's time to take me to the emergency room or take Eugene to the emergency room," but he had said, "I want to die in my own home." We talked about that to the hospice doctor who visited us, and she was supportive of his wish and was very honest with us about what we could expect ahead. So as things got worse, he and I just rode them out as best we could. He slept a lot. By the twenty-first of December, Eugene hadn't come downstairs in three days. He had gone upstairs because he said, "I don't want to sleep in the hospice bed. I want to sleep in my own bed. That's my quality of life and as long as I can make it I'm going to do it." Then he was stuck upstairs in the bedroom by sheer weakness and difficulty in breathing.

But on Saturday, the twenty-first, he came downstairs in the late afternoon and said, "I can shower!" Eugene loved showers. We have a wonderful, big shower, and he hopped into the shower room, and I stood outside the door listening to him. He was cooing and purring like a big animal; "Ooh! Oh my! This is so good... This feels so wonderful!" He did go on and on, and I finally opened the door and said, "Do you have a man in there?" He laughed and said, "No, this is even better!"

About two minutes later, he turned the shower off and stepped out of the shower, and I handed him a towel. He dried the top of his chest quickly and handed it back. I dried the top of his shoulders, and he said, "I'm dizzy...," and fell back naked in my arms and died. Like that. Boom.

By the time I had angled him down on the toilet, he was dead. There were the three final exhalations that made me know for sure he was gone. I had to lean him against the wall a little bit, sitting on the toilet, and made a call to one of my students, who's a psychiatrist and a physician, and he said, "I'll be there in a moment." Dr. George is a dear friend who lost his lover to AIDS ten years ago.

I sat for twenty-five minutes and looked at Eugene with love and just drank in how beautiful he was. I covered his nakedness with a little towel because I knew there would be police and fire people in later and I took his one arm that had fallen down and put it in his lap and wrapped a Buddhist rosary around his wrist. I said some of the things that we Buddhists are supposed to say to people as they die, which really are instructions to the living on how to feel about what's going on; with tenderness to be sure, with caring and compassion to be sure, but also to see the larger picture that everyone dies and everyone who loves experiences separation.

Dr. George and five policemen and four firemen came and milled around and did things and asked questions. Because George is a physician, we didn't have to wait for a medical examiner, and then they carried Eugene and put him in the bed in the living room under the sheets and left. One of my other Buddhist students came up and the three of us sat with Eugene for about three hours talking, talking about him, and I'd get up and go over and I'd kiss his lips and his nose and his brow and then put my cheek against the top of his head, where I could feel the heat still coming from his body.

He got colder and rigor set in, and my one student friend went home. Dr. George stayed and slept in the house that night so I wouldn't be alone.

We both got up early and came and sat with Eugene for about two hours and went out for breakfast. Now Eugene and I had already planned for that Sunday a Buddhist liturgy, a commemoration service.

He had said, "I really want to have a commemoration service while I'm alive," so we had planned it. We did the liturgy, people brought food, we talked, we laughed, I kissed Eugene a lot. He became more beautiful as the rigor set in. He became like a beautiful sculpture, and I will always remember the dignity and the rest and the repose, and also the coldness of his body, which was not repugnant or distasteful to me.

After everyone except Dr. George left, the men came from the crematorium, and with authentic care and concern, they wrapped Eugene up and took him. The cremation occurred a few days later, and I have the ashes sitting in a box on a chair here in the dining room with me. I have no idea what I'm going to do with them.

I've been surrounded by caring people who loved Eugene and loved us, more than I ever expected. The biggest surprise has been at the gym. We have an enormous number of friends at the gym, and over fifteen years, we had built a really close friendship with people who come there to do sports.

Ever since the first newspaper article came out about us a couple years ago, it seemed to make the guys more friendly in the locker room, I suppose because we didn't have to pretend anything. I think they appreciated that we were willing to be ballsy enough to be open about our love for one another.

But, oh my gosh, I've had tears and arms around me over Eugene's death. Men have come up to me crying and one man cried and told me how much our relationship meant to him and his wife. That's been the biggest surprise. When someone says to me, "My wife died five years ago," as a man at the gym said the other day, I finally know what he was going through and probably still feels, where I didn't before. So it's because of our willingness to share with one another and to share in a way that makes it clear, "Look, I'm not expecting you to solve this, but let me share my heart and then maybe you'll feel like sharing yours."

In some way I'm fine, and that's real, not a stiff upper lip. It's an honest appraisal of how I am. I am fine and I'm full of grief, and it comes and goes in waves. One of the things that my first Buddhist teacher taught me, that I find is absolutely true in my experience, more and more as I get older, is that there's room in one's heart for contradictions. So instead of experiencing those as in conflict, I'm fine and I'm overwhelmed with grief. Somehow there's room in our heart for both of those. Sometimes one is a little more apparent and sometimes the other, but they seem to kind of balance each other out. I don't know if that makes any sense, but it's very, very true and strong for me.

There's one other thing that I want to say, though I'm probably going to sound like I'm preaching... In my lifetime I've seen some men take more ownership for their enormous capacity for tenderness, gentleness, and nurturing. Men and women have been limited for centuries and made to believe that their qualities were limited to limited roles. But Eugene and I have been around long enough to see that some of these artificial limitations are softening or disappearing.

Gay men and lesbians have been lied to in a particularly toxic and destructive way. We have been taught that we can't love. This new generation is learning that that's quite a bit of nonsense, but for us older generations—going back many centuries—we have been taught that we cannot love, that we are corrupt, sinful, willfully evil, psychologically damaged beings. We have been taught that we cannot love and have been told that God hates us and wills our destruction. We've been taught that plagues and famines and bad weather—à la Jerry Falwell and others—are the result of our being permitted to live. But most cruel of all, we've been told that we cannot love, that we are merely sexual beings, distorted and sick and damaged and sinful.

What these generations of children and LGBT young men and women have had laid on them for generation after generation is that we cannot love one another and we cannot love God. It pisses me off that we have been lied to, and it also is a joy to me to see that things are changing. The fact that you and I are having this conversation tonight about the man I've loved for so many years and what was it like demonstrates that we're in the midst of an enormous and important change. I want to go up and down the street and knock on every door and say what I just said.

I remember a conference I was at some years ago for gay Catholic people. I was long since a practicing Buddhist, but it was not far from my Kentucky monastery, so since I was visiting there I went. There were several speaker-presenters and one of them was a retired bishop. What can be very interesting about retired bishops is they can afford to tell the truth. They've paid their dues and have gotten their rewards, and this one was clearly a good man. He said, "You know the Catholic church has these teachings on sexuality that appear so noble or so cosmic almost. But they don't work because they're written by people who have not had enough sex to be able to reflect on it and say something intelligent about it."

I nearly fell out of my chair. He didn't say it was because they were written by celibates—men who didn't have sex—but rather he was acknowledging by implication that there are some who are celibates, but there are vast numbers who simply have not had enough sex without guilt that they can reflect on it and say something intelligent. I do know that the world of an intimate relationship—and sex is only a part of it, although at the beginning it often seems that it's nine-tenths of it—is an environment, if we're willing, to face our early childhood wounds, our difficulties that have developed over the years as a result of that, and to do really serious, downright spiritual work by learning to love one another and be patient with one another.

One of the difficulties for Eugene and me is that we've become the objects upon which people can project their hopes and fears about how wonderful it is to be in a long-term relationship. Some people seem to be called by life to have short-term relationships and they can learn and they can care and they can be giving. The only advice I'm willing ever to give anyone really is to cultivate a love of love.

In relationships, there come those moments of boredom and difficulty and feeling separate, and those can be challenging. So it's difficult, but then that's what it is to grow together. Don't hesitate to seek counseling from people who specialize in couples therapy; there's a great rich world out there. When Eugene and I were young, we felt we had to hide. It never would have occurred to us to say, "Well, let's find a couple's therapist..." We simply had to work things out the best we could but trust in the love of each other, even when we weren't feeling that love especially deeply.

I still have my own death eventually. I don't know how long I'm going to be able to hang on. I really don't. I don't feel like I'm dying but I feel more vulnerable than I've ever felt in my life, since I was seven or eight years old, and that's not a surprise. I check in every morning with one of my students and every evening with one of my students because I don't want to die and have the bird left alone in his cage and starve to death.

PART TWO – JANUARY 15, 2014:
NEARLY ONE MONTH AFTER EUGENE'S DEATH

I'm really quite astonished at the degree of warmth and affection I'm getting from people. I'm getting lots of hugs everywhere. Lots and lots and lots of hugs. There's a rather smart grocery store with a marvelous delicatessen we've gone to for many years. When I told the owner of Eugene's death, he burst into tears, and we sat at a table while he cried and I cried with him. His daughter-in-law, who works in the store, came along and promptly fell against me and started crying. They're very kind people and they've been kind to us for years.

As you know, people who just lost someone talk to their loved one, and I said to Eugene today, "I'm very glad that I'm doing this, and you aren't. I wouldn't want you to experience these moments of extraordinary longing that I have for you..." The reason that I—self-centeredly probably—say that this experience is easier for me than it would be for Eugene—if the shoes had been reversed—is that my nature as a therapist and a person is to take pleasure in finding models of understanding what's going on and how to work with it. In fact, I have to be cautious not to have simply turned this into an occasion to get philosophical and use philosophical and spiritual language. But it's part of my nature to look at patterns and to try to make them of value to myself and to other people. In a very real way, it gives me something to do with what I'm experiencing.

I don't feel distance from the feelings. I feel intimate with it, but my missing him isn't just beating on me. I'm noticing what the "strokes" are about and what they feel like and how fast they come and can talk about that, which I think gives me a safe and healthy distance from being absolutely embattled by my grief. I don't want to fall into that.

My Buddhist teacher said years ago that one of the problems he perceived apropos the death of someone we love dearly is that the Christians too easily mutter on about "They're in a better place now," and Buddhists have a tendency also to miss the direct raw poignancy of the death of our loved one by saying, "Well, they'll be reborn under other circumstances," and so on. I was struck by the clarity with which my teacher saw that that can lead away from the experience of grief over losing this particular person right now.

My first meditation teacher once said to me, "About this rebirth thing... Maybe it is and maybe it isn't. If it is, fine. If it isn't, we won't be there to know it. Nonetheless, this is the most reasonable and rational way to live my life." Over the years, I've come to the very same conclusion. There's a rational side to Buddhism that enables me to live a life with more equanimity, by getting used to the impermanence of things and the unclingability of things; I can't really hold onto them, no matter how hard I try.

The Zen community has been very helpful, doing things for me, and being there for me emotionally. So I am well supported. I would say the hardest thing right now is the periodic recognition that Eugene is not coming back from anywhere. On the one hand, the house is still full of his presence, but it can seem particularly empty when I get these periodic recognitions of, "Oh, there's no one else here but me." I'm not afraid of being alone. I'm just not used to being alone. We enjoyed being together very much. We enjoyed just saying nothing but doing whatever we were doing around the house.

I've begun to realize that there are things that I need to do that I'm learning from this experience, and I need to make them a part of my teaching for a while. One of the wonderful things about Buddhism is that it is about working with tools that open our hearts, and each generation and probably every teacher tries to nuance the teachings so that they fit the human beings that they're coming to reside in. So I'm not suddenly developing a great love of life but there are things that I know I need to say as a teacher and to do and to be with friends and students of mine.

In the '70s, Eugene and I went into some very intensive and long lasting interpersonal growth group work. These experiences were often ferocious, really ferocious, and the trainers really drove many of us into terrifying situations as a way to help us step out of our cautious and lazy attitudes and fears. So the two of us, along with a lot of other people, learned how to he present in the world without it being an act of heroism any more.

When the newspaper here, *The Oregonian*, years ago did a three-day series on gay people and asked us if we would be featured, we ended up on a front page with a large photograph of the two of us and a lengthy interview. Then a few years later something similar happened, and then on our fiftieth anniversary, we decided to renew our vows that we had taken on our fortieth, and the paper covered it rather extensively. So we've been of value to people by being visible, but we really have not been courageous in being visible. We were creatively hammered into a willingness to do that sort of thing earlier in the '70s, and I'm so incredibly grateful to the trainers we had, who forced us out of our timidity. So that explains what Eugene and I have been willing to do all these years.

Our memories are built into us; they're part of our biochemistry. They exist in us here and now, right now. I can evoke a memory here in the present, noticing both what's going on around me and making room for my loneliness for my lover, and at the same time feel his kiss on the back of my neck or his holding me. Or seeing in my mind his hands, which I loved to reach over and touch. As long as that isn't an escape from what else is true around me right now, I really think I'm using the memories as nurturing, as nourishing, here in the present, and not running from the present.

Eight years ago, on one of my stays at the monastery in Kentucky, Brother Stephen asked me, "Eric, do you still find Eugene sexually exciting? He's saggy and baggy like you are." I was sitting at the reception desk in the abbey when out of the blue he said that to me.

I said, "Stephen, I know for sure that it's just been revealed to me from another plane that you're never going to be a diplomat working for the Vatican. But on the other hand, if you think that I can't tell the difference between how exquisite his body was the first time he took his clothes off in front of me in a room filled with the light of his beauty, and how his body is now, you're wrong. I can, but he's still beautiful and still emotionally moving to me in a different way, in the same way that when my garden begins to go down in the fall I don't dislike it. It's still full of the memories and the connections with the beauty that was there earlier, so my lover's body—and mine, I hope, to him—these are the fall gardens that we love."

And actually, here I am, an elderly man who until a few weeks ago was overweight, and Eugene would come up from behind me in the bathroom while I was shaving and naked and put his arms around me and say, "You're so beautiful." He did it frequently. And I found myself looking over at him as an old man and finding not just the memory of what he looked like earlier but how he looked now, which would partake in exactly that beauty of the past. He's still beautiful. In fact, sitting at Starbucks and looking around, I would sometimes find my eyes looking at someone and thinking, "Well, he hasn't aged well..." But if he were my husband, I'd say, "What a nice-looking man!"

As I was thinking about this, I came across a short saying from a very important medieval Zen monk named Dogen yesterday: "Every phase of the moon is the entire moon." Every memory I hold of Eugene is in some way the entire Eugene, and it can nurture and feed me now, along with all the other things I am feeling here in the present.

PART THREE – JUNE 12, 2014:
SIX MONTHS AFTER EUGENE'S DEATH

I'm still receiving an abundance of hugs and affection from people. The guys at the gym are amazingly warm and loving and affectionate. I go to the same restaurant almost every day for breakfast and sometimes for lunch instead, and three of the waitresses bring their big bosoms from the far side of the restaurant and engulf me every time I arrive.

Yesterday was Eugene's and my sixty-first anniversary, and I celebrated it by taking chocolate chip cookies into the gym class. When I brought them, I made a short introduction and said that Eugene and I had been in this exercise class for fifteen years—about a third of the class has been there for the same fifteen years—and that I was very happy to celebrate this with them. All the people who were still there from years ago were at our Buddhist wedding ten years ago, and they are not people who had ever been in a Buddhist temple before nor had they ever been to a relationship ceremony for two gay men.

My words were well received. There's one man in the class who always has been and always will be very narrow-minded religiously, but he always takes more than two cookies. I almost said to him, "You realize, Howard, that when you're eating these cookies, you are sharing the sacramental presence of Eugene's and my relationship..." But I decided that my intent was to be snide and I would do better to shut up and let him savor the chocolate.

Not long after Eugene died, I was in his room looking at all the piles of paper he had been sorting through. There was a homemade, bound 8 1/2 x 11 book sitting on top, and I opened it and read a poem on the first page. Then I read a poem on the second page and then one on the third page. It turned out there were thirty-four pages of poems. On the fourth page, it said, "Eric, there are some corrections in the back here. Please insert them between page such-and-such and page such-and-such." This was sitting right next to a page that, because of the inscription on it, indicated that he had written it for me during the first week we had known one another. As I looked further and read the poems, I realized he had written all of them. I tell you, I went through about ten minutes of doubt, saying, "It couldn't be, it couldn't be....," before I finally realized he'd been writing these over the years. I couldn't have been more stunned if I'd learned that he'd had four children with the woman down the street.

It was a whole side of Eugene he never articulated. He was not a shy person in general, but he was very shy about articulating his feelings. He was very reticent that way. With all the pieces I know about his early childhood, he would be very shy about sharing a poem or an essay that had come straight out of his own mind and heart. There had never been anything that we didn't share with one another, I thought. But I am a loudmouth and I always have an opinion about things, and even though I know for sure in my heart that he totally trusted he could share anything with me, on some level, it was probably beneficial for him that he didn't.

I have several friends who are very literate and who said to me, "These poems really could or should be published. And it's not because I loved Eugene, but this is a side of him none of us ever guessed was there, and they are really good." Although I had the same feeling after reading them, it's been interesting to have people in the academic world who are professionally qualified to judge the quality of literature say that.

Soon after finding the poems I looked at a picture of him on my desk and I cried and said, "You son of a bitch! You make me so raw with love, and then you're not here to hold!" And I laughed and cried as I swore at him. I still feel the same way. Well, that's how we men tell one another we love one another, isn't it? We swear at one another.

It's still difficult inhabiting this house. I love my home. I enjoy being alone but I'm not used to Eugene being gone. It's very much like losing an arm or a leg. But in a very real way I'm glad that I'm the survivor. I would not want Eugene to be dealing with all this. He would manage it, but I think it would be much more difficult for him.

A friend named Jim and his husband are longtime members of the gym, and we see each other almost every other day in the shower and sometimes sit and chat afterwards. Jim and Eugene used to grab ass and grab dick with each other very playfully. Jim and I were talking the other day and I said to him, "I want you to know how happy that made me to see the two of you being like two little kids who were just having a fun, sensuous time. That was a great gift not only to Eugene, but to me as well.

Jim cried and said, "I really loved him as a friend and I miss him a lot."

One of the women in my exercise class came to me the other day and said, "I've been thinking about you a lot because of my own process." She said, "It took me a year before I could simply cry tears, and not roar with grief."

I still want to be able to hold Eugene again, and I moan and cry out with grief for him. Grief is in a way incredibly sweet and very, very painful at the same time. It sweeps in unsolicited and overwhelms, and there are certain aspects of the grieving process as it sweeps in that have the quality of an orgasm engulfing one. There are similar changes in the breathing and skin and surface temperature. I said that much to a friend at the gym the other day, and then what came out of my mouth was, "So that's how Eugene and I make love now."

The top row, center photo on the cover features an embracing Eugene (left) and Eric (right) in 2003, during their fiftieth year together as a couple.

ABOUT THE AUTHOR

Jazz pianist and writer Tim Clausen grew up in Oconomowoc, Wisconsin, where MGM's *The Wizard of Oz* received its world premier in 1939. He spent his childhood drawing monsters and learning to play piano by ear. In addition to recording three solo CDs, Tim has played solo engagements at many of Milwaukee's top hotels and restaurants. In his work as an oral historian, he has conducted hundreds of interviews over the past two decades, and was honored to interview dozens of jazz legends while putting together musical histories on jazz greats Erroll Garner and Dave Catney.

Tim founded and facilitated the Milwaukee Gay Fathers Group for its ten-year run, from 1995 to 2004. In his spare time, he enjoys cooking, travel, hiking, writing puns, meditation, swimming, movies, gardening, abstract painting, and spending time with friends. Open to a possible long-term relationship, Tim especially likes younger men who are altruistic, funny, passionate, handsome, and spiritually oriented; extra points if you also have a great smile and like pets.

Visit the author's website at www.timclausen.com.

Made in the USA
Lexington, KY
18 February 2015